The Making of a Mom
My Unexpected Journey through Birth & Adoption

Kimberly Severn

Published by Longest Day Press

Cover design by Matthew Pantoliano (matt.pantoliano@gamil.com)
and Rob Williams (fiverr.com/cal5086)
Photography by Nataliya Khan - www.nataliyakhan.com

Library of Congress Cataloging-in-Publication Data
Names: Severn, Kimberly, author.
Title: The Making of a Mom – My Unexpected Journey through
Birth & Adoption
Identifiers: LCCN: 2019901608
Subjects: motherhood, adoption, parenting

ISBN: 978-1-7337035-0-5 (paperback)
ISBN: 978-1-7337035-1-2 (ebook)

Longest Day Press
14201 SE Petrovitsky Road
Suite A-3-218
Renton, Washington 98058

For Q-man and Lu-Lu who continue to teach me about motherhood.
Love you both forever and for always,
Mom

And with love and gratitude to my partner on this wild journey.
Hang on babe, there's more adventure to come!

Author's Note

Thank you to the family and friends who were part of my journey and who will see themselves in these pages. To protect the privacy of the people involved, I have changed individual's names and identifying information about the experiences we shared.

The events that I share in this memoir are based on my personal memories, legal documents, email correspondence, and other documentation I retained throughout the adoption process and its aftermath. Nonetheless, some of the events I describe are narratives of my own perceptions of a deeply personal event that involved many different people, with perceptions of their own. It has not been my intention to hurt anyone or misrepresent anyone in any way, and to the extent I may have done so, I apologize.

Contents

Prologue

By the time I was twelve, I had created my life plan: go to college, marry my high school sweetheart, have two kids and a career — most likely as a nurse or a teacher. I figured if I did everything right, my plan would become reality.

My quest for the perfect life started early. I was the second of four children, all of whom — except me — sailed through school, earning great grades with minimal effort. I was the odd kid out.

Each day, during the five-block walk to and from school, I struggled to figure out how to get from the bottom of the class to the top. It was up to me to figure it out, since no one at my school knew how to help a kid with dyslexia. My biggest obstacle by far was reading; a single page took forever. It was humiliating.

"Okay, boys and girls, pull out your books and turn to page 20," said my second grade teacher, Mrs. Campbell, beginning the instructions for an assignment that would ultimately leave me feeling defeated. I groaned as I reached inside my desk. "Please read the story and then answer questions one through four."

With both elbows on the desk and my forehead resting in my hands I started to read. After only a few minutes, the rustling of paper and scratching of pencils told me many had already finished. My stomach sank in despair as I counted how many pages I had left to read. I considered closing the book and telling Mrs. Campbell I couldn't do it. There simply wasn't enough time. But if there's anything worse than not finishing, it's quitting. I was not a quitter.

"Okay, time's up," Mrs. Campbell announced. "Make sure your name is on the top of your paper and pass it forward."

The next morning we got our assignments back. I stared at the half-inch long red dash in the upper righthand corner of the page. I knew I'd be called up to talk to the teacher before recess to explain why I hadn't finished and she'd question me about whether I'd understood the assignment. The thought of being called out yet again made my jaw clench and my cheeks burn. *I'm not stupid. There just wasn't enough time! I'm smart. I just gotta read faster.*

But no matter how hard I tried, I never finished in the time provided. Mrs. Campbell didn't treat me like I didn't understand. It was even worse, she treated me like I wasn't trying. I wanted her to know I was doing the best I could, that I was smart, and that I belonged at the top of the class. I hated the experience of failure.

Second grade and already enough was enough. If I was going to succeed, I needed a plan.

First, I tried reading faster. Sliding my eyes across the page like a speed skater racing around the rink only got me to the questions faster; it didn't help at all with finding the answers. But it did provide the insight I needed to create a successful strategy: *start with the questions.* If I read the questions first, I'd know what to look for. I could stop and write down the answers as I read. Eureka!

The confidence my academic successes provided eventually helped me read faster too, and, with more time, I started to show off my smooth cursive writing skills, which also improved my grade.

By the end of sixth grade, I'd found a formula for success I could apply to any situation: identify a goal, build a plan, execute it. Although I never made it to the top of the class, I graduated high school with honors and was accepted to the top university in my state. So far, so good. My plan was on track.

During my sophomore year of college, I was set up on a blind date and, two years later, Nate and I got married. Life was turning out better than I had planned. By the time I was 25 I had a university degree, a good job, and we had bought our first home. I was on top of the world. The stars were the limit and I couldn't imagine anything slowing my momentum.

What I didn't recognize in my youthful naiveté, however, was that life doesn't operate like a classroom — it's uncontrollable and unpredictable, and one formula can't solve all problems. When it came time to having children, Nate and I faced challenges we had never imagined. And the very skills that had been key to my past success would prove my Achilles heel.

Despite a decade's worth of data proving I could achieve anything I set my mind to, the next decade would test even my deepest held beliefs as I set out to become a mother.

Chapter 1

Next Phase of the Plan

"Hold onto your kibble, Chinook, the ride's about to get bumpy," I said to our fifty-pound husky who lounged across the backseat as we turned onto the narrow gravel road that led to the Christmas tree farm. I glanced over at Nate, who sat behind the wheel of our Subaru station wagon. With his unshaven face and dark blue raincoat over a red and black flannel button-up, he looked part yuppie, part lumberjack. After seven years of marriage I still had a deep crush on him.

The mottled grey skies threatened rain and the wind rustled the branches of the evergreen trees that filled the rolling landscape. We were only a few miles from home, but it felt like a world away from the manicured lawns of our suburban neighborhood.

"You ready for this?" I asked, pulling on my gloves and grabbing Chinook's leash.

"Yep. Let's do it."

"What kind of tree are we looking for?" I asked as I negotiated a puddle and met him at the back of the car.

"A live one?"

"Oh really?" I raised an eyebrow. "Everyone loves a smart ass, Charlie Brown."

He smiled and reached for my hand. After receiving a saw and instructions on how to safely cut down a tree, we headed into the nearest field. Chinook and I followed a few steps behind Nate as we tried to decipher the difference between Noble Firs, Grand Firs, and Blue Spruce.

It was a busy day at the tree farm. Giggles and excited screams filled the air from every direction. A father helped his young son maneuver their saw back and forth through the trunk of a tree. The father's encouragement interrupted by the *vrr-rup, vrr-rup, vrr-rup* of the saw slowly cutting through the wood. A high-pitched "Timber!" accompanied the satisfying crack as the last of the wood gave way.

A mom, bundled-up baby strapped to her chest, tried to get her husband's attention so she could point out the perfect tree. "Hey, sweetie, over here," she bounced slightly, arm raised and pointing in the direction directly opposite her husband's current path through the trees. A moment passed and she whistled, "No, babe, this way. That one over there, between the two shorter ones."

I glanced in the direction she pointed and saw a slender pine, standing at attention between its two squatty neighbors. It looked barely wide enough to stand up without toppling over, but the joy in her face said it all – that tree would be at the center of their Christmas celebrations.

"Excuse me, would you mind taking our picture?" another woman asked as the teenage boy standing next to her rolled his eyes. She elbowed the boy in the side and handed Nate her camera as she said, "I saw that."

"On three say, Merry Christmas," Nate said, brandishing their camera. "One, two, three."

"Merry Christmas!" each member of the family of five responded, some sounding more excited than others. Nate took several pictures, hoping to catch the teen smiling in at least one.

As Chinook and I stood watching, I wondered if a picture at the tree farm was part of their annual holiday tradition. I imagined the family using the photo for their Christmas card and placing a copy in a frame, replacing the one from the year before. Every December the parents would take a moment to reflect on how much their children had grown. It was an idyllic and sappy tradition that I unexpectedly realized I wanted to be mine. But years before we'd agreed not to have children.

My thoughts were suddenly taken over by the memory of sitting in the sparsely furnished office of the Pastor we'd chosen to marry us. She was a friend of Nate's mom and had agreed to officiate at our wedding on the condition that we met her for three pre-marital counseling sessions.

We were young and had fallen in love fast. During our courtship, it had never occurred to me to ask Nate where he saw himself in ten, fifteen, or twenty years. I just assumed, since we had so much in common, that our expectations for the future were compatible too.

Imagine my surprise when, during our second pre-marital counseling session, Nate said he didn't want children. *How could you not want kids?* I had thought. *How could you be happy without children in your life? What would you do on weekends, vacations, and holidays while everyone else was spending time with their families?* I simply couldn't imagine it.

"What do you think about that, Kim?" the pastor asked, raising her eyebrows above her round tortoise-rimmed glasses.

"I, well, uh..." I wasn't sure how to respond. "Well, it's not as if we're going to have kids any time soon. There's a lot to accomplish before we could even think about becoming parents." I smiled and looked from the pastor to Nate.

"It sounds like something important for the two of you to talk about." Her tone was matter-of-fact, despite the potentially ruinous disclosure. She allowed the silence to linger, the time morphing her suggestion into a warning.

It was three months before our wedding, I loved Nate, and I couldn't imagine life without him. We both agreed that we weren't ready for children, so I let it go. There was plenty of time to change his mind later. *Why worry about something before it's even a problem?*

A burst of wind chilled my cheeks and the fresh, pine-scented air brought me back to the present. The constant buzz of activity as people pointed, chopped, and lugged evergreen trees back to their cars sent the memories of the past into the recesses of my mind. The excitement and energy of the present moment echoed my satisfaction with the life Nate and I had built together. Even the bickering that broke out between a set of nearby siblings had a note of warmth to it.

Chinook and I followed Nate through the trees. Stepping over stumps and hopping over puddles in the mud, we continued our search. As we wound our way through the evergreen forest it was impossible not to notice that we appeared to be the only kid-free couple in the area. I wondered if we were missing out, having only our four-legged baby in our life.

Eventually, we found a mostly symmetrical Blue Spruce about seven feet tall with branches extending four feet in diameter at the base. Nate and I took turns sawing through the trunk, making slow progress with the well-worn saw in dire need of sharpening. Chinook joined the fun by providing the occasional bark of encouragement. *He's our four-legged baby, we should snap a picture with him before we go,* I thought as Nate made the final cut through the trunk. I shrugged off the thought, feeling uncomfortable with how sentimental the outing had become for me.

We worked as a team to get the tree back to the car, tied it to the roof, and then, after stopping at the pay station, we headed home.

* * *

The rain fell in fat, round drops that burst into hundreds of droplets as they hit the road. Illuminated by our headlights the water looked like glitter erupting from the pavement. As Nate drove us to our friend's house, I thought about all the families we'd seen at the tree farm, each one flashing through my mind like a slideshow of Norman Rockwell paintings. I'd been pushing the thought away for hours but could no longer resist its power. I wanted Nate and me to be the subjects of one of those paintings. As much as I'd grown used to our comfortable life and family of two, I couldn't shake the feeling that Christmas would be a lot more meaningful with a child to share it with.

"That was fun at the tree farm," I said, glancing over at Nate. "The house is gonna smell so good with a real tree." I tried to sound casual before dropping what I feared would be a bomb.

"Yep, we found one good lookin' tree." He said with a fake southern drawl that made me laugh. "I'll trim the trunk tomorrow and we can decorate it."

"Be sure to check for spiders before bringing it in from the garage, okay?" I'm seriously afraid of spiders.

"Don't worry, honey," he said as he reached over and set his hand on my leg, "I got your back. I'll make sure it's spider-free." He flashed me a smile that reminded me how much I loved him.

"I hope Chinook won't knock it over. Remember the year Lucy knocked the tree over so many times, we had, like, two ornaments left?" Lucy was a cat we'd adopted shortly after our engagement, nine years earlier.

"He'll probably leave it alone." I could tell by the wrinkles that had suddenly appeared at the corners of his eyes he knew I was headed somewhere with this conversation.

"There sure were a lot of families there today." I paused, stared straight ahead, and slowed my breath before continuing. "Did you see how happy they all looked with their kids? How cute the babies looked all bundled up?" Nate's smile broadened as he glanced over at me and squeezed my leg again. I laced my fingers through his. "Wouldn't it be great if that was us next year?"

"Ya think?" *Why is he being so casual about all this? Does he seriously not get what I'm hinting at?*

I took a deep breath and decided to get to the point. "I think I'm ready to have a baby." There. I'd said it.

"Okay."

"Okay?" A huge smile spread across my face and my breath caught in my throat. *Did he truly mean it? Was he really ready?*

More importantly, was I?

Chapter 2

Preparing for Success

Why am I so nervous? I thought as I waited for Susan Worthington, my nurse practitioner, to enter the room. Since the first time I met her almost a decade before, she'd made me feel so at ease that I felt safe asking her almost anything, no matter how potentially embarrassing. This time I felt different. I knew the only way to get what I was after was to tell her that Nate and I had decided to get pregnant. But mentioning we were ready for kids, meant talking about sex – and I suddenly realized that wasn't something I was comfortable talking about with anyone.

I was in her office for my annual exam, but what I really wanted was her reassurance that I was ready to be a mom. Or more accurately, that my body was up to the task. *Why shouldn't it be?* I was twenty-nine, healthy, and strong. Both my mom and my two sisters had had easy pregnancies and deliveries. This exam was just a routine precaution. But like taking a reading test, deep down I feared I wouldn't pass it.

Once she entered the room, however, she put me immediately at ease and my fears faded. Getting pregnant would be no big deal. People do it every day.

Once the exam was over, she left the room so I could get dressed. After a few minutes, there was a quick knock on the door, Susan entered and sat down across from me. With her elbow resting on the laminate countertop, I felt as if we were meeting for a cup of coffee, not discussing my reproductive organs.

"So, here's some information on getting pregnant." She handed me a small booklet. "It covers the basics, most of which you likely already know."

"Thanks." I paused and took a deep breath. I felt my cheeks begin to pinken as I summoned the courage to ask the only question I wanted her to answer. "I guess what I really want to know is," I paused, "How long will it take?"

She smiled before responding as if she'd anticipated my question. "For healthy couples your age, it could take anywhere from a couple months to a year." She leaned toward me a few inches before continuing, "If you're not pregnant after twelve months of trying, make an appointment and we'll talk about options."

A year? Since when did it take a year to get pregnant? We were a healthy young couple who wanted a baby. *Why would it take a year?* The women in my family never had a problem getting pregnant. Furthermore, if it took a year just to get pregnant, it would be almost two before we had a baby! I knew it wasn't rational, but we'd made our decision, and it was go time. Time to move on to the next step. I felt a sudden rush of disappointment and embarrassment at my uninformed expectations.

"Wow, that long? I thought if it took more than six months, that was a long time."

"You know, Kim, someone once gave me a card that read, 'The only way to ensure you get pregnant right away is to be two sixteen-year-olds in the back of your parents' station wagon.'"

"Well, at least we own a station wagon." I laughed, easing the tension I felt. "I guess we'll have to be patient and just start trying."

"Good luck and call me if you have questions." Susan stood up to leave. "Oh, and it's not a bad idea to start taking prenatal vitamins now. It won't hurt and you'll know you're getting plenty of folic acid from the beginning of your pregnancy."

I thanked Susan, grabbed my bag and followed her out to the reception desk. As I walked down the hall to the elevator, I stuffed the booklet into my purse and decided to stop at the drug store in the lobby. Although, clearly I'd never been a Boy Scout, I did subscribe to their motto "Be prepared!" There was no better time than the present to begin preparing my body to make a baby.

* * *

Two months later and a few days late, I grabbed the home pregnancy kit from the back of the bathroom cabinet. Nate was already at work. I followed the directions, placed the little white stick on the back of the toilet and jumped in the shower. The results would be ready by the time I was done.

With a towel wrapped around me, I stepped out of the shower and grabbed the stick. There were two pink lines in the small recessed oval. I compared what I saw with the pictures on the brochure. Under the diagram showing two pink lines I read the word PREGNANT in thick bold letters. I must have looked from the stick to the diagram and back again a dozen times before I was convinced.

I grabbed my cell phone off the counter and called Nate.

"Morning babe. What's up?" he said sounding cheerful.

"I found something out this morning!" The excitement took my breath away.

"What are you talking about?" Followed by a quick laugh.

"I found out we're pregnant!" I started laughing and bouncing up and down, still wrapped in a towel.

"Whoa babe, congratulations!"

"Congratulations to us! I can't wait to talk more when you get home tonight." I knew his coworkers were likely nearby as we talked. Nate was a private person and I didn't want to put him in an awkward situation.

"See you tonight. I love you, babe." Despite his casual response, I could tell Nate was excited and a little nervous, too. This would be a big change for both of us.

"Love you too, babe." I stood in front of the bathroom mirror and placed my hand on my still firm, flat stomach trying to envision how my reflection would change in the months to come. I turned and walked into the closet to find some clothes. *I'm pregnant!* I repeated it silently over and again as I pulled out a pair of black slacks and a blue pinstriped blouse. I couldn't believe it. Ten months short of a year. *How's that for fertile?*

I was now running late for work, so I had to hustle to make the train. I worked as a project manager for a transit agency located in the heart of the city. It was an intense job that easily took up fifty hours a week, with an additional ten-hours of commute, and I loved it. The challenge of bringing together experts from multiple disciplines to deliver our projects on time fueled my passion. I was always learning. Everyday there was a new problem to solve, a new opportunity to capture, new people to meet. Juggling motherhood with my career wasn't going to be easy, but I knew that I'd find a way to master it. After all, most women figured it out, right?

I spent the train ride thinking about what would happen next. My mom had taught us not to announce a pregnancy until after the first trimester because of the risk of losing the pregnancy in the first three months. How in the world was I supposed to hide my excitement for another seven or eight weeks? But my mom, a mother of four, had a lot more experience at this than I did. So I decided to keep my mouth shut and trust her advice. For the next two months, it would be a secret for Nate and me to keep.

On my lunch break, I locked myself in a conference room and called the doctor's office to schedule my first prenatal appointment. When the receptionist explained they didn't make the first appointment until ten weeks, my heart sank. The first milestone in my pregnancy was already delayed. I wrote the appointment in my date book, then sat at the long table imagining the excitement the next eight months would bring.

I pictured myself having an idyllic pregnancy — gaining a couple pounds per month, my stomach growing only until it looked like I'd swallowed a beach ball. I'd have a beautiful pregnancy glow and my hair would grow longer, thicker, shinier. Nate and I would work as a team to decorate the nursery in a music theme. We would paint a piano keyboard on the lower half of the wall with the hope of inspiring our baby to love the piano as much as Nate did.

My idea of the perfect pregnancy would culminate in an on-time delivery. Our baby would be born on his or her due date, after only a few hours of drug-free labor. We'd bring our little bundle of joy home with smiles on our well-rested faces, the baby in an adorable outfit, me in my pre-pregnancy jeans. It would be perfect.

* * *

I treasured these images as my pregnancy advanced. However, as the months passed, life dealt me an altogether different reality. The first three months weren't *too* bad. My breasts, which had been throbbing initially, eventually stopped hurting, replaced by mild morning sickness. I was tired after a full day's work and would routinely doze off on the couch before nine.

At the beginning of my second trimester I found myself needing new clothes — not because of my growing belly but because of my rapidly widening butt. I didn't look pregnant; for the first time in my life, I looked fat.

All my life, I'd enjoyed a trim, fit figure. I never had to worry about what I ate or whether or not I exercised. As if having a human growing inside me wasn't strange enough, my quickly expanding size left me feeling rudderless. I no longer stood to wonder at my growing belly in the bathroom mirror after I stepped out of the shower. Instead, I headed straight to the closet to cover myself up as quickly as I could.

One afternoon, while walking back to my cubicle after a meeting, a male colleague came rushing up behind me and grabbed the door.

"Let me get that for you, Kim," he said rather gallantly.

"Oh, hi Scott. Thanks."

"So, how's the pregnancy going?"

"Fine, thanks." My pregnancy had become common knowledge and I often felt awkward when coworkers mentioned it.

"Well, you look great. But don't you usually see it in the stomach first?" Scott elbowed me like we were buddies at the bar after work.

"One would think." I responded with a weak laugh. *What the hell?* I wondered as I tried to maintain my composure. "I just remembered, I need to stop by and talk to Stacie." I turned and walked in the opposite direction. *What kind of remark was that?* As if I'm not perfectly aware my butt looks like it's expecting its own offspring!

* * *

After four and a half months, I finally began to show in my belly. In the middle of my twentieth week, Nate joined me for my first ultrasound. "You're having a boy!" the technician announced. We looked at each other and smiled.

A boy. I'd always imagined having a girl. I wasn't close to my only brother, Greg, who was six years younger than me. I'd moved across the state to attend university when he was twelve and hadn't visited my family for more than two weeks at a time ever since. I quickly convinced myself I'd figure it out. I had my mom to lean on, and my mother-in-law had survived raising four energetic boys.

My pregnancy had a few more surprises in store. One hot summer night, as I sat on the couch watching HGTV, I noticed my shirt was wet. Assuming it was just condensation from the glass of ice water I was holding, I ignored it. A few minutes later, I looked down to see two large wet circles the size of saucers spreading across my chest. Something was leaking. I looked at Nate in a panic as I realized it was me!

"Nate, what the heck is going on?" I asked as my cheeks began to burn.

"I have no idea." He jumped up from the couch to grab *What to Expect When You're Expecting* from the bookshelf.

"What are you doing?"

"Seeing what the book says."

This is so embarrassing! We'd been married nearly a decade, but we were in uncharted territory. Nothing we'd read or heard included anything about leaking breasts before the baby was even born!

Turned out, I'm one of a small percentage of women whose colostrum comes in early. In my case, three months early.

* * *

By thirty-five weeks, I was over sixty pounds heavier and had high blood pressure. So much for a couple pounds a month and only showing in my belly. My weekly visits to the obstetrician became twice weekly with routine non-stress tests. I'd lie with fetal monitors strapped to my belly, clicking a button every time the baby moved. If he didn't move enough, the nurse would click spoons together over my belly to coax him into motion.

Alternating between nervousness and annoyance as my dream pregnancy disintegrated with each passing day, I had to constantly remind myself not to be dramatic and that the baby was perfectly healthy, which was all that mattered.

Except, it wasn't all that mattered to me. I felt I was letting myself, my husband, and my family down. I'd worked hard for a successful career, saving up five years' worth of vacation and sick time so I could stay home for three months without a break in paychecks. Still, all the planning, attention to detail, and determination wasn't enough. It felt like I'd lost myself — and I wasn't sure I'd ever find her again. There was nothing I could do but ride out the storm and hope for the best, whatever that might look like.

* * *

Late on a Friday, as I approached my thirty-eighth week, my doctor had me stay late to await the results of some tests. She didn't like how my weight had once again risen, my belly had shrunk and my blood pressure spiked from high to borderline alarming. I sat in the small exam room, reading a well-worn copy of *Better Homes and Gardens* and trying hard not to freak out as I thought about the rush-hour traffic I'd be forced to endure on my drive home.

"Thanks for waiting, Kim," the doctor said as she walked into the room. "I wanted to review your blood work before you left."

"Okay. What's up?" I tried to put aside my annoyance, so I didn't raise my blood pressure even more.

"As you know, you've gained a lot of weight and your blood pressure is steadily rising. I think it's best you stop working and go on bedrest. We want to give the baby as much time to develop as possible. These last few weeks are so important."

"When you say 'bedrest,' what exactly do you mean?" I felt my chest tighten and tears begin to sting the backs of my eyes.

"I mean, you'll stay lying down, except to go to the bathroom or to eat."

"Seriously?" I couldn't believe what she'd said. None of this was in the plan. And I had so much work to get done before going on leave.

"Yes. We want to get your blood pressure down for the remainder of your pregnancy. If it gets too high, we'll have to induce. And there's an increased chance of cesarean section with induction." She paused, allowing me time to process. Softening her voice, she continued, "And since I know you want a natural delivery, we'd like to give you a chance to go into labor naturally."

"Okay." I slumped back and rested my head against the wall. I was concerned and also angry — mostly at myself, for not being able to control my body or work harder to ensure I had the pregnancy I had dreamt of. It felt better to be angry than afraid.

"I'm sure you're disappointed. Do you have any questions?"

I shook my head. Thoughts were buzzing around my brain like bees in a hive under attack. I'd waited almost 30 years for this pregnancy. Nate and I had worked hard to create a stable life for our future family. My excessive weight gain had contributed to the hypertension necessitating the impending bed rest. *If only I'd eaten better. If only I'd taken time throughout my pregnancy to exercise. If only I'd practiced the breathing we learned in our birthing classes.* There was a long list of 'if onlys.' I felt responsible for what was going awry in my pregnancy. And I was wracking my brain to figure out exactly where, when, and how I'd made the critical mistake that led me to my current predicament.

Pregnancy was one thing my body should be able to do without difficulty, right? These things are hereditary and nowhere in my family tree is there any hint of the troubles I was experiencing. Therefore, it had to be my *choices* that caused the problems I was experiencing.

It felt like I was back in my second grade class, trying to find the answer to why I'd failed. How was I going to explain this latest development to Nate? And, more importantly, convince him not to tell anyone? I didn't want to raise any alarms — or let anyone know what a failure I was.

I felt sad, frustrated, and embarrassed as I left my doctor's office and waddled to the elevators. *One of life's most important experiences and I'm blowing it!* I willed back the tears that still threatened to soak my cheeks.

* * *

Nothing could have prepared me for the difficulty of bedrest. It was hard knowing someone was picking up my work when I hadn't had the opportunity to organize everything first. There were important decisions scheduled and I wanted my recommendations and intentions clearly laid out. I wanted the quality of my work to speak for itself so I wouldn't come back to a mess.

While Chinook loved every minute lounging beside me, soaking in the hours of attention, I grew increasingly bored and frustrated. Even with a hundred channels to surf and months of *Architectural Digest, Vogue,* and *Sunset* magazines to thumb through, nothing captured my attention for longer than ten minutes at a time. I couldn't wear any of the clothes in *Vogue*, couldn't do any of the gardening suggested in *Sunset* and, most surprisingly, didn't feel inspired by any of the homes in *Architectural Digest*. I wondered if Nate was up to preparing one of the dishes in *Bon Apettit*. At least my sense of humor remained partially intact.

Where was my appreciation for this time to completely relax? I was on doctor's orders not to raise a finger — was this not something most women dreamed of? Not me. With feelings of boredom and frustration, there was also relief that by following the doctor's orders I was keeping our baby safe.

A week and a half later, my blood pressure no better, we scheduled an induction. I'd made it to thirty-nine weeks. The nurse told us to wait for the hospital to call around six the following morning, unless the maternity ward was full.

The next morning, at six o'clock sharp, the phone rang and I reached over to answer.

"Hello?" I was already awake. Between the discomfort of pregnancy and having to pee every couple of hours, I'd given up trying to sleep.

"Kimberly? This is Stephanie from the labor and delivery unit. I'm calling to let you know we're ready for you to come in and have your baby." She sounded so chipper and excited for us, I suddenly felt excited, too.

"Okay, sounds good. We'll be there as soon as we can." *I'm going to meet my son today!*

I hung up the phone and rolled over to wake Nate. Just rolling over was so much work for my swollen body, I was nearly out of breath. *Thank God this will all be over soon.* I immediately felt a hot rush of guilt burn my cheeks. I was both excited to meet our son and desperate for my body to feel familiar again. I just wanted to hold him in my arms, cover his cheeks with kisses, and put the last several months behind me.

As we left the house, I felt confident that no matter what happened our baby would be born healthy. But I couldn't shake the feeling that my body might not make it through the experience unscathed.

Chapter 3

Labor, Delivery, and A New Life

I slowly maneuvered my clumsy body into the car and pulled the seat belt around my enormous belly. In nine months, I'd ballooned from a fit 130 pounds to a nearly unrecognizable 207. There wasn't an inch of me that wasn't stretched, swollen, and aching. I felt like the Stay Puft Marshmallow Man and I wasn't happy about it.

"You ready for this?" I asked Nate.

"Yep, let's do this." I looked over at Nate to gauge how he was feeling. His hair still damp and his cheeks newly shaven, he sat back straight, shoulders set, hands at nine and three on the steering wheel. Over the past decade, I'd gotten pretty good at measuring his stress level by his posture and the set of his jaw. I could tell he was putting on a brave face for my sake. He was anxious and ready for the day's big event to conclude — hopefully without any complications.

It was seven o'clock on a Tuesday morning. Rush hour. Despite the carpool lane, we rarely got over 30 miles an hour on the freeway. During our hour drive, I called my mom and assured her Nate would call with updates throughout the day.

Once we reached the hospital, we were given a spacious suite with a large soaking tub in the bathroom and a view of the snowcapped Cascade Mountains. It was a beautifully clear, sunny October day forecasted to hit 80 degrees. I loved the delightful surprise of a warm fall day, but I'd be spending it in the hospital, under fluorescent lights.

"Here are two gowns," our nurse, Stephanie, said, laying both on the bed. "Take everything off and put one on, tied at back. Layer the other over it, like a robe. Might as well maintain your modesty for as long as possible!"

"Okay, thanks. Is it okay if I keep my bra on? My colostrum has come in so I'm already wearing nursing pads," I felt my cheeks flush in embarrassment. I was extremely self-conscious of my gigantic body that now included stretch marks from the top of my thighs to an inch above my belly button. The leaky boobs I'd had for the past couple of months were the icing on the cake.

The idyllic pregnancy I had dreamed of had never materialized. I was sad and embarrassed by how things had developed. If I didn't stay in a constant state of anger, I was afraid I'd dissolve into a puddle of tears and despair. I'd read so much about how women felt powerful, excited, and fueled by love for their unborn child. I yearned to feel that way. Instead, I felt incompetent, out of control, and filled with impending doom. *What if I've hurt our baby?* I wondered. *What if I can't do this and die giving birth, and Nate is left to raise our son alone?* I fought to control my racing thoughts.

"I'll leave you to get changed. Be back in a few minutes." Stephanie turned toward the door. "Oh, and Nate, here's a bag for Kim's clothes. She won't be needing them for a while."

"Just set the bag on the bed, Nate" I snapped. "I can fold my clothes myself." I needed to feel in control of something. Then I blushed as I remembered I couldn't reach my feet. "But could you untie my shoes for me, please?"

"You okay, babe?" Nate did his best to hide the vein of worry woven through his overly casual tone as he bent down to untie my tennis shoes. "Everything's going to be fine."

"Yeah, I'm fine. It's just really hitting me now." My eyes suddenly started to water.

Stephanie returned with another nurse in tow. "This is Sam. She recently graduated and she's completing her labor and delivery rotation. She'll be working with me today."

We exchanged greetings and Sam prepared my IV. But sure enough, there was a problem. Neither Sam nor Stephanie could find my vein. After several minutes, Stephanie left to go get another nurse. "She's the best we have," Sam smiled.

"And if she can't do it?" I had a growing sense of dread.

"Then we'll call an anesthesiologist. We'll take care of you, Kim, don't worry."

After several minutes, Stephanie returned with a nurse they introduced as the IV wizard. But she wasn't having much success, either. Just when she was about to give up, she slid the IV into place — and my induction medication started to flow.

* * *

I was finally settled in bed when my doctor came by to check on me.

"We're getting a bit of a late start," she said, glancing from her watch to my chart. It was already almost nine. "Let's check you out and see where you're at."

"Well," she determined, "everything looks fine. Why don't we break your water and that should get things moving."

"Okay, let's do this." I squeezed Nate's hand. He reached over, smoothed my hair back, and kissed my forehead.

With my water broken, I decided a soak in the tub would help pass the time. I sat in the warm water chatting with Sam while Nate went to Starbucks for a coffee and some breakfast, and to give the first round of updates to our families.

By the time he returned the skin on my fingers and toes had turned to raisins, so I decided it was time to get out of the tub and walk around a bit. My labor was progressing, however slowly. We hoped changing positions and increasing my activity would speed things up. The nurses brought new gowns — I'd refused to sit naked in the tub in front of strangers — and Nate helped me change. To maintain some semblance of modesty and control, I kept on my soggy bra.

Just as I turned to leave the bathroom, a bone-splitting pain radiated through my pelvis. It felt like giant hands had grabbed my hip bones in an effort to slam them shut like the cover of a book. A cold sweat covered my forehead and I felt nauseous and faint.

"Whoa, Kim. You okay?" Nate asked with panic in his voice.

"Oh my God it hurts!" I choked as I reached for his shoulders to steady myself.

Nate and Sam helped me maneuver out of the bathroom and sat me down on the edge of the bed. My hands still on Nate's shoulders, my head hanging, my body curled around my belly as if trying to protect my baby. I had never been so scared. Nothing I'd read included anything about labor pains that felt like someone was breaking your bones.

"I need an epidural," I whispered. "Now. Please?"

"Are you sure?" Nate knew I wanted a natural birth.

"You can try walking around or sitting on an exercise ball," Sam offered. "Changing positions often brings relief."

"No, I want the pain to stop." Tears filled my eyes as the crushing pain took my breath away.

"But you wanted to try to deliver naturally," Nate reminded me.

"I did, but this is too much." Tears spilled down my cheeks and onto my chest. "I need this to stop."

I was in too much pain to care about my birthing plan.

The anesthesiologist arrived a few minutes later and administered my epidural. "Let me know if you feel any pain shoot up or down one side of your body. And if you do, try not to move."

"Okay." I tightened my grip around Nate's neck. "Ouch!" I felt a zing run down the right side of my body. The doctor backed off a bit and readjusted his equipment.

After about 15 minutes, I was blissfully pain-free and relaxing in bed. It was early afternoon. I drifted off to sleep while Nate sat in the chair next to me watching a movie on his laptop.

The nurses woke me an hour later when the doctor arrived to check on my progress.

"We're concerned that the baby's heartbeat is slowing during your contractions," she said, looking at the data captured by the monitors. "It might just be where the external monitor is placed, but we'd like to put an internal one on him just to be safe."

"You need to do what? Are you going to hurt him?" I was tired and could no longer hold the stress of the last few weeks inside. I was losing confidence, including confidence in my doctor. This just wasn't how it was all supposed to happen. I felt I was in way over my head and totally out of control.

"No, we place the monitor on the top of his head," she explained with a reassuring smile. "He'll be fine."

"Okay. How much longer before I can start pushing?" I was ready for all this to be over.

"You're about eight centimeters now, so I would guess you'll be pushing in an hour or two." She attached the fetal monitor, readjusted my blankets, and patted my numb leg. "I have another patient just getting checked in so I'll check on her and then be back to see how you're doing."

An hour later, my doctor returned. I'd progressed another centimeter but there was another complication: while the baby was positioned head down, his nose was facing up, which was not an ideal position for delivery. My doctor tried to turn him, but he just wouldn't stay facing the direction she wanted. However, she reassured me all would be fine and that the nurses would let her know when I started pushing.

I couldn't help feeling like I'd just received another cruel punch. Things just didn't seem to be going our way and I wasn't accustomed to feeling so helpless. I'd always tackled problems head on. I always had a plan. I never sat back helplessly and let things happen to me. I was the one who made things happen. I was strong, capable, in control. Now, I was completely helpless, and there wasn't a thing I could do to change the course of events. Whatever was going to happen, was going to happen regardless of my actions. It was an unfamiliar and disturbing state to be in, and all I could do was hang on for as long as it took to deliver my baby.

* * *

I pushed for over an hour and was getting increasingly more uncomfortable with every contraction. I told the nurses I could feel the contractions coming on just above my left hip. We tried changing positions and pushing through the pain, but it only got worse. I had what the nurses called a "window," which is an area of the uterus where the epidural had worn off. They called my doctor and the anesthesiologist, who increased my medication.

Time felt suspended as I focused on breathing, pushing, and recovering from each contraction. I opened my eyes and noticed it was dark outside. *How late is it?* This was taking too long. Something wasn't right.

"Please call my doctor," I sobbed to Nate and the nurses. What I didn't realize was that Stephanie had already quietly left the room and made the call.

"Here's what's happening, Kim," my doctor explained after she'd arrived and worked with me through a few pushes. "Each time you push, you're doing a great job moving the baby down the birth canal. But the umbilical cord is wrapped around his torso, just under his arms, so when you stop pushing, he's sliding back up."

Why is this happening to me? This never happened to my mom or sisters. What am I doing wrong? I was trying desperately to understand the overwhelming series of events. I was more frightened than I'd ever been. The fact that I'd done nothing wrong and, like a million other women, was having a difficult delivery, didn't occur to me. In the moment, I wanted to be the perfect woman, just like in second grade when I wanted to be the star student. I knew, intellectually, that it wasn't my fault I was having a difficult delivery, but emotionally I felt like I was defective, as if other women were entitled to have normal deliveries, but I just wasn't good enough to merit that experience.

And on top of it all, I was running a fever. Another punch.

After adding antibiotics to my IV, my doctor coached me through more pushing, her voice calm and reassuring. But eventually, her tone changed.

"I can tell you're getting tired. I think it's best if I use forceps to help him out."

I'd read a couple of articles about the damage forceps had done and cringed. I didn't want my baby to enter the world with his head clamped in a set of forceps.

"Aren't forceps dangerous? I'm not tired, I can do this. I can try harder." I pleaded. I didn't want to be weak, I didn't want to be a quitter. I had to put my baby's needs first, try to ensure he was born healthy.

"Forceps are safe when used properly and I have years of experience," my doctor said patiently. "Your baby is experiencing some signs of stress and we want you to deliver him soon. "

I looked at Nate for reassurance. He had been a trooper through the entire day. He helped support me through every push, and constantly reminded me that everything was okay and that we were at a great hospital with the best doctors. But I could see the stress was taking a toll on him. His shoulders were tense, the lines around his eyes deep set, the corners of his mouth curved down.

"Okay," I told the doctor. "I trust you."

But the forceps didn't work either. And on top of everything else, the pain from a couple hours earlier was coming back through the 'window'.

"Okay, Kim, here's the deal," the doctor said. "We need to move you into an operating room in case you need a cesarean section. I'm concerned about you and I'm concerned about your baby. I know this isn't what you wanted, but we need to keep you both safe. Okay?"

"I don't want a C-section," I said pleadingly, starting to cry. Another punch, and this was a big one. I reached for Nate and pulled him onto the bed next to me. I buried my face in his chest as he rubbed my back.

"I know you don't, Kim," he said. "But we need to do whatever it takes to keep you two safe, okay? This means we'll meet our boy soon."

I continued crying into Nate's chest, defeat flooding me. This was not the woman I wanted to be when I met our son. I wanted our son to meet a strong, capable, powerful mom. And I felt exactly the opposite.

"I'll go make sure the operating room is all set up and Sam and Stephanie will get you ready. Nate, they'll bring a gown and mask for you to wear."

A few minutes later, I was rolled into the operating room with Nate walking beside me wearing a yellow hospital gown, blue booties over his shoes, a mask over his nose and mouth, and a disposable cap over his hair.

The room was bright, cold, and full of people buzzing around. Medical equipment lined the stark white walls.

My doctor, her voice filled with authority as she talked to the O.R. staff, asked where the anesthesiologist was. I needed another dose of medication as the last epidural was already wearing off, and I had to be covered in case I needed a C-section. The anesthesiologist arrived a minute later and administered a double dose. Within two minutes, I could feel absolutely nothing from the waist down.

The day had gone nothing like I'd planned and was becoming scarier by the second. I did as the doctor and nurses instructed and pushed a few more times to no avail. The only evidence of my effort was the burning in my cheeks.

"Okay, Kim, one more push and then we need to get this baby out." My doctor sounded stern.

"Okay." I cried. And I prayed. *Dear God, please help me get this baby into the world alive and safe. Be with me now. I need you!*

I took a deep breath, closed my eyes, and pushed as hard as I could.

"Stop pushing! Stop pushing, Kim. I have him!" The relief in my doctor's voice was a shock to my exhausted system.

I'd pushed so hard, the baby came out past his shoulders. The doctor maneuvered him the rest of the way.

"You have a beautiful baby boy!"

I looked up at Nate and smiled weakly. "We have our boy. Look at him, make sure he's okay?"

All I wanted in that moment was for our baby to see one of his parents. "I can see him Kim, he's fine." Nate kissed my forehead. "The nurses are just taking him over to weigh him."

"Go with him, make sure he's okay. Please?" A new kind of panic was setting in. *Was our baby truly perfect? Had Nate counted his fingers and toes to make sure they were all there? Was he breathing normally?*

The nurses cleaned up our son, weighed and measured him. After he was tightly swaddled with a blue knit cap on his head, Nate brought him to me.

"Here's our boy," he said in a gentle tone I'd never heard before. "Seven pounds, three ounces. Twenty inches long." Nate knew these details would have a soothing effect on my shredded nerves.

I looked at our baby boy. His face was dark pink with large, dark blue eyes peering back at me. His brows knitted together in a look of great concern as his lower lip jutted out in a giant pout. I craned my neck and gave him a kiss on the forehead. "Happy birthday, buddy." My voice was hoarse.

"You can hold him," said one of the many nurses. I was shaking badly as I reached up for my baby. Nate sat on a stool next to my head and wrapped his arms around both of us.

We were now a family of three.

I was overcome with relief at surviving childbirth and delivering a healthy baby. I figured the worst *had* to be over and it was now time to focus on what came next. I had no idea there were more punches yet to come.

Chapter 4

We Have a Baby

We named our son Theo Alexander. After his eventful delivery, I had a couple minutes to hold him, while the doctor stitched me up. With that last push, I had avoided a cesarean section, but incurred a nasty third-degree tear. Thanks to the additional medication added to my epidural, however, I was blessedly numb from the waist down. It was time to settle in to my first moments as a mom. There were people to call, photos to take, breastfeeding to try.

It was after nine p.m. when we were all back in our labor and delivery suite. Nate sat in the chair beside the bed to call family. When he reached my mom, he handed me the phone.

I ached to have her at the hospital with us.

"Hi Mom," I said and instantly burst into tears. "Theo's here," was all I could manage to choke out. Everything I'd been through over the last several months, and the last twelve hours, in particular, caught up with me the moment I heard her voice.

"Oh, sweetie, are you okay?" Just the sound of my mom's voice calmed me.

"I'm fine," I lied, continuing to cry. I gave her the particulars of Theo's weight and length, my voice trailing off as I tried to gather my thoughts. I'd never felt more desperate to have my mom's love and understanding. "But he's doing good. He has some dark hair and very dark blue eyes."

"Delivery is hard work, isn't it honey? I'm glad to know everything's okay. We're looking forward to seeing you guys and meeting Theo." We chatted some more and she assured me that as soon as she and my dad got off work on Friday afternoon, they'd make the long drive to meet their grandson.

As I hung up the phone, an orderly arrived with my food. I tried to sit up and noticed I was having a hard time getting my lower body to cooperate. I was forced to push my fists into the mattress to move myself into a seated position. *That's strange, this epidural is taking its time to wear off.*

After I managed to get myself propped up, I finished half a sandwich, drank some ginger ale in an effort to settle my increasingly queasy stomach. "I'm ready to try to nurse him now," I told Amy, our new nurse. I was Theo's mom and I was ready to dive in.

"Perfect timing," she said. "Let me just get him swaddled and I'll help you get him latched on."

Nate sat on the bed next to me while Amy arranged pillows behind my lower back and under my arm. Theo wasn't initially interested in nursing but when we finally got him to latch on, I jumped. The pain was unbelievable! I had no idea nursing could hurt so much. I tried not to grimace and was determined to wait it out for as long as it took. I figured that's what good moms did. Theo needed this nourishment, and if Theo needed it, I was going to ignore the pain and deliver.

After fifteen long minutes, he finally released and I felt like I could breathe again. I handed him to Nate while I got myself situated. I tried to sit up straighter and rearrange the pillows behind my back, but I still couldn't move my legs. No matter how many times I willed my legs to move even the slightest bit, nothing happened.

I tried to bend my knees. When nothing happened, I tried to wiggle my toes — still nothing. *Bend, right leg. Come on, bend.* Nothing. It was the most surreal feeling. I was telling my legs to move and getting absolutely no response. *Okay toes, wiggle.* Still nothing. It was getting increasingly more difficult not to panic. Trusting the medication would soon wear off, I turned my focus to my new baby boy. He was absolutely perfect.

* * *

It was close to midnight when Amy returned to let us know it was time to move to the postpartum floor. "Nate, why don't you gather your things together and Kim, why don't we see if you can empty your bladder."

I tried again to move my legs, but nothing happened. "I don't think I can go yet," I told her. "I still can't feel my legs."

"They might still feel a bit numb, but just go ahead and swing your legs over the edge of the bed and I'll help you into the bathroom."

"No, you don't understand, I can't move my legs."

"Well, you did have a really big last dose of medicine in the operating room and it can sometimes take a while to wear off," mused Amy. "Let's give you a catheter so your bladder can drain and we'll get you moved upstairs."

And the punches just keep on comin'.

* * *

It took two nurses, and Nate, to get me into the wheelchair the orderly delivered. We were a mini caravan as we travelled toward our new room. A nurse pushed Theo in a bassinet, I came next in a wheelchair, followed by Nate with our bags. The halls were dimly lit and quiet. I could hear the faint beeping of monitors, the squeaking of shoes on recently mopped hallways, and the dinging of elevators as they came and went.

Nate and the nurses helped get me into my new bed, beside which Theo slept in a clear acrylic bassinet sitting atop a small wooden chest of drawers. After exchanging whispers with Amy, the two postpartum nurses disappeared into the dimly lit hallway.

Nate changed into a pair of sweats, gave me a kiss, and settled into the convertible chair that would be his bed for the night. He promptly fell asleep. I, on the other hand, lay wide awake as worry coursed through my body. I still couldn't feel anything below my belly button. I simply couldn't move, not even the slightest wiggle of a toe or flexing of a muscle. I rustled the rough hospital sheets against my bare legs and felt nothing. I poked my thighs with my index fingers. Still nothing. I pinched my right thigh so hard my fingers hurt and a welt appeared on my skin. And still felt absolutely nothing.

I lay there, listening to Nate's soft snores, and stared out the window at the empty top floor of a parking garage with hot tears streaming down my face. What was I going to do?

* * *

It was nearly two days before I could move my legs enough to maneuver myself out of bed and go to the bathroom. I had to use my arms to push myself up and then lock my knees so I wouldn't fall. It took complete focus just to do that. I visualized a taught string running from my shoulders down the front of my body to my kneecaps. Making sure not to release that image, I willed my legs to move me forward, feeling only the movement at my hip joint as first my right leg shuffled a few inches forward, followed by my left. I looked like a swollen Frankenstein's monster as I lumbered to the bathroom, sweat pooling under my arms and at my brow. I'd never worked so hard, or been so frightened, just to walk ten feet.

I finally reached the toilet and tried to calm my nerves as I tried to pull down the gigantic, disposable underwear that held my industrial-sized menstrual pad in place. I knew there was no graceful way to sit. Once I released my knees I'd fall and hope to land on the toilet seat.

Getting back up was another matter. I could have pulled the cord and summoned a nurse but, worried my continued disability would mean more nights in the hospital, I twisted myself sideways until facing the wall. Then, with both arms on the cold metal safety bar, pulled myself up to standing.

The numbness continued for another day until I was finally getting ready to go home. Then, while I was shuffling from the bed to the sink to brush my teeth, I momentarily forgot to lock my knees. They buckled, and I fell to the floor.

"Kim! Are you okay?" Nate rushed over to help me up.

"I'm fine, I'm fine. Please don't tell the nurses!" All I wanted to do was go home. I was done trying to keep it all together while feeling nearly helpless.

Since Theo's birth, I'd asked repeatedly about my inability to move, but no one gave me any real answers. I felt like everyone was blowing me off and that the anesthesiologists were more concerned about covering their butts than helping figure out what was wrong.

The day after Theo was born, a senior anesthesiologist came to my room. "You did receive a high dose of medication, Mrs. Severn," he told me. "We had to make sure you were covered in case you required a cesarean section." His defensive tone made me bristle.

"Yes, I know. But the nurses said it should have worn off last night before I was moved."

"Do you drink, Mrs. Severn?"

"What does that have to do with anything? I was pregnant. Of course I didn't drink!"

"Before you were pregnant, how quickly did alcohol impact you? I ask because your system may just be slow to metabolize medication and that's why it hasn't fully worn off yet."

"I see," feeling deeply offended by the question, "I haven't drunk in years, so I couldn't really tell you."

"Well, we could give you a CT scan to see if there's something there. But I doubt it." There was no way to miss the condescension in his voice.

"No, I'm sure I'll be fine," I lied. The thought of a CT scan was more than my frayed nerves could take. And I didn't think I had the strength to handle a diagnosis if there was one to be provided. If there was something wrong, the doctors would *tell* me I needed a test, not *ask*. Right?

* * *

Two and a half days after arriving at the hospital, we strapped Theo carefully into his car seat and the orderly wheeled us down to the car. As I slowly maneuvered myself into the passenger seat, I peered over my shoulder to watch Nate place the car seat in with a loud click.

"Did you double-check everything? And can you pull the sun shade down in case it shines in his eyes while we're driving home?"

"Yep, he's good." Nate gently patted my leg.

"Let's go home."

I rested my head against the headrest and closed my eyes. When I re-opened them, we were ten minutes from home.

"Sorry for falling asleep on you. I'm just so tired." I looked over at Nate; he looked tired, too. His shoulders were slumped forward and I could see dark circles under his eyes. His cheeks were rough with the brownish red of a three-day-old beard. Though he'd stayed pretty silent, taking his lead from me, I knew he'd been worried about both Theo and me.

I didn't know how to wrap my mind around all that had happened in the past few days. I decided to devote all my energy to settling in at home and beginning the Norman Rockwell family life that had captured my heart at the Christmas tree farm nearly a year before.

Chapter 5

Settling In

Oh crap! Panic struck the moment Nate pulled the car into our driveway. As he put the car in park, I tried to quickly figure out how I would maneuver my still enormous, and now malfunctioning, body out of the car and up three steps into the house. I could barely walk and had no idea how to negotiate stairs. Every time I bent my knees I collapsed.

"It might take me a minute; you guys go first," I said, trying to sound light.

"Need me to help you in first? Theo's sleeping, I can come back out and get him."

"No, no, please get Theo." I didn't want Nate to see me struggle. It was both embarrassing and scary. And he was so tired and stressed out, I didn't need to cause him even more concern.

Nate retrieved Theo from the backseat, car seat and all, so as not to wake him. In preparation for his arrival, we'd taken classes covering everything from breastfeeding to infant first aid to diapering. We'd read books and blogs, and received copious amounts of advice. There was only one suggestion he and I had made a pact to ignore: we would not wake our sleeping baby.

After they left, I opened the car door. *Slowly. I'll just go slowly.*

"Alright legs, work! Right leg, up and out!" I said aloud, giving my leg a pep talk. It didn't move. I felt sweat bead on my forehead.

I took a deep breath, put my hands under my thigh, and lifted my right leg out. I swiveled toward the door, then lifted my left leg out. With one hand on the back of the seat and one on the top of the open door, I braced myself, then half-pushed, half-pulled myself up. I was standing! I breathed a huge sigh of relief. Locking my knees so I didn't fall, I closed the car door. With one hand on each of our two cars, I took a few slow, stiff-legged steps forward, my eyes focused firmly on the ground as I concentrated on not falling.

"You okay, Kim?" I was so focused, I didn't hear Nate come back out. I felt my cheeks burn as a new burst of embarrassment washed over me. *How much had he seen?*

I felt alien in my body. The powerful woman who was in control of her life and destiny had disintegrated, and every time I tried to grab control back, a new part of me seemed to break. It was bad enough I was one and a half times my size, my mid-section covered in stretch marks, but now I couldn't even stand properly.

"I'm fine." I blinked hard as I concentrated on my breathing. I had to find a silver lining to focus on, I had to be strong and not allow pity and weakness to take over. *Stop whining! You know what to do — lock your knees and take slow steps. Focus on the improvement; 48 hours ago, you couldn't even stand! Just focus.*

"How can I help you?" Looking up at Nate almost broke my heart. This wasn't how our homecoming was supposed to be.

"Really, sweetie, I'm fine. It's just slow going." I gave what I hoped was a convincing smile. "If you could get the bags, that'd be great. Where did you set Theo?"

"He's still sound asleep, so I put him in the center of the dining room table."

The thought of our sleeping baby strapped into his car seat atop our dining room table made me chuckle. It seemed at the same time both absurd and totally logical.

I got stuck at the stairs. There was nothing to hold on to and I was scared to take that first step without being able to use my arms to brace myself. Nate must have continued watching because, before I knew it, he was at my side.

"Here, let me help you up the stairs at least." He took my arm in one hand and wrapped his other around my waist. "I got you."

"Are you sure? I weigh a ton and I don't want to fall and crush you."

"I got you, don't worry about it." He squeezed his arm tighter around my waist.

After a couple nervous steps, we were in the house and I was at the table checking on the still-sleeping Theo. He looked so peaceful bundled in his car seat with the blue knit cap on his head and a light blue fleece blanket tucked around him. *At least our boy is okay; things could be so much worse.*

We spent the evening relaxing in front of the TV. It felt good to be able to fall into a familiar routine; maybe that's what my body needed to find its equilibrium. With the evening news playing in the background, we both sat on the couch, eating pizza and admiring our son. I was already in love with his sweet face, his eyelids capped with long, dark, perfectly curled lashes. I leaned into Nate's strong shoulder as he wrapped his arm around me. The only thing missing was Chinook, who was still at Nate's parents' house while we settled in.

When it was time to go to bed, the panic returned.

The bedrooms were upstairs. There was no way around it — I'd have to tackle the thirteen stairs that stood between me and my bed. Luckily, the stairwell was narrow enough that I could use one arm on each wall for support. It was slow going but, bracing myself between the wall and the stair rail, I was able to make it to the top. And then it was time for the bathroom.

After locating the sanitary pads that more closely resembled adult diapers, I lumbered into the bathroom. Everything went well until I tried to stand up. I couldn't do it. The toilet was situated between the wall and the bathtub. Without something to use on both sides to push myself up, I was stuck.

"Um, Nate. I need you."

"What do you need? Are we out of toilet paper in there?"

"I can't get off the toilet." Tears of frustration and shame streamed down my face. *This is insane!* It was all too much and none of it made any sense. Nobody warned me that anything like this could happen. *What in the hell is going on?*

Nate was a total champ. He grabbed a tissue from beside the sink, wiped my tears, and helped me up off the toilet like it was the most natural thing in the world for a husband to do.

"It's going to get better," he whispered in my ear as he embraced me.

"God, I hope so."

I could tell Nate was trying to stay strong for me. I wasn't sure how he did it, but I was grateful. Meanwhile, I was trying to convince myself that within a couple days, we'd be just like any other new parents and life would return to normal. But deep down inside, I wasn't convinced.

Just as we were getting ready for bed, Theo began fussing and an increasingly familiar damp pain began to spread across my breasts. Feeding time. After I nursed and burped him and Nate changed his diaper, we settled him into his bassinet. With our baby safely swaddled just a few feet away, we collapsed into bed. I snuggled next to Nate, with the familiar smells and sounds of our home, my body relaxed for the first time in days.

Two hours later, I was woken by soft squeaks, followed by a more urgent, high-pitched cry. With Nate still snoring softly, I decided to try take care of this feeding on my own. Nate wasn't going to be around all the time and I needed to figure things out. I hoisted myself out of bed, locking my knees as I stood.

As I carried Theo to the recliner, I considered how I was going to sit. Having little other choice, I backed up to the oversized leather chair and, holding Theo close to my chest, unlocked my knees and plopped down with a thud.

Wiping the sweat from my brow, I gently rocked my newborn son as he nursed. I'd regained enough movement to move my feet up and down. Staring into the darkness, I tried to raise first one leg, then the other. Nothing. *Okay, Kim, start smaller. Just concentrate on trying to flex your thigh muscles.*

I tried to do so, but still, nothing. I could no longer control even my own legs.

Realizing I couldn't stand up while holding Theo, and too tired to figure out a solution to this latest problem, I reclined the chair as far back as it would go and, with my son nestled between my chest and arm, I fell asleep, wondering if I my body would ever work normally again.

Chapter 6

Motherhood

"You have everything you need?" Nate slid his laptop into his backpack.

"Yep, we'll be fine. We'll just hang out, maybe watch a movie." I wasn't quite sure what to expect over the next few hours.

"Okay. Remember, you can call Jodie if you need anything." Jodie was our next-door neighbor and one of my best friends.

"I know." I didn't know why I felt irritated by his suggestion. *He's just trying to make sure you're okay,* I reminded myself. I'd been experiencing a seesaw of emotions over the prior few days. I wanted to be fiercely independent and in control but between my legs not working and my body healing from the delivery, the simplest tasks were a burden. Just going to the bathroom was an enormous pain. I couldn't move very fast so I had to plan in advance because, on top of everything else, I had near zero bladder control. Once, I'd waited too long and all I can say is, *thank God for those gigantic sanitary napkins.* I constantly felt disgusted with myself and my new constant companion, embarrassment.

"You better get going. We'll be *fine!*"

"Love you guys." Nate gave Theo a kiss on the forehead and me a peck on the lips. "See you around eight." A few months earlier, Nate had stopped working and enrolled in an evening degree program to earn his teaching certificate and he was off to class.

I wish I was the one getting out of here, I thought as I waved to Nate, jealous he got to escape the house for a few hours. I wasn't just stuck in the house; I spent most of my time upstairs. Not having to navigate the stairs made things easier, but I was feeling increasingly isolated, bored, and frustrated.

* * *

The first months of Theo's life were extraordinarily difficult. I was so tired, I felt nauseous. He slept only when I was awake; the longest stretch I could get from him at night was a couple hours. And on top of it all, my legs still didn't work.

The doctors had finally conceded that something was indeed wrong with them. The final, double-dose epidural had put pressure on the nerves in my lower back, which controlled my legs. As a result, I had femoral neuropathy, a fancy-sounding name for legs that I couldn't feel and wouldn't reliably work. The treatment was twice weekly physical therapy to retrain my nerves to fire and build up strength in my legs.

Gradually, I became steadier on my legs, but I was slow and worried constantly I'd fall or get myself into a position I couldn't get myself out of. The weather didn't help much, either; it was rainy, cold, and dark by dinner time.

While pregnant, I'd envisioned spending hours gazing lovingly at my beautiful baby, breathing in the sweet smell of his freshly bathed skin, and listening to his soft coos. I pictured myself carrying him around in a front-pack as we got things done around the house or strapping him into his stroller for long walks through the neighborhood. While he napped, I'd work on his baby book, read, maybe take up knitting. Instead, I didn't know what to do with myself. I'd sit on the couch for hours holding Theo, waiting until he needed something – a diaper change, a feeding, a little entertainment.

I'd long stopped trying to get any projects done; it was just too hard. I felt out of control and feared I didn't even know who I was anymore.

I was also growing increasingly resentful toward Nate. His body still worked, he slept through Theo's cries at night, he got to escape and be around other adults every day. I began to hate him as much as I hated myself. And I hated that I felt that way. Why should Nate have to hurt like I was hurting? Wasn't it a blessing only one of us was falling apart? Shouldn't I just be grateful our son was happy and healthy?

Feelings of failure began to wash over me like waves; as the days went by, the waves would come in faster and stronger until there was no reprieve. My only break from the constant pounding of surf was the few hours' sleep I managed to grab in the middle of the night.

I needed to shake myself out of the funk I was being submerged beneath. Perhaps it was just a reaction to my isolation. I decided what I needed was an outing.

"Nate, Theo's one-month check-up is Thursday morning. Why don't we stop for lunch somewhere afterwards?" It wouldn't be a big trip, but it would be something — a chance to see other people, enjoy a change of scenery, show off our son.

"What time's his appointment?" I could tell by the edge in Nate's voice he was trying to find a hole in my plan.

"10:30. We could stop by Red Robin for burgers on the way home. Nothing fancy."

"I need to get my paper done Thursday before class."

"Or we could stop at Taco Time. That'd be fast; we'd be home by 12:30."

There was no convincing Nate to take time off for lunch; he wanted to come straight home and get his homework done — and not risk having to deal with a crying baby in public. My resentment and despair deepened. *This is not what I signed up for.* I loved our son, but I missed being around other adults, I missed my work, and I missed my slender, physically capable body.

* * *

One afternoon at the end of November, I decided to venture out to the mall. Surely the holiday decorations, festive music, and some retail therapy would brighten my mood? I was nervous, so not wanting to be dissuaded I kept my plan to myself.

After Nate left for school, I strapped Theo in his car seat and we hit the road. As luck would have it, there was an open parking spot directly across from the mall entrance. *This is a sign!* I loaded Theo into his stroller and headed inside. It felt great to be out of the house. I was excited to be surrounded by people and part of the real world for the first time in what felt like an eternity. The attention Theo received was a salve for my aching soul. For a few hours, I wasn't broken; I was simply a new mom to a beautiful baby.

"How old is your son?" the saleswoman at the fragrance counter asked.

"He'll be six weeks on Tuesday." My heart swelled with pride.

"Oh, look at those big, dark eyes!" said a woman with a soft voice and shimmering silver hair.

"Thanks so much!"

He's been a dream, I thought, after wandering around for an hour, *I should do this every day*. The thought was quickly followed by, *He's been asleep for an awfully long time. What if he freaks out on the way home?*

That was me, unable to find contentment for longer than an hour at a time, constantly on the lookout for another shoe to drop and pound me further into the ground. I had thought that having a family would make me feel calm and content. Instead it was filling me with anxiety every minute of the day. *What was wrong with me?*

Theo and I made it home that night without a meltdown from either of us. And once it was over, I felt a dash of pride at what I had accomplished. I'd gone out into the world with my newborn son and returned. Baby steps.

It was the first of several outings that got more manageable as the weeks passed. I only hoped life would get appreciably easier by the time I returned to work after the holidays.

Balancing a full-time job and motherhood was a challenge I had to be ready for. I didn't have a choice. Still, I doubted my body and mind were up to the challenge.

I'd lost myself over the past year and I didn't know whether I'd be able to find myself again. Would I have the strength to hide my struggles? Would I be physically able to meet the demands of my long commute? Would I be fit to address problems and find solutions like my career demanded? As I lay awake at night, my body on high alert for sounds from Theo's nursery, all my mind would tell me was, no, no and no!

Chapter 7

Back to Work

"Ugh, *seriously?*" I said loud enough to wake the dead. I rolled over and looked at the clock, 5:12 a.m. I secretly hoped my audible disgust would wake Nate and he'd go get our son, but he continued to sleep soundly. Sighing loudly, I rolled myself out of bed. *At least I'm starting to get around easier,* I thought. *I'm supposed to be happy today,* I reminded myself, *its Theo's first Thanksgiving.*

Theo's cries grew louder and more insistent. It was going to be a long day. With an average of four hours sleep a night, I moved through our holiday preparations like a zombie. I wanted our first Thanksgiving and Christmas to be extra special. I yearned for the joy of the holidays to warm my increasingly chilled spirits.

With Theo fed and dressed, we settled in to watch the *Today Show,* followed by the *Macy's Thanksgiving Day Parade.* I smiled as I remembered spending Thanksgiving morning as a kid laying on the living room floor watching the parade while my mom was busy preparing the turkey and pies for dessert. I looked down at Theo as he slept soundly in my arms and hoped he would grow up loving the parade as much as I did.

This was my chance to create a lifetime of happy holiday memories for our family.

* * *

As I stood at the bathroom sink brushing my teeth on Christmas morning, I thought back to that day at the Christmas tree farm. It had been a little over a year since I first felt something was missing in our holiday celebrations, that there was a hole in my life only a baby could fill. It had only been a year, but it seemed like a lifetime ago. The woman who stared back at me in the mirror was a stranger.

There'd been so many dark, lonely days in the few months since Theo's birth, I was desperate for this one to be filled with light, laughter, and hope. Like a poker player going all-in in a desperate attempt to break a losing streak, I had everything riding on this day. I needed to prove we'd made the right decision and that all the struggles of the past year had been worth it.

I sat with Theo propped up against my stomach as we opened the gifts piled beneath the tree. Theo, who got the most, had no idea what was going on, and sat happily staring at the twinkling lights.

We'd forgone our trip to the Christmas tree farm. The weather had been ugly and we were loath to take Theo out in the cold, wind and rain, so we settled for the most realistic artificial tree we could find. One thing I wasn't willing to compromise on, however, was our first Christmas photo. I wanted the perfect picture of the three of us in front of the tree, so we could begin our own set of Norm Rockwell-esque memories.

* * *

After a quiet New Year's spent watching college football games, it was time to return to work. I was still carrying the majority of the seventy pounds I'd gained during my pregnancy so I left Theo with Nate and went to the mall. I was crushed to find that my once size-eight body was now a 14/16.

Surrounded by a pile of discarded clothes, I slumped to the fitting room floor and gave in to the despair and self-pity that had been building for months. I let the big, hot tears run down my face and land on my swollen breasts, now the size of large cantaloupes sitting atop what resembled a sad, partially deflated beach ball. I stared at my reflection in the full-length mirror, once again mystified by the unfamiliar woman staring back at me. The disconnect between how I felt on the inside and how I looked on the outside was overwhelming and confusing. Another example of something broken I couldn't figure out how to fix.

* * *

My alarm went off at six. I'd set it as a precaution, since Theo normally woke at five for his first feeding. *Wow! He actually slept four hours in a row! Maybe he knows today's a big day for me.*

As the steaming hot water ran over my head and down my back, I took long deep breaths, trying to energize myself for my first day back at work in three months. Rinsing the shampoo from my hair, I heard the first rustlings from Theo's room. My heart raced as adrenaline coursed through my veins; my breasts ached as my milk let down. I took another long, slow breath to calm my racing heart. *Three months and my body still panics whenever I hear that cry.*

My hair wrapped in a towel, I retrieved Theo from his crib.

"Good morning sweet boy," I said, covering his cheeks with kisses. "Thanks for letting me sleep in this morning." I changed his diaper, nursed and coaxed tiny burps from his belly. I loved the feeling of his soft hair against my neck as I gently patted his back.

I carried him into our room to wake Nate so I could finish getting ready. Standing over our bed, a now all too familiar wave of jealousy rushed over me. I hadn't had a peaceful night's sleep in months and yearned for it like an addict yearns for one more hit. I took a deep breath and forced a smile on my face.

"Hey babe, it's time to get up. I gotta get ready to go."

"Uh, what time is it?"

"A quarter to seven; I have to go soon or I'll miss the train."

"Okay, I'm up, I'm up."

"Theo's changed, fed and burped."

"Why don't you try to put him down again? It's still early."

"He's not tired, babe; it's almost seven. You need to get up and take him. I gotta go!" The last thing I needed today was to miss my train!

"Okay. Let me just get some sweats on. I'll meet you downstairs." Nate's voice had an edge as he walked into the bathroom and closed the door.

Tears welled up in my eyes. *Why is he giving me attitude? Doesn't he understand what I have to try to do today?*

I needed Nate to step up. I was putting my needs last at every turn and I needed him to put my needs first just this one morning.

"Let's make Mommy's coffee while Daddy gets dressed. Okay, buddy?" I said to Theo as I quickly pulled my hair into a low bun, then carried him down the stairs and into the kitchen. I'd taken to talking him through everything I did; I'd read that it helped kids with language and connection. It also helped me feel connected to the world too.

"Let's use the new travel mug you and Daddy got me for Christmas."

One handed, I got my briefcase ready to go and double checked I had everything I needed to pump breast milk. Satisfied I was ready, I grabbed my coat, poured my coffee, and handed Theo off to a still sleepy Nate before heading out the door.

You can do this! You can do this! I repeated the mantra over and over as I drove to the train station with a lump in my throat.

* * *

My desk was just as I'd left it three and a half months prior. I hung up my coat and wandered down to the IT department to find someone to reset my password. Too much time away and too little sleep had erased all recollection of it.

Throughout the morning, people stopped by to welcome me back, ask about Theo, and look at the pictures I had in a small album I had created. I scanned through e-mail after e-mail, all documenting decisions that had been made while I was away. One in particular caught my attention. As I read it, I became increasingly concerned about the direction things had taken. The logic presented was sound, but it lacked the reality of the lessons learned from two previous projects.

For weeks before returning to work I had worried about how I would learn to balance being a mother, wife, and career woman. Back only a few hours I began to wonder if I'd made the right decision in coming back to work. *Where would I find the energy to address the issues I foresaw — on only four hours' interrupted sleep a night? Where would I find the patience for the difficult conversations that were certain to come? Where would I find the motivation to fight for what I believed was right?*

Despite my relative youth, I'd risen through the ranks quickly, and had one phenomenally successful project under my belt. Before my leave, the success of that project had buoyed my confidence. Now that I was back, I felt unrelenting pressure — I'd set the bar high and feared I wouldn't be able to achieve it again.

As the days went by, I found it increasingly difficult to manage everything, from rising early in the mornings, to pumping three times a day at work, to making dinner and caring for Theo until Nate got home from school at night.

I wanted to feel like the confident, intelligent, pulled together person I was before my pregnancy. Instead, I felt dumpy in my ill-fitting clothes as I struggled to put together a logical argument to fight for what my projects needed. I was emotional, exhausted, and easily distracted.

I still hadn't admitted to myself, or anyone else, that I was depressed. The thought had occurred to me, many times, but admitting it would have amounted to admitting yet another failure. To me, the fact that I wasn't brimming with joy could only mean one thing: I was doing something wrong. I thought if I only tried harder, was more focused, less selfish, everything would be okay.

* * *

Months passed and we all limped along. Theo got bigger, smiled more and began to interact with us in increasingly dynamic ways. We formed new routines that helped us get through the days. After work, to brighten my mood and energize my body, I'd sing Theo the baby songs my mom used to sing my younger siblings. When I couldn't remember the words, I just made them up.

When Theo was crying or crabby, I sang to him. And to my delight, I found it helped us both. In an exhaustion induced bout of silliness, I made up what came to be called the "What's a Matta You?" song, which I sung like an elderly Italian man spinning dough in a pizza shop. It went like this:

What's a matta you?

Oh, what's a matta you?

I want to know, what's a matta you.

Theo is great, Theo is fun.

We are so very glad, you're our son.

What's a matta you?

Oh, what's a matta you?

I want to know, what's a matta you.

Theo is strong, Theo is loud

He makes us so very proud.

Ohhhhhh, what's a matta youuuuuuuu ….

It was just a silly thing, but it seemed to make the tears go away a little quicker, for both of us.

* * *

By late spring, I'd dropped about half the baby weight. I'd even found the energy to squeeze in 30 minutes of exercise several days a week, though I could never manage to maintain a regular routine. By August, when Theo was ten months old, I'd finally lost most of the weight. And I'd almost made peace with the fact that I'd never get my pre-pregnancy body back. My figure was just different: my waist was thicker, much of my mid-section covered with stretch marks and my once full breasts more like helium balloons the morning after a party — slightly shriveled and fallen to the floor.

At work, things had also turned a corner. After a great deal of effort, my projects were on firmer footing and I felt more than a passing glimmer of hope that I could deliver successfully on all of them. I felt less like a fraud, a lucky one-hit wonder, and more like a professional who knew what she was doing.

I didn't know if it was the additional hours of sunlight, the final rebalancing of hormones or sheer force of will, but things felt like they were beginning to fall into a semblance of order. A sense of security and control, missing for nearly two years, began to return.

On a sunny Saturday morning nearing Theo's first birthday, I bundled him into the car and headed off to the mall. It was time to treat my new body to properly fitting clothes. As Theo played quietly in his stroller, I tried on a new pair of pants. The size ten glided right over my hips and zipped up, even as I exhaled. I smiled and turned to look at myself in the mirror. Catching Theo's eye, I smiled and said, "Well buddy, this is your mom. Not bad, huh?"

It had been a crazy couple of years, but together the three of us had figured it out. I wasn't sure what was up ahead for us, but I was beginning to feel like I was once again strong enough to handle it.

Chapter 8

Career Woman & Mom

It was our second Christmas Eve night as a family. We'd celebrated at Nate's parents' house, arriving home just after nine. Theo, 14 months, was on the second day of a fever of 101. Nate and I worked together to get him into his red fleece Santa pajamas. He looked so cute, his cheeks flushed a bright crimson, his coffee-colored eyes sparkling in the light, his nose, reddened from the constant wiping, reminiscent of Rudolph.

"Poor little buddy," I soothed as I carried him into the kitchen, where Nate stood at the counter with a bottle of Tylenol, using what looked like a big syringe to suck the red liquid out of the bottle. The pharmacist recommended using it to ensure Theo got exactly the right dose. After filling it, Nate tipped the syringe upside down, open end facing the ceiling, to get the air out so he didn't shoot the medicine into Theo's mouth too fast and make him gag. We'd already made that mistake. But the plunger wouldn't budge. A few seconds — and a little more pressure — later, Nate got the plunger unstuck and the medicine shot up into the air, splattering the ceiling and raining down on all three of us, covering us in sticky red goo.

"Well, aren't we festive?" Nate deadpanned, and we both dissolved into fits of laughter. To this day, I have no idea how one teaspoon of medicine could make such a huge, sticky mess. It was everywhere!

Theo looked back and forth from one to the other of us, as if thinking, *"Yep, they've lost it. I thought I had at least a few more good years with them. But they've cracked."*

"Well, looks like it's working now," Nate said through tears of laughter.

"Yep, guess so. I'll get our boy cleaned up while you ready another dose." I walked out of the kitchen still laughing and shaking my head. A drop of Tylenol dripped from my bangs onto my cheek. "Guess we need to clean Mommy up, too, huh buddy?"

That beautifully imperfect moment was the highlight of our holiday — it made it richer, not ruined. I realized I was beginning to roll with life's punches rather than constantly trying to battle against them and make everything perfect. Life, I'd learned, had always been a balancing act, there was just more to balance now.

The gulf between pre- and post-baby Kim had finally narrowed. For months, I'd awoken to the feeling of heavy curtains hanging around me, blocking the light that might brighten my mood. Though still constantly exhausted, I was now waking to glimmers of brightness on more mornings than not.

Before my pregnancy, I had prided myself on my ability to always anticipate what needed to happen next. I was quick on my toes and always ready to respond when something wasn't headed in the right direction. As my body slowed during pregnancy, however, my physical and mental agility did too. As a sleep-deprived mother of a newborn, it took all my concentration just to do basic tasks like holding my baby in one arm and pouring a glass of water with the other. Nothing came like second nature as it had before.

With time, I slowly regained my ability to navigate my day and manage everything that fought for my attention. The puzzle pieces of my new life began to fit together as I figured out how people related to me not just as a career woman *or* a mother, but as a career woman *and* a mother.

Before Theo, I was the first to volunteer for overtime at work or for a community event on the weekend. After returning to work, it took a few months before people stopped swinging by my desk to inquire why they hadn't seen my name on the volunteer sign-up sheet. At first, I'd apologized and explained that I didn't have the same flexibility I had before Theo. Eventually, I stopped apologizing and simply said I wasn't available. I had done my time in the years prior to my son's arrival so my coworkers with kids could enjoy time with their families. It was my turn now.

I began to understand personal success demanded that I respect myself as a mom and a career woman at all times. There was never a moment when I was completely one *or* the other.

I was closing in on 18 months of motherhood. I was regaining my professional confidence. And I was hitting my stride as a mom. I was learning, growing, and changing along with my son. Each day was a little less scary and a lot more fun. But I had no way of knowing how much I would need my newfound wisdom to survive the surprises life had in store for our family.

—

Chapter 9

An Unexpected Feeling

I slammed on my brakes nearly missing the rear bumper of the car in front of me. "Whoa!" I yelped as I looked in my rearview mirror to see if the driver behind me was as surprised by the sudden stop as I had been. A thick mist fell onto my windshield blurring my view of the cars around me as we crawled along the interstate. As the last of the adrenaline passed, I realized I had been distracted by thoughts of having another baby. One hand on the wheel, the other had been rubbing the spot on my belly where Theo used to press his little foot against my hand.

More and more often during my commute, I had found myself wondering what life would be like with another baby. I wasn't sure I was ready, I didn't even know if I wanted another child, but the idea continued to interrupt my thoughts with increasing frequency.

Theo was a healthy, cantankerous, over-achieving toddler who had needed only 18 months to hit the terrible twos. He was equal parts charmer and tyrant. We'd have a marvelous time running around outside, pushing cars around the living room floor, snuggling in his rocking chair with a book before bedtime. And there were also the times he'd manage to make me want to throw myself down on the ground, kicking and screaming with frustration as he battled us for control and the freedom to rain down his special blend of toddler chaos and terror. Luckily, the fun and cuddles outnumbered the temper tantrums many to one.

I was in my early thirties, so if we were going to have another baby, we needed to do it soon. I knew that many pregnancy-related risks increased after 35 and given how my first one went, I wanted to avoid as many incremental risks as possible. I was ready to try again.

I finally decided to broach the subject with Nate during a rare night out alone.

"It's nice to be out, just the two of us." I smiled at Nate before taking a bite of my salad. "I kinda miss our boy already. I just can't believe how big he's getting. No baby left for us."

"Nope, no baby left. Just gotta get the kid toilet trained and we'll be set."

"I kinda miss the baby phase, though. A little crazy, huh?" I raised an eyebrow at him and noticed that, though there was still a smile on his lips, there was no trace of it in his eyes. Not a good sign.

"Um, yes, that *is* a little crazy." His voice was serious and he'd placed his fork on the side of his plate. Definitely not a good sign.

"I've just been thinking a lot about a second child." I wanted an opportunity to explain myself before being shut down. "Theo will be three soon, and I don't know if I want him to be an only child."

"Kim, things are finally getting easier. He's sleeping through the night, he can tell us what he wants, he's almost out of diapers." There was an edge to his voice, and his jaw muscles twitched.

"I know, Nate. It's not necessarily logical. I just keep thinking about it. A lot." If I'd been on the fence before, I wasn't anymore. I dug in my heels. "I really want another baby."

"Kim...."

I interrupted before Nate could continue. "Stop using my name, *Nate*. You only do that when you're trying to shut me up. I don't appreciate it. I'm trying to have an open conversation." Although, in fairness, I knew I was no longer open to the idea of *not* having a second child. I was now in convincing mode.

Nate took a deep breath. "Don't you remember your pregnancy, Theo's delivery, and everything that happened afterwards? You really want that again?" He looked down at his plate and used his fork to push a piece of lettuce from one side to the other.

"Are you *kidding* me? You think I could forget?" I stopped myself; an argument was not what I wanted. I took a long, deep breath and held my hands up asking for a truce. "I'm sorry. Listen, I'm surprised by these feelings, but they just aren't going away. The doctor said second pregnancies are usually easier. And my legs... that was a freak thing. Super rare." The last part was as much to convince myself as Nate.

"Uh-huh."

"This is really important to me." I nearly whispered and decided to leave it at that. I knew it was better to stop before I ruined more than our evening out.

I thought back to what he'd said about not wanting kids during our pre-marital counseling. There was a part of me that felt guilty and manipulative for trying to talk him into having a second child. But I wanted two kids so badly, and he loved Theo so much. . .

We had a few more conversations over the following weeks and Nate eventually gave in. The issue having finally been settled, I set about enjoying our family of three even more thinking we'd soon be a family of four.

Months passed and I didn't get pregnant. I began to worry and wonder what we were doing wrong. It had only taken two months with Theo. At six months, I scheduled an appointment with my obstetrician.

"Hi Kim, nice to see you. How're you doing?" My doctor leaned against the counter in the examination room.

"I'm doing well, thanks."

"What can I do for you today?" She glanced over my chart. "How's your son doing?"

"Theo's doing great. He's three and pretty amazing."

"About time for number two?" She had a twinkle in her eye.

"Actually, that's why I'm here. Nate and I've been trying for over six months with no luck. I'm not sure what's going on."

"How quickly did you get pregnant the first time?"

"It only took two months."

"Well, we can take a look and do some tests. But don't worry, it's still early."

Everything checked out as perfectly normal and I was told to 'keep doing what you're doing' for a few more months. I was frustrated but figured sometimes things just take time.

* * *

Another month passed. I kept myself busy at work, and busy at home, confident that it wouldn't be long before I was pregnant again. Then in an instant, everything changed. I was just sitting in my car, waiting for the light to change when another car slammed into me. It was a minor accident, but enough to rupture three discs in my lower back. Once again, I was back in physical therapy. And once again, I began to heal. And once again, shit happened.

I was transferred to a new project with an incredibly tough client. Both the client and the project were high profile, and I would be one of only two senior program managers overseeing the largest development project our company had in the western United States. It was a tremendous opportunity—but also a tremendous amount of work, and my commute time doubled. I had to work long hours, often ten-hour days with two hours in traffic and work to take home. I was under constant stress. But I persevered, certain that I would get through it.

Then, one afternoon, I was sitting on our front lawn, taking a rare break to play with Theo, when a neighbor came by to say hello. As I stood up to greet her, I felt something pop in my back. I nearly fell over, the pain was so intense. The just-healed discs had ruptured again.

A week later, I sat in the doctor's office, discussing the results of my MRI.

"Wow, you have quite a history, Kim." He was young, only a few years older than me. Tall and slim, with thinning brown hair, he was kind and a good listener. We'd spent twenty minutes talking about what had happened to my legs during Theo's delivery and my current back injury. "We have a few options to consider."

After talking through my choices, I decided to opt for physical therapy again. I was wary of too much medical intervention, and physical therapy had already worked once.

"I have one more question," I said tentatively. "My husband and I are trying for a second child. Will this injury impact that?"

"Well, there's a possibility the discs will heal quickly, and if you keep your core strong, you'll probably be okay. But if the discs rupture again during your pregnancy, you'll have few treatment choices and you could be left in quite a bit of discomfort."

"I see." Frankly, I was no longer ready to get pregnant again. My body just hurt too much.

* * *

Eight months of physical therapy and two rounds of steroid injections later, the three ruptured discs hadn't healed. So, five days before Theo's birthday, I underwent a micro-discectomy, a procedure that would remove the portions of the discs that were putting pressure on the nerves in my back. With back surgery successfully behind me, I felt ready to begin trying to get pregnant again. I met with my OB to talk about our options. She suggested hormone therapy.

The last year had taken a physical and mental toll on both Nate and me. Between my new job and back injury, I was constantly exhausted and stressed out, and the hormones didn't work. They only made me short-tempered. I'd do my best to care for Theo after work and on the weekends, but there were days when all I could do was lay on the couch and watch TV or play Lego Star Wars with him on the Xbox.

With my OB's recommendations in hand, I met again with my back surgeon to discuss the risks of pregnancy to my body. Armed with information, and Theo playing at his grandma's house, Nate and I had time alone to talk things over.

"This year has pretty much sucked." I looked at Nate across our dining room table. "I mean, seriously, it's not at all how I planned it."

"I know it's been tough, babe. But there were good things, too." He gave me a half smile.

"Nope, it sucked," I said not willing to expend any energy putting lipstick on the proverbial pig.

"Yep, it sucked," he agreed.

"I've been thinking about our inability to get pregnant." I paused, watching for a reaction. To my surprise, he stayed relaxed and leaned back in his chair. "After talking to my doctors, I think it's best if we just stop trying."

"What do you mean, stop trying?"

"Admit it, I'm a bitch when I'm on the hormones and they haven't worked anyway. And Dr. Givens thinks it's probably best I don't put my body through another pregnancy. It would be pretty risky for my back."

"Okay..."

"I just don't think it's gonna happen, babe." Tears streamed down my face as the reality of what I was saying hit me. I knew once we had this conversation the chance of another pregnancy was as good as gone.

One of the things that got me through the tough days following Theo's birth was the idea that I'd have another chance to have the pregnancy and delivery I'd dreamed of. I yearned for a second chance to make it right. Forfeiting that dream was devastating.

It was frustrating to have so much go right in life, to catch so many lucky breaks, to create so many opportunities. Then, when it came to the one thing my body was supposedly built for, I couldn't do it right. And then, when I wanted to try again, I couldn't do it at all. It wouldn't happen. I felt defeated, inadequate, and tremendously sad.

As the year drew to a close, Nate and I put the subject of a second child to bed. I was trying to understand everything that had happened over the past year, and what it meant for my future and for the future of our family. Although he had been willing to try for another, the truth was that Nate was content with our family of three, just as it was. But I felt very alone.

None of my friends had struggled with infertility and getting pregnant had never been a problem for any of the women in my family. I knew of women who'd struggled to have a first child, but I'd never heard of someone who'd conceived once having to struggle the second time. I wasn't sure what to do or who to talk to.

I just wanted to stop feeling sad. The only way I could think to counteract the sadness was to take action. First, I needed to figure out if I could I be happy with our family of three or if my happiness depended on becoming a family of four. In order to find peace, I had to find a way to decide.

Chapter 10

One Decision Leads to Another

'Vroom, Vroom, Screetch!" Theo roared as he raced cars around the living room floor. I hopped over invisible race tracks while I finished organizing his toys, trying to make room for his Christmas haul. I like to start the new year with the house clean and organized.

Since my postpartum depression had lifted, I'd noticed a new richness to life. I was able to find joy in smaller moments. I often glimpsed the world from Theo's perspective, as he learned to navigate through it. And I experienced an intensity of both happiness and sorrow as we celebrated his accomplishments and kissed away the pain of everything from hurt feelings to scraped knees. It had taken time, but I felt the love and comfort for my life that I'd envisioned when we decided to have a baby. The daily sacrifices of motherhood helped me remember to be thankful for the good times and that the tough spells don't last forever.

And at some point, without noticing, I'd felt a growing void, an emptiness in my heart. I'd spent hours trying to make sense of what I was feeling. Then, like a light turned on in a dark room, I saw it, or, rather, I felt it — the yearning to have another baby.

But all of that was months before and we'd travelled unsuccessfully down that path. Why did organizing Theo's toys bring on a wave of regret? The connection was simple. While I organized the living room to make room for the new toys, puzzles, and books Theo had received for Christmas, I had slowly filled a box with the ones he had outgrown. Theo wasn't a baby, or even really a toddler anymore. He was a little boy. How is it possible that your heart can be both overflowing with love and broken by the same person, all at once?

I put down the stack of books I was organizing and sat down next to Theo on the floor. We began racing cars in increasingly larger paths around the living room furniture, giggling as we bumped into each other and I pretended to crash into the couch.

A few minutes later I had made my decision. We would have a second child and adoption was the answer.

* * *

With my decision made, I began formulating a plan. Nate and I had never talked about adoption and I felt it was important to do some research before even bringing it up with him. I wasn't sure how he had interpreted my decision to give up trying to have another baby. Did he realize I was still thinking about another child? Did he consider the conversation closed? Would he be open to adoption?

Tensions were high between us. The past twelve months had been stressful what with my new job, my back surgery and Nate's graduation from college. He hadn't enjoyed substitute teaching and wasn't working full-time and with Theo still in daycare, finances were tight. Neither of us was doing a good job communicating, especially around emotionally charged topics related to family.

I started my research with a checklist. As a project manager, this is how I approached all new projects, and it was the easiest way to manage my emotions. The disappointment surrounding my first pregnancy and the failure of having a second was still raw. I'd managed to bundle up my feelings and tuck them in the back of my mind, although just one Johnson & Johnson commercial was all it took for the hurt and sadness to come tumbling forward. Treating adoption as a research project helped me manage the regret, disappointment, and fear that threatened to overwhelm me whenever I thought about moving forward with it.

My checklist, written in a spiral notebook, included: type of adoption, cost, application process, timeline and additional decisions to be made. If we moved forward, I figured the first decision was domestic versus international. Until I understood more about the different types of adoption, I couldn't begin to research agencies and, until I chose an agency, it would be hard to determine expenses and timelines.

Without a better idea of where to begin, I Googled "adoption." My search generated millions of results. The Internet, like many things, can be both a blessing and a curse. I was instantly overwhelmed. As I scanned through pages and pages of links, I discovered it wasn't just a matter of international or domestic adoptions, but also public or private. There were adoptions for newborns, infants, and older children. I'd never even heard of "foster to adopt," whereby a child first joins a family through the foster care system and is then adopted. For foster care, we could contact the state or one of several local agencies. For adoption, we could use an attorney, a non-profit, or a for-profit agency. If we chose a domestic adoption, we'd need to familiarize ourselves with applicable laws in each state. In our own state, I discovered the rules differed depending on what county the child resides in and where the adoption is finalized. *This is all too much! Where is the page with the definitive Starter's Guide?*

I wasn't prepared for the level of complexity I immediately uncovered. I couldn't even figure out how to organize what quickly became a complicated set of terms and concepts, benefits and risks.

Not wanting to be a quitter, I continued researching every night after work, but would quickly get overwhelmed by the abundance of information and flood of emotions. Resisting being pulled behind a new curtain of darkness was more challenging because I was often exhausted after a long work day, followed by an evening of entertaining a busy preschooler. Once Theo was in bed and I sat down in front of my computer, I struggled to find the energy to turn up the volume on soothing, positive thoughts. Instead, the negative voices would blend together in a cacophony of doom, rushing toward me like a river bursting through a dam. All at once, the swirling waters of sadness, frustration, anger and disappointment threatened to pull me under.

Shutting my eyes, I'd lay my hands on my belly and feel it rise and fall as I took long, deep breaths in an attempt to slow my racing heart. *You're going to be okay. You're a strong, capable woman and a loving mother. You're smart and resourceful, you'll figure this out.* I silently repeated this mantra for as long as it took to feel calm again.

After a couple weeks, I decided I needed to take a step back. Jumping into the raging river of emotions headfirst and trying to swim upstream wasn't going to work for much longer. It had nothing to do with being strong enough; I needed to work smarter. There was just too much information out there and I felt too fragile.

One evening, with Nate out and Theo tucked in for the night, I sat down on the couch, turned off the TV, and sat quietly with my eyes closed. After a couple minutes, I realized I was giving myself a silent pep talk. *You can figure this out. You're an intelligent woman. You want this and where there's a will, there's a way.* I took several deep breaths and noticed I was smiling. "It's going to be okay," I said aloud to Chinook, who'd wandered over and placed his head on my lap. "Let's start with what we know."

I wrote a list of people I knew who had experience with adoption. When I was in high school, a couple at our church had adopted three kids from different countries. I hadn't talked to them in at least twenty years, so they were out as a potential resource, but they were a happy family. I figured that was a point for international adoption. Also, our neighbors had a school age child they'd adopted from Guatemala. They were a lovely family and their son was an intelligent and kind boy. Another point for international adoption. On the negative side, I didn't like the idea of having to choose a country and all the unknowns that came with it, from changing governmental policies, to language barriers, to the extended time away from home. Travelling to a foreign country at such a stressful and emotionally charged time frightened me. A couple points against international adoption.

Then I remembered my sister telling me about a childhood friend who, when Theo was a few months old, had chosen an open adoption for the baby she had conceived. *Why didn't I think of her earlier?* Stuck in the midst of postpartum depression, I'd felt a lot of compassion for what I imagined my old acquaintance was experiencing. I had hoped she found comfort in knowing that the baby was with a couple she'd had the opportunity to meet. I didn't know much about the details, but I did know that in the three years since her baby was born, the adoptive parents had kept in touch, and that her relationship with them and the baby was good. Score one for open adoption.

As I thought more about that story, I became increasingly interested in open adoption. I knew I could easily find out what agency she had used, which would kill two birds with one stone — choosing the type of adoption and an agency, all at once. The more I thought about it, the more sense it made, until finally I decided to take a leap of faith and talk to Nate. If he agreed to consider adoption, I'd ask my mom to find out more, since our families had remained in touch.

"I think I know where to begin!" I said to Chinook, who was now soundly asleep on the couch next to me. I flipped on the TV to relax and distract myself before heading to bed. An hour or so later, as I brushed my teeth, I felt excited for the possible path I'd cleared for us. Even though I wanted to wait up and talk with Nate that night, I knew it was best to wait until the weekend.

During my lunch break the next day, with my curiosity getting the better of me, I sleuthed online for the adoption agency my friend had used. I figured there couldn't be that many agencies in my hometown. It only took a couple of clicks to find what I assumed was the right one. The website had information about the agency, their services, and testimonials from both birthmothers and adoptive families. It didn't answer all my questions, but it answered some. And I now had a number to call for information. Most reassuring of all was that, unlike all the other agencies and attorneys I'd researched, I knew someone who had worked with this one.

* * *

The rest of the work week dragged on as I tried, unsuccessfully, to think of anything other than adoption. Unable to wait any longer, I decided to create an opening over dinner Friday night.

"Crazy week! I thought it was never going to end." I twirled spaghetti around my fork with one hand and handed Theo a piece of bread with the other.

"It was kind of a slow one," Nate replied.

"Do you know if your parents have plans this weekend?"

"I doubt it, but I can ask. Whatcha thinkin'?"

"There's something I'd like to talk to you about, and I was hoping we could drop Theo off for a few hours sometime this weekend." I met his eyes and smiled. *Why all the nerves? Come on, Kim, he loves you. You're making a big deal of nothing. You're only wanting to have a conversation.*

"I'm sure it won't be a problem. I'll call my mom and ask." Nate returned my smile but it wasn't the full-mouthed kind that told me he was happy; it was the close-lipped kind meant to put me at ease while wondering what I was up to.

The next day, Nate brought Theo over to his parents' and returned with take-out.

"Thanks for grabbing lunch, babe! We haven't had Thai in a while." As I grabbed a couple of plates from the cabinet, I worked on building up the courage to start the conversation.

"No problem. What's on your mind?"

"Let's dish up and sit down first." I gave myself a few more seconds to figure out how to begin. As I pulled out my chair and sat down, I took a deep breath and decided to just dive in.

"I wanted to talk to you about adoption."

"Okay, what about it?" Nate's casual tone caught me off guard.

"Well, we agreed to stop trying to get pregnant. But I just can't let go of the thought of another child." He didn't recoil, didn't shake his head, he just took another bite of pad thai followed by a gulp of soda. "So I've been doing some research on adoption."

"Okay." Nate's shoulders were still relaxed, arms resting lightly on the edge of the table, fork poised above his plate.

"I'd like to seriously consider it." I was beginning to feel frustrated at how hard I was working to go from monologue to dialogue. I had wanted to have a conversation. I peered over Nate's shoulder at the tall evergreen trees in our backyard swaying in the light winter breeze and decided to just cut to the chase. "And I'd like you to consider it."

"What have you learned?"

"Will you consider it?" I was confused by my growing irritation. Nate was reacting positively and seemed completely open to the idea — why was I on the verge of inviting him to fight? "There's no point in talking about it if you aren't open to the idea."

"Come on, Kim, just tell me what you learned. I wouldn't have asked if I didn't want to know." There was a hint of irritation in Nate's voice. He wanted me to cut to the chase and tell him what I wanted. He knew I'd hear him out — and he also knew that if I really wanted us to adopt, I'd find a way to make it happen.

"Sorry, it's just that this is super important to me. And I don't know what I'll do if you don't agree." I looked down at my plate, feeling ashamed at my defensiveness. "I know you're happy just having Theo, and I know you would've been fine never having kids. But I'm not. I *really* want another child and this is the only practical way I see it happening." I held my breath as I waited for Nate to respond.

"Kim, you and Theo are the two most important people to me in the world. I can't imagine life without you." He leaned across the table, extending his hand towards mine. "If it's this important to you, I'm willing to consider it."

"Seriously?" I was stunned. I'd convinced myself Nate would say no and I had tried to prepare myself for that eventuality. "Thanks babe, this means a lot to me." I reached out and squeezed his hand.

Over the rest of our lunch, I told Nate what I'd learned so far. We agreed a reasonable next step would be to call my mom and ask what she knew about the agency based in my hometown.

It was a huge relief to have Nate's agreement and support. It was nice to have a partner along on the journey with me, someone to help figure out what to do next. With him on board, and an agency to seriously consider, I was confident we'd soon be able to formulate a plan.

I thought all I needed to do was call my mom, confirm the name of the agency, and everything else would fall into place. But that call would turn out to be barely a blip on a gigantic radar screen tracking our journey through adoption.

Chapter 11

Making Contact

With shaking hands, I sat on the edge of my bed and dialed my mom's number. What had felt for days like the logical next step in adopting a child, suddenly felt like a leap out of a plane in a prototype parachute.

When she answered, her cheerful voice calmed my nerves. After some pleasant chitchat, I decided to cut to the chase and told her we were considering adoption and wondered if she could find out the name of the agency our acquaintance had used. She was more than happy to help out and as we talked I became aware of my dad's breathing as he listened on the other phone. I was relieved I hadn't known he was there. The subject wasn't meant to be a secret, but I wasn't comfortable openly talking about the fertility troubles Nate and I had experienced. Hearing at least part of the conversation with my mom would save a lengthy explanation.

We talked for a few more minutes and I waited to hang up until I heard the click on the other end of the line. My mom had also mentioned another agency one of her coworkers was using. I was excited to have leads on a couple potential adoption agencies; options are rarely a disadvantage.

However, my excitement was soon smothered by the all too familiar feeling of regret over not being able to experience a second pregnancy. I tried to convince myself it was all okay. *There are children coming in to the world who need parents, and we're meant to be parents to one of them.*

The truth was, however, that while adoption was a way to bring another child into our family, a way to give Theo a brother or sister and a way to fill the hole in my heart, it wasn't the salve to soothe the ache of never being pregnant again.

I shook my head to shake free the dark curtain threatening to close over my mood and I set my sights on success. There was no time to wallow in self-pity when I had agencies to contact and a plan to create. I glanced down at the paper on which I'd absent-mindedly doodled during the call. I didn't remember picking up the pen and paper I always kept on my nightstand. The page was filled with spirals. Life had felt exactly like that lately, spiraling downwards with one challenge after another, with me trying to make the choices necessary to fight my way back up. With two solid agency leads, I hoped we'd managed to reverse the trend and begin to make meaningful upward-bound progress.

* * *

A few days later, my mom emailed me the names of the two adoption agencies. I'd been right about the first one when I searched the week before. The agency had been operating in my hometown for a couple of decades. The other was a global agency with a Christian affiliation.

Staring at the website for the global agency, I was struck by the gravity of the arrangement we were seeking. What had at first felt normal, although rare, now made me marvel at the complexity of it all. I was surprised by the philosophical questions that hit me as I readied myself to send an email introducing Nate and me and asking for additional information. How would we know if the birth parents were treated well and furnished with the services they needed? What should we expect in terms of support? What could the agency dictate to us? Were we comfortable agreeing to parenting choices like one parent staying home or specifics of dividing parenting responsibilities? And the global agency required the child to be raised Christian. Were we comfortable having religion as a condition of adoption? While I choose to go to church on a regular basis, I don't think it's a requirement of raising healthy, happy children. And would the fact that I worked fulltime and Nate worked part-time, be an issue? I don't think it's necessary for one parent to be home fulltime with the children, and I don't believe parenting is the mother's sole responsibility. I believe it's important that both parents share caregiving duties; people excel at different things and a parent's strengths should be taken into account.

As I drafted an email enquiring about the services offered, the process, timeline and costs, I reflected on the tension between the deeply personal decision we were making to move forward with adoption as contrasted against the practical, business-like aspect of the process. I was facing questions I'd never pondered before and for the first time was examining beliefs I'd held without a second thought as I considered how our family would be judged. But I knew I had to consider these issues if I wanted to adopt.

With the first email sent, I moved on to the second agency. There was no email address listed on their website, so it would have to wait until I had time to call on my lunch hour.

A few days later, just before noon, I grabbed my coat and cell phone, and headed outside. My office was a cubicle in a construction trailer I shared with ten other people and afforded absolutely no privacy. I couldn't find a free conference room in the building next door, so I headed outside. It was a cold but sunny January day. I leaned against a retaining wall as I dialed the number I'd scribbled on a Post-It note. The support was comforting. I instinctively turned my face toward the sun and closed my eyes. I loved the contrast between the chill of the air and the warmth of the sun. As the phone rang, I worried the agency was closed for lunch. Then, on the fourth ring, I heard, "Good afternoon, Alto Family Support Network, Lynn speaking."

"Hi Lynn, I'm calling for information about your adoption services?" My greeting came out sounding like a question rather than a statement.

"We'd be happy to help," she responded. "Barbara is our adoptive parent counselor and she can provide you information. Let me see if she's available. Can you hold for a minute?"

"Yes I can, thank you." I listened to the smooth beats of the golden oldies, feeling the cold of the concrete seep through my back. As the minutes ticked by, I wondered if they'd forgotten about me and considered hanging up. To combat my growing restlessness and warm my quickly chilling body, I decided to do a lap around the building.

As I was rounding the north corner, I heard a click, the sound of shuffling papers, then a woman's voice saying, "Thank you for waiting, this is Barbara O'Donnell. I'm the adoptive parent counselor."

I introduced myself and explained about the research I'd done on various kinds of adoption and how I'd been referred to her agency.

"Well," she began, "we've been offering open adoption services in the area for over twenty-five years. With open adoption, prospective parents share information about themselves and the birth parents choose who will adopt their baby. Everyone meets prior to the birth and stays in contact afterwards."

"I see." I squinted my eyes as I tried to imagine what it would be like getting to know our child's birth parents. I hadn't thought much about that before.

Barbara went on to describe how the agency screened prospective adoptive parents as well as birth parents. She assured me they had a high success rate because of their thorough screening process, experience, and the support they provided after the baby's birth.

"If you're interested, I can send you an initial screening application. We'd need this, along with a check for $500, to get started."

"Thank you, that was a lot of information." I said, trying to soak in everything she was telling me. "I do have two additional questions, and I apologize if it's rude to ask them at this point. The first is how long does the process usually take?"

"Good question. We keep a limited number of adoptive parents on our wait list at one time. We find that twelve to fourteen prospective families enable us to make placements faster. So, it's typically twelve to eighteen months after completing the application process. Luckily, we have a couple open spots right now."

"Wow, that seems fast." Based on my research, anything under two years was quick; many adoptive parents waited up to five years.

"My second question is, what's your fee?" My cheeks burned with embarrassment. *The money shouldn't matter; this is a human life you're talking about.* But the fact of the matter was, money did matter. I had to ask about the expenses because the costs I read about during my research varied wildly from a couple thousand dollars to several tens of thousands. And we only had a small rainy-day fund saved; we'd never factored the expenses of an adoption into our financial plans.

"There's the initial screening fee of $500, which I just mentioned, and the portfolio fee of $2,500, if you pass the initial screening. The adoptive fee is $18,000, which doesn't include the legal fees for the adoption finalization. If you use our attorney, that's an additional $3,000."

"Okay, thank you." My stomach fell and I felt a rush of adrenaline — not owing to excitement; it was the all too familiar rush of an impending panic attack. I took a deep breath, hoping to calm my nerves. Barbara had just mentioned close to $25,000 in fees. I had no idea where we'd get that kind of money. *The process is a long one*, I reminded myself. *We have time to scrimp and save. This is important, we'll figure something out.*

"And as you may know, the federal government offers a tax credit of $10,000. Again, that's a tax credit — versus a deduction — so you get some of the money back," Barbara added. "Do you have any other questions?" The fact that she included this information gave me the sense that I wasn't alone in worrying about where the money would come from.

I thanked her for her time and gave her our address so she could send us some more information. Then headed back to the office, my head swirled with all the new information and a tangle of competing thoughts. It felt good to have more information, and twelve to eighteen months was a lot shorter wait than I was expecting. On the other hand, $25,000 was a lot of money. *Where would we come up with that kind of money? Will Nate change his mind when I tell him how much the adoption could cost? And why would we pay their attorney to advise us? That seemed like a conflict of interest; if we went through with it, we would want our own attorney.* I decided to wait for the other agency to send information before deciding what to do next.

As I walked up the wooden steps to the trailer, something Barbara said came back to me: "Our process helps us ensure that our adoptions don't make good *Lifetime* movies."

Oh God! Please tell me my life hasn't turned into a script for a Lifetime *movie!* None of this was what I had imagined for my life. My chest tightened and I was suddenly filled with dread.

Chapter 12

Proving We're Worthy

I dropped the mail on the kitchen counter with a loud thud. The pile included the latest issues of *Vogue* and *Architectural Digest* along with an envelope, the size and thickness of which reminded me of my college admissions packet. As I turned over the envelope to see the return address, I was surprised by the jolt of fear that left me feeling weak and slightly out of breath. I'd thought a lot about this moment and had expected to feel excited, like I was being handed the keys that would unlock the door to my family's future. Instead, it felt like I was about to unlock Pandora's box.

Since the call with Barbara I had received a response from the global agency and decided it wasn't the right agency for us. The agency required adoptive families to agree to raise the child Christian. Even though I was raised Presbyterian and Theo was baptized in a Catholic church, Nate and I couldn't sign their contract. We didn't believe Christianity was a prerequisite to being either good parents or a good person and we couldn't support an agency that did.

* * *

I read the cover letter and skimmed the next few pages, which repeated the information Barbara had covered during our phone call. When I came to a section titled "Agency Requirements," my heart skipped a beat. Barbara hadn't mentioned any requirements. My pulse quickened and I felt a little light headed. I felt a *gotcha* coming but had no idea why.

"What's that, babe?" Nate asked as he wandered into the kitchen with Theo on his heels.

"What? Oh, it's the info packet from the agency. I'm just looking it over." I turned my attention to Theo. "Hey buddy, are you and Daddy goin' outside to play?"

"Yep," he replied, smiling widely as he jumped up and down. "I need shoes!" Theo loved to play outside, even in the damp, cold January weather.

"Okay buddy, just a sec, I'll help you find them." I put the papers on the table and went in search of Theo's fireman replica rubber rain boots. The faster I got him outside with Nate, the faster I could get back to reading through the information from the adoption agency.

Leaning forward, my chin resting in my hand, I read down the bulleted list of requirements. We easily qualified for the first two. We'd been married longer than the agency's three-year minimum and we were both under 45. The third, for applicants over 40, didn't apply to us. My breath caught in my throat as I read the fourth requirement.

I looked out the window and willed myself to inhale deeply to slow the rising tide of emotions. *It's going to be okay.* To adopt a newborn or infant, I read, a couple had to be considered infertile or the woman unable to carry a pregnancy to term. *Do we qualify?*

Technically, we'd stopped trying to conceive before exhausting all infertility treatment options. And even though my doctor strongly recommended against another pregnancy due to the risks to my back or legs, he didn't say it was impossible. He had left the final decision to us. Nate and I believed we were making the right decision for both my health and our family when we stopped trying to get pregnant, but was there a chance the agency would see it differently? Would we face another dead end?

Nate and I talked a lot about the child we hoped to welcome into our family. We didn't have a preference for the sex or race, but we both wanted a baby. I'd read about the potential challenges of adopting older children, from lengthy adoption finalization processes to an increased risk of attachment disorder, to struggles with birth order if we adopted a child older than Theo.

I was open to a lot, but there was very little wiggle room when it came to age. After all, this journey had begun with a desire for another baby. I'd already relinquished my hope of experiencing another pregnancy. I didn't want to lose the opportunity to parent another baby, too.

I sat considering the matter. Should we reconsider our decision and go for an older child instead? Tears stung my eyes. Chinook got up, stretched, and walked over to me. "Hi buddy," I said as he sat down next to me and laid his head in my lap. His eyes were filled with a sorrow mirroring my own. Combing his soft fur with my fingers, I let the tears fall. I felt another loss on the horizon. I lay my head on my folded arms and gritted my teeth as a torrent of frustration and anger rose up from my belly. I'd held the emotions back for months, and then three sentences in twelve pages of information brought me to my knees. *I'm just not tough enough for this. It isn't meant to be.*

I stayed seated at the kitchen table with my head in my hands for what felt like an eternity. I seemed to travel through all five stages of grief before I summoned the strength to lift my head.

After taking several deep breaths, I sat up straight, wiped my eyes, and said aloud, "You want this, Kim, and you *will* make it happen."

I was shocked by the determination in my voice. I heard a quiet whine and looked down to see Chinook's concerned face staring up at me. "Nobody promised life would be easy, did they, buddy?" I decided to give Barbara a call the following day; if I couldn't convince her I was biologically infertile, I would at least convince her that we met the *intent* of requirement number four. Meanwhile, I'd finish reading through the packet.

* * *

There were four steps to complete before officially making it onto the wait list. First, we had to pass the initial application. This entailed both Nate and me answering several questions about our backgrounds, as individuals and as a couple, gathering references from three people unrelated to us, and passing an FBI fingerprint check. Once the agency received all our information Barbara and her partner would then decide whether to accept us into the adoptive parent pool. It was ultimately up to two strangers whether we could adopt.

I began considering who we'd ask to write our references. We had lots of friends who fit the criteria; what I struggled with was having to share our decision to adopt.

Our friends knew we'd been through a tough year. Which is to say, they knew about my back injury and subsequent surgery; they didn't know we'd been trying to conceive. We considered that part of our life private and, since the problem appeared to be mine, it felt deeply personal.

There were questions we couldn't answer, like when was the baby coming. There were others we didn't want to answer, like why were we adopting. There were potentially so many opinions, no matter how well meaning, we just didn't want to hear. With so little we could control on this new adventure, we found comfort in the few things we thought we could. With whom and when to share our news was something *we* wanted to decide.

I reminisced about the excitement and joy of being the only ones who knew we were expecting Theo. I was disappointed that this time, we couldn't share our news on our own terms. I also didn't like knowing, even in the smallest way, that our friends would play a part in the decision of whether we were worthy of becoming parents again. It was clear in the agency's information that their feedback would carry heavy weight in whether Barbara and her partner would approve us.

Yet if we wanted to move forward with expanding our family, I knew I'd have to pack away my sadness and focus on what we were gaining, not what we'd lost. I could only hope that whomever we chose as references wouldn't ask too many questions and would hold our dream in confidence.

I looked up to see Nate and Theo at the back door, stomping mud off their boots. I bottled up my churning mix of emotions as I gathered the papers from the table and put them back in the envelope. I'd wait until after Theo went to bed to discuss it all with Nate. For now, I'd focus on our son and making the most of our evening together.

"Night, night, sleep tight," I whispered to Theo later, as I tucked the covers tightly around him and kissed his forehead, "Don't let the bedbugs bite."

"Or tickle," he giggled as I tickled him softly.

"Sweet dreams, I love you." I leaned in to lay more kisses on his soft, still-pudgy cheeks.

"Sweet dreams. I love you too, Mommy."

"See you in the morning, sweet boy."

I flicked off the light and walked slowly down the stairs with a smile on my face. My heart was filled with love for our son. We were so lucky to have such a fun, energetic, and caring boy. I was over the moon in love with him. I cherished our bedtime routine and the way it magically brought life into crisp perspective.

"How'd it go?" Nate asked as I joined him in the living room.

"Just fine. I think he's pretty tired. Want anything to eat?"

"Nope, I'm fine."

"I took a look at the information the adoption agency sent." I sat down on the couch and tucked my feet under me, wrapping my arms around my chest in an effort to comfort my aching heart.

"What did it say?"

"There's quite a bit of information. I didn't make it through all of it, but we do need references."

"Okay, I figured we'd need some."

"And it can't be family." I reached out to grab his hand and capture a little more of his attention. "We should talk about who we tell."

"Who we tell?" Nate finally stopped channel surfing and turned to look at me.

"Yeah, if we're going to ask people to be references for us, we have to tell them we're pursuing adoption. I really wanted to keep it to ourselves." I felt my cheeks flush. I blamed myself for both insisting on a second child and being unable to carry another pregnancy.

"I know you did, babe, but we can ask people not to say anything. And besides, it's not a secret."

"Really, you don't think so?" I raised an eyebrow in confusion. I thought we were both on the same page. "But nobody knows we were trying for another baby and I don't want anyone to know we decided to stop."

"You might be overthinking this. All they need to know is that we're interested in adopting and we'd like them to be a reference for us. It's nobody's business why." He made it sound so simple.

"Thanks babe, I needed to hear that." I leaned over to kiss him. I knew it wasn't logical, but the thought of explaining our decision to friends and family felt as uncomfortable as talking with my nurse practitioner about getting pregnant had over five years before.

I snuggled next to Nate hoping the TV would distract me from the many thoughts dancing through my head.

* * *

Over the next couple of days, we selected the people we'd ask for references. We chose our next-door neighbor, Jodie, a former coworker who'd become a trusted friend, and our friends Christina and Alex. I'd worked with Christina in college when she was dating Nate's best friend, Alex; they had set Nate and I up on our first date. They all knew us both as a couple and as parents, would answer questions honestly, and were the least likely people to probe.

I still needed to call Barbara to discuss requirement number four and confirm that our circumstances wouldn't prevent us from adopting an infant. Not wanting to hear bad news that meant beginning our search for an agency again, I held off calling her for almost a week. Work had been unexpectedly hectic, but I knew I could've made time if I'd wanted to. I also knew that if we were going to move forward, I shouldn't hold off any longer. The agency only had a few open spots, and if those got filled, who knew how long we'd have to wait to even get on the list. I was optimistic, but wary; I didn't know if I was ready for any more bad news.

Chapter 13

Approval to Parent

I sat in the driver's seat and took several long, calming breaths as my nervousness grew. It was four-thirty and I hoped to catch Barbara before she left for the night.

Searching through my purse I found my headset, popped the earbuds in, and dialed her number.

"Good afternoon Kim, what can I do for you?" Barbara asked.

"Thanks for sending the information, Barbara. If you have a few minutes, I have a question." I looked both ways before pulling into traffic.

"Sure, how can I help you?"

"It's about your requirement that a couple must be infertile to adopt an infant." I paused trying to gather my courage. "As you know, we have a biological child. When we tried for a second, I was unable to get pregnant. Then I injured my back and had to have surgery."

"Yes, I remember you mentioned your son," Barbara said when I paused to take a breath.

"Well, long story short," I started again, wondering why I was having so much trouble getting to my question, "We tried several interventions that didn't work. And then my back doctor told us it was best not to risk another pregnancy. Even if I managed to get pregnant, I risked doing permanent nerve damage. So we decided not to try further interventions." I breathed in quickly before she could respond. "We really want to adopt an infant." I could hear the pleading tone in my voice and hoped I didn't sound as desperate as I felt. "So, bottom-line, our question is: do we qualify to adopt a baby from your agency?"

"Yes, based on your medical history, your family would qualify if everything else on your initial application checks out. Anything else I can answer for you?"

Her tone caught me by surprise. She sounded so clinical, her tone devoid of emotion. I felt a little foolish for working myself up about the possibility of hitting a dead end. Relieved, I hoped it wouldn't take long for the agency to approve our initial application.

* * *

On each of the following three nights, after putting Theo to bed, I reached out to one of the three people we'd selected to write a reference. I started with my friend Jodie. Jodie and I had become good friends after we moved in next door to her and her husband several years before. Leaving Theo with Nate, I hurried across our damp front yard and knocked on her door.

"Come in," I heard through the bright blue door.

"Hey Jod, it's me. Gotta few minutes?" I said as I opened the door and took off my shoes.

"Yep, I'm in the kitchen. What's up?"

"Not too much. What's up with you? How's work?" Jodie was an investigator for an insurance company. I enjoyed listening to her work stories, her work so different from mine. We'd both chosen male dominated careers and I could relate to the challenges that brought with it.

"It was good, kinda slow day. Same old, same old," she said with a grin. Jodie worked hard and I took the reply to mean she didn't really want to recount the details of her day.

"So, you know how I told you we were thinking about having another baby?" I paused and she nodded. "And how we had to stop trying?" Other than Nate, Jodie knew the most about what I'd been through over the past year. "Well, we've decided to adopt."

"Wow, you sure you want another baby?" she said as she raised her eyebrows at me. Jodie was the mom of a pre-teen son. When it came to parenting, she was well beyond the baby phase.

"I know, there are days that I think I might be a little crazy." I gave her a tight-lipped smile. I was beginning to really enjoy the benefits of having a kid with an attention span longer than 5 minutes, who could tell me what he wanted or when something was wrong. But I really wanted another baby.

I explained about the agency, the references we needed, and my concerns with having to open up our lives for judgment from so many people.

Jodie listened as only a close friend can and didn't hesitate to agree. After explaining that the agency would contact her directly, we chatted for a few more minutes then I wandered back across the yard to my house.

As I opened the door, Chinook jumped off the couch and barked as she ran to greet me. "Quiet Chinook," I admonished, "No barking. Geesh dog," I shook my head as she followed me over to the couch and I shared the good news with Nate.

The next night I called Christina to ask if she and Alex would be references. The conversation went even more quickly, partly because I caught them in the middle of the bedtime routine for their four kids. Christina was surprised by the request, but said they'd be happy to.

Finally I called my friend Mary. She and I had worked together for six years. She had two adopted daughters who were now in their late teens, and gladly agreed to provide a reference for us.

It hadn't been as hard as I thought it would be to share our plans with these people. They were all trusted friends and none of them asked questions, other than when to expect the reference form from the agency. Nate had been right; it wasn't a big deal. My fears of prying, personal, or unanswerable questions hadn't become a reality.

I still struggled with the unanswerable questions about the process, however. The unknowns felt even more real now that more people could potentially ask them. I felt the burden of these unanswerable questions. I wanted to not only take away the uncertainty I was feeling, but I also wanted to create the sense of comfort that knowing what to expect *and when to expect it* brought.

The inability to answer the myriad of questions was frustrating. I was a planner and excelled at building a plan and taking the actions necessary to achieve it. A big part of my professional success had come from my ability to do thorough risk assessments, setting my imagination free to create as many possible problems and outcomes as possible, assigning each one a likelihood, and then developing ways to mitigate or even possibly avoid them. These habits had served me well professionally but quickly began to wear me down when it came to personal matters.

I had instinctively planned our adoption process like I would a work project. But instead of doing a single risk assessment and then adjusting based on what happened, I was stuck in a cycle of constant worry. There were so many questions that didn't have an answer. Each unanswerable question added to the emotional weight of the situation. Asking our friends to provide references unexpectedly brought my fears to the surface. With a work project, I had a specific role —I was the composer and conductor. I was responsible for orchestrating all the moving parts and getting the job done. But in my personal life, I couldn't maintain the emotional distance necessary to keep potential problems from becoming potential defeats. Asking my friends for references may have seemed insignificant, a minor task to check off my list of things to do. But the stakes were so high that it had felt like a looming catastrophe. Any one of those friends could have pulled the plug on my dreams, and realizing that fact, I had focused on my worries, and not my goal. It was time to get back on track and focus on the goal—adopting a beautiful newborn baby.

* * *

Now that we knew who would provide our references I turned my attention to the initial application. It was Saturday morning, and Theo and Nate had gone out to run errands. With a few hours to myself I once again sat down at the kitchen table, poured a hot cup of tea and opened the seven-page application.

There was an initial section either one of us could complete and then identical sections filled with questions, one for Nate and one for me.

There were the easy questions, name, date of birth, employer, and profession. There were questions about our finances: gross annual income, total debt, and savings. And then came the hard questions: how do you describe yourself, what do you find most challenging in life, how would you describe yourself as a parent, and what will your parenting philosophy be.

While reading the questions about parenting I noticed each assumed we were childless. I smiled and felt comforted by the knowledge that this wasn't our first time around the parenting block. We had learned a lot over the past three years as parents and were thankful for our lessons learned. At the same time, I felt a sense of foreboding, as if the application didn't really apply to us, and as a result the agency wasn't asking the right questions to truly learn what they needed to know.

We must just be in the minority, I thought trying to reason my way through my growing discomfort. As the minority of adoption cases for their agency, they probably didn't see the value in having different applications for prospective parents who were already raising children. I figured my discomfort was just nerves and would lessen after they met Theo and got to know our family better.

Then I hit the crushing questions. My discomfort became an anxiety-laden, failure-punctuating, sadness-filled tsunami of emotions. I read over the final three questions and my mind went completely blank. The sounds of the occasional neighborhood traffic, kids playing outside, and dogs barking fell silent and I couldn't hear anything but my thundering heart. The silence lingered, and was then followed by a crushing wave of emotion and the screaming roar of "I have to prove I am worthy to parent!"

The anguish was overwhelming as I raised my arms in frustration, my fingers curling into fists like the Incredible Hulk, my head thrown back in despair before it fell to the table. Even before I could move my arms down to protect it, my head hit the table with a dull thud. Pain radiated across my forehead.

The agency wanted us to describe how we would teach and discipline our child, describe how life would change after adopting a child, and what strengths and experiences we had to help us be a good parent. They even wanted us to project into the future to the rigors of parenting through the teenage years.

The last three questions broke me. They were asking me to provide proof that I was worthy to parent. For some reason, those questions ripped me from my emotional foundation, undermining all the strength I had fought so hard to build since becoming pregnant with Theo four years before. No, that wasn't right, it attacked something I'd been fighting for even longer than that.

Those final questions hit upon the foundation of every decision I had made since high school when I had finally gained a tenuous belief in myself, a belief that I was free to dream and could achieve whatever it was I set my mind to.

I had a college education from an excellent university, a marriage of nearly twelve years, a career on the rise, and most importantly a wonderful son who couldn't be more perfect. We lived in a good suburban neighborhood, drove safe cars, and had families who loved us. *Just look at our life,* I thought. *Just look!* I couldn't think of the words to describe what I knew to be true. I sat sobbing at the dining room table, unable to crawl from beneath the emotional rubble the wave of devastation had created. I couldn't even pick up a pen and provide the written proof of the truth that I lived every day.

I knew I was a strong, kind, and determined woman. I was a good wife and a good mother. But there are times that even with the best materials it doesn't make sense to rebuild. I may have hit the end, even before crossing the starting line. If three reasonable and seemingly innocuous questions could bring me to my knees, was adoption really an option for me? Was I kidding myself? Was this the sign I was meant to see – the one that told me I had hit a dead end and should be happy with what I had?

Chapter 14

Moving Forward

I rolled out of bed and trudged into the shower. The day after the application process threatened to crush my spirit, I woke up physically sore, feeling battered and bruised, my nerves raw.

For decades the fear of failure has been a strong motivator for me. First as I tried to reach the top of the class and then as I pushed myself to create incontrovertible proof I was smart, successful, and competent. For as long as I could remember fear of failure had kept me on my toes and driving forward. Trouble came when it combined with my other primary motivator, the desire for control. The two came together to create a toxic mix that brought me to the deepest moment of despair I had ever experienced.

I had a choice to make about whether or not to continue with the agency's application process. If I didn't want to lose the momentum I'd worked so hard to gain, I needed to make a decision and it needed to be final. Was I in or was I out? Was I going to throw myself fully into the effort to adopt a child or was I going to learn to be happy with the one wonderful kid we had?

I had been at this crossroads before and it was my decision to make. Nate had made it clear he supported pursuing an adoption. And I also knew he was happy being the father of one. From my point of view, he couldn't lose either way.

For me, it was more complicated. Taking the lead on pursuing the adoption had already taken a toll. The combination of coming to terms with not having another pregnancy, trying to make sense of mountains of information, and making choices about the best way to move forward was energy draining. On top of all of life's other responsibilities, letting go of this major one was at times tempting.

On the other hand, it was nearly impossible to picture myself at peace with one child. I also couldn't imagine explaining to Theo he was an only child because I let a long process and intrusive questions get the best of me. I held the cards and it was my turn to either go all in or to fold.

As the hot water washed away the soreness, I gave myself a pep talk to cement my resolve. *Today's a new day,* I reminded myself as I hurried to get dressed, trying to be ready to go before Theo woke up. I was just pulling a sweatshirt over my head when I heard him in his room talking quietly to himself. As I walked out of the bathroom, I felt a spark of inner resolve as it relit a fire of belief in who I was and how I wanted my life to be. I had never wanted something so badly as I wanted this. I was all in.

Entering his bedroom I began to sing "Good morning to you, good morning to you. It's so good to see you ... and I love you too!" I smiled, remembering the many mornings my mom woke me up with the same song. Theo sat up and smiled at me, his dark brown eyes sparkling.

Kissing his soft, round cheeks, I pushed thoughts of the adoption application from my mind. I knew he would keep me busy all morning so there was no point in thinking about the application again until he was down for his afternoon nap.

As Theo and I sat at the table eating cereal, Nate wandered downstairs and grabbed a cup of coffee. I had managed to pull myself together before he and Theo returned from their errands the day before so he had no idea of my short-lived emotional breakdown.

I turned in my chair to face him as he leaned on the kitchen island. "I started filling out the initial adoption application yesterday. There's questions I can fill out for the both of us, but there's some that we have to do individually."

"Okay, sounds good," he said as he walked over, gave me a quick peck on the lips, and kissed Theo on the top of his head before joining us at the table. "When do we need it done by?"

"I'd like to get it done as soon as possible. There are also some forms we need to sign and send to our doctors. They're medical references. It's our consent to release medical records along with a couple questions. There's one for each of us and one for Theo," I took another bite of cereal as he drank his coffee. "Oh, and we need a check for five hundred bucks for the agency to process our application."

"Five hundred bucks for an *application*, wow," he said as his eyes got wider and he raised his eyebrows. "And then we're good to go?"

"Nope," I said setting down my spoon and leaning over the table. "Then we wait for them to review our written application, our references, and our medical information. And if they approve us and the FBI fingerprint check comes back clear *then* we're good to go to the next phase."

"The next phase?"

"Yep. We need to attend a weekend workshop."

"Okay," he said his eyes growing bigger still, deep wrinkles appeared in his forehead. I could tell the ride he'd agreed to go on was finally beginning to sink in. Until then, he was completely happy to let me take the lead and hadn't felt the need to engage.

"Oh, and the workshop is another couple hundred bucks. And then after the workshop if we agree we want to move forward," I paused, "there are a couple more fees to pay so we can begin the home study process. It isn't until after we pass the home study that we're good to go."

"Gotcha," he took another drink of his coffee, picked a Fruit Loop off Theo's shirt and popped it in his mouth. "That good cereal buddy?"

I noticed Nate was shaking his head slowly side to side and I knew he was adding up the amount of money we would spend just to be approved. Not a great sign.

* * *

The second time through the application was easier than the first. And when I say easier, it's all relative since this time instead of drowning in feelings of inadequacy and failure, I merely felt frustration and annoyance. I channeled this energy into finding the best possible words to describe what I liked to do, how I pictured myself as a parent, and my hopes and dreams for my children. Several times I wrote sarcastic answers as a way to take the sting out of the injustice that continued to creep to the surface.

One question asked about my hopes and dreams for my child. *Our child will be a popular, straight A student who will excel scholastically, artistically, and athletically. There will be no bounds to our efforts to nurture his or her interests. We will travel the world, provide private lessons for all extracurricular activities, and only the best school will be good enough for our little angel.*

The real answer, and the one we submitted, was pretty simple. I hoped to raise happy, healthy, compassionate children. I hoped our kids would learn how to dream and be courageous enough to work toward achieving those dreams. I hoped our family enjoyed spending time together and we had each other's backs. Most of all, I wanted my kids to grow up feeling loved, nurtured, safe, and wanted.

After hours of work, and several revisions, Nate and I were satisfied with our responses. As I placed the application into a large envelope and prepared to return it to the agency I resisted the urge to drop in a wallet size photo of Theo with the words "enough said" written on the back.

With the application returned, personal references mailed, releases sent to our doctors, and fingerprints on the way to the FBI for processing, there was nothing more for us to do but wait. The next decision was out of our hands. The agency would now decide whether we were good enough to become parents for the second time.

* * *

I was sitting at my desk answering email when my cell phone rang. I looked down and saw the agency's number on the screen. I quickly clicked answer and stood up. This wasn't a phone call I wanted my co-workers to overhear.

"Kimberly Severn speaking." I answered the same way I answered all my business calls hoping not to attract attention as I walked quickly out of the construction trailer.

"Hi Kim, it's Barbara, from Alto...."

"Yes, hi Barbara," I said accidentally cutting her off. My heart raced as I hoped she was calling with good news.

"We received your application and two of the three references have already come back," she said. "We have an adoptive couples' workshop in two weeks and we'd like to invite you to attend."

"Does this mean we're approved?" I asked as a flock of butterflies took flight in my stomach. I walked over to the retaining wall I had leaned against during our first conversation over a month before.

"Assuming your FBI check comes back clear, and we've no reason to assume it won't, yes, you're approved."

"Absolutely it will come back clear," I said in case she had any amount of doubt.

"Yes, Kim, we have every reason to believe it will be." I could tell by her tone she was laughing at me.

"Wow, what good news." I quickly tried to visualize our calendar to figure out if there were any potential conflicts. "I'll get back to you tomorrow to confirm we'll be there."

"We look forward to hearing from you."

The sense of relief was overwhelming. For the first time in weeks, I felt tension release from my body. With the burden of waiting for the agency's approval lifted, I stood taller, my spine straight and shoulders back, as I quickly dialed Nate's number.

After sharing the good news, I hung up the phone and walked in the door smiling ear to ear. *What a relief!* I thought as I settled back at my desk. *Now, get back to work girl.*

Chapter 15

When Does the Waiting Start

The adoption agency was located in an early twentieth century house along a busy arterial in one of the oldest parts of the city. The majority of the rooms were still intact, although all now served a new purpose. The architectural details that once graced this house had been removed decades before, traded in for practicality and durability. With venti mochas from Starbucks in hand we walked through the front door. Sunlight flooded into the room from several large leaded glass windows that lined the front and side of the house.

I was a bundle of nerves as I wondered what to expect. The workshop was scheduled to begin at nine and as usual we were fifteen minutes early. Nate and I both hated to be late, so we always left plenty of time to get where we were going.

"Good morning, Nate and Kim Severn," I said as I extended my hand in the receptionist's direction and we exchanged greetings.

Looking over her shoulder, I noticed we weren't the first to arrive. There were two other couples already seated in folding chairs set up in a tight circle in the workroom behind her. I did a mental eye roll and hoped the weekend wouldn't include anything close to the group therapy session the furniture arrangement seemed to imply.

"Go ahead and have a seat," the receptionist said, gesturing toward the circle of chairs. "We're still waiting on Joyce to arrive and we're expecting two more couples." Joyce was Barbara's partner and the birth parent coordinator.

We chose a pair of seats that provided us a view of the front door. It was comforting to be able to see who was coming and going. *We're also ready for a quick exit,* I thought. As we waited to get started, I was trying hard to keep my nerves under control and knowing I could make a quick escape if my anxiety got too high helped to calm me down.

Shortly after, the last two couples arrived followed by Joyce, who kicked off the morning by greeting each couple energetically. In her late fifties, Joyce was part drill sergeant, part school teacher. Her smile was warm, but there was an edge to her voice that let you know she meant business and expected compliance with her requests.

To get the workshop started, she asked each couple to introduce themselves, share where we lived, and why we had decided to adopt.

There were five other couples in total ranging in age from the mid-twenties to mid-forties. Two had never been able to conceive, two had conceived but miscarried. There was one other couple who had a child, but their situation was much different from ours. It was a second marriage for both of them; the wife had a teenage daughter; the husband didn't have kids of his own. They had decided they wanted to have a child together but hadn't been able to conceive.

Nate and I quickly introduced ourselves, sharing that we had a three-and-a-half-year-old son and had been unable to have a second pregnancy.

The morning was spent talking about how adoption had changed over the years, what was unique about open adoption, and the process the agency used to place children with adoptive families. We were briefed on the services the agency provided to birthmothers, how adoptive families were selected, and the dos and don'ts throughout the process.

As the morning session came to an end, instead of feeling like I was surrounded by fellow travelers on a similar journey, I began to feel a growing sense of isolation. We certainly all shared the desire to be parents, but unlike most of the other couples, we weren't first time parents. We didn't have the questions about caring for a baby. We knew how to prepare our home, what diapers to buy, and what equipment and supplies were essential to have at the house the first night baby came home. I also felt an unexpected mixture of guilt and selfishness since we had experienced the conception and birth of a biological child that all but one of the other attendees had had. Was I asking for more than I deserved?

I felt like a second-class citizen in this community of prospective adoptive parents. Did we have a right to be there? Was I going to inadvertently say something stupid or waste other people's time with the questions we had? I had questions about how to talk to Theo about when he was going to be a big brother. I wanted to know the best way to talk to a preschooler about adoption. I was anxious to understand if there was a difference in how to parent a biological and an adopted child. Would I offend the other couples if I asked my most burning questions?

My biggest worry was the fear of feeling a difference between the love I felt for Theo and the love I would feel for the new baby. How much did a biological connection matter in the love and commitment a parent felt for a child? Would I feel different as a mother between my biological and adopted child? Would I feel more like a father to our second child since I didn't carry the baby in my womb?

I sat patiently and listened as the morning session wore on. We followed along in the three-ring binder they'd given us. The binder was filled with the same information we were being told. I wrote notes in the margins of the pages in an effort to pay attention as Joyce and Barbara slowly covered each section. It was hard to focus as my questions danced around in my head and competed for my attention.

During the morning break I leaned my head on Nate's shoulder. "Everything alright babe?" he whispered quietly in my ear as he kissed the top of my head.

"Yeah, I'm fine," I replied as I lifted my head and kissed his cheek. I just needed to feel the support of someone else who was on a journey similar to mine. I began to wonder if it was possible to find another woman to build such a kinship with. I yearned for someone who could understand and truly relate to my experience. I realized I had hoped to find her during the workshop that weekend, but I knew by noon that wasn't going to happen.

The agency had scheduled three birthmothers to come in and share their stories after lunch. Each of their experiences was unique, all part heartbreaking and part life-affirming.

The first birthmother was a boisterous woman in her mid-twenties. She'd gotten pregnant in high school seven years before. She was an entertaining storyteller and you could tell she was a lovable handful for the ladies at the agency. She now had a pre-school age son she was raising on her own. She talked a mile a minute and we all felt a little exhausted as she thanked us for listening and left. Overall it sounded like everything had turned out well.

The second birthmother's story broke my heart and I couldn't help wondering how she had the strength to come and talk to us. She had a tough time in her teens and had landed in a rough crowd. Soon after she found herself addicted to drugs and pregnant. The father of the baby abandoned her as soon as he found out she was expecting. She found prenatal care and got clean. She wanted to turn her life around and raise her baby girl. But after giving birth, she once again fell on tough times, had no place to live, and no job to pay the bills. When her daughter was three months old she made the agonizing decision that adoption would be best for her daughter. It had been six months since the baby was placed with her new family. Through her tears she showed resolve and pride in her strength to make the decision she felt was best for her child. She spoke lovingly about her baby's new parents and was excited to tell us about the baby's nursery and her dreams for her. My chest ached as I listened to her story. The pain she felt was palpable. We could all tell how much she was hurting, still mourning the loss of her child, and struggling to take care for herself. I was struck by her courage and determination. I couldn't help thinking about how cruel life could be and wished there was something I could do to help. I was not alone in my concern. There were a lot of questions from the other couples about what would happen to her.

The first birthmother's story had sounded like it had a happy ending. The second was crushing in its sadness. Joyce took the opportunity to talk with us about what they called the Birthmother Assistance fund. It was an account the agency had set up years before to help birthmothers before and after the adoption to pay for food, shelter, and the services they needed to get back on their feet. She explained that we would all pay into the fund at the end of the workshop as part of our agreement to move forward with the adoption process.

I certainly hoped it was enough. What these women were doing for their children was heroic and took an incredible amount of courage and determination. As a result, I let the surprise of writing yet another check slide. Some of the women who used the agency clearly needed a helping hand but I couldn't help wondering why Barbara hadn't mentioned it before.

The third birthmother never arrived. So after recapping the day, going over the next steps of the adoption process a second time, including the remaining costs, we were dismissed an hour early.

Nate and I couldn't get out of there fast enough. I wanted to get away from the sadness, uncertainty, and anxiety I felt. It was exhausting trying to focus on all the information that Joyce and Barbara had provided, while at the same time trying to figure out if the answers given to the other couples' questions were even helpful to us.

The next morning, three other couples joined us, to share their experiences adopting a baby through the agency. They talked about writing their portfolio, what it was like taking their baby home, and how they were managing the relationship with the birth parents.

Each of the couples had waited less than six months before being chosen by birthmothers. Two of the three families had smooth adoption processes. They had been selected quickly, had positive relationships with the birthmother during her pregnancy and now had intermittent contact with their child's birth parents. For both of these couples, the birth parents had decided to stop contact.

The third couple's story was sad and heartbreaking. They hadn't waited long before a birthmother, relatively early in her pregnancy, had chosen them. The birth parents were a young, unmarried couple who had decided they weren't ready to be parents. The adoptive couple spent months getting to know both birth parents, went to doctor appointments with them, and even invited them to Thanksgiving dinner at their family cabin in the mountains. It sounded like they had developed a strong relationship and had all tightly bonded. There was only one odd detail to the otherwise idyllic match.

Throughout her second trimester, the birthmother refused to have the standard ultrasound her doctor recommended. Even when encouraged by the agency, she wouldn't change her mind. Due to the closeness of the relationship, the adoptive parents figured it was better not to push the issue, and besides, based on what they had heard during the doctor visits, there was nothing to worry about. Finally, after months of anticipation, they received a call that the birthmother was in labor and they rushed to the hospital. But within minutes after the baby girl was born, it was clear she had a very serious birth defect. The defect was so severe that the adoptive family couldn't go through with the adoption. As much as they wished it were otherwise, they knew they didn't have the skills necessary to provide adequate care for the baby.

They later learned that the birthmother had feared something was wrong with the baby and was too scared to say anything. After her daughter was born, she cut all ties with the adoptive couple. The adoptive parents were crushed at the loss of the baby they had thought of as their own, and the deep friendship they had built with the birth parents. Yet to have gone forward with the adoption would have been more than they could handle. The baby needed life-long, around the clock care.

What would we have done in a similar situation, I wondered. Hearing their story brought home the reality of adoption – just as in birth, things can go wrong, but unlike in birth, there is an element of choice, for all the parties involved. It is the element of choice that so often leads to worries and heartaches – what happens when one of the parties changes their mind?

In this case, as tragic as it was, everything worked out. Another family, accustomed to raising children with serious medical conditions, adopted the baby and a few months later, the adoptive parents received a call about another baby girl who was waiting to be released at the hospital. The birthparents already had three children, had become pregnant unexpectedly, and didn't feel prepared to raise another child. If the couple was willing, they could go to the hospital to meet their new baby daughter. They never met the birth parents who had wanted to remain anonymous.

As their beautiful six-month old daughter sat bouncing on her dad's knee, we could see the love and pride they had for her. But when they finished their story, I realized that they still felt a bond to the child they'd had to let go. I knew that I would probably have made the same decision – what kind of parent would that make me? The question gnawed at me.

After hearing the adoptive families' stories, I wanted to hear more about how to manage the birth parent relationship. Joyce explained that the standard open adoption agreement stated birth parents would see the child twice a year and adoptive parents would send pictures twice a year as well.

"Building a relationship with the birthmother as you wait for the baby to be born is important," Joyce explained. "We encourage birth parents and adoptive couples to meet in person as often as possible before the baby is born to get to know each other."

"What if we don't live close," one of the women asked.

"We encourage you to see the birth parents as much as possible and you can, of course, talk on the phone. Birthmothers may want you to attend doctor visits with her, some may not. That is one of the things you should talk to her about."

My mind began to wander as I looked around the room taking in my surroundings again and trying to figure out what the other couples were thinking. I was trying to imagine how to have the conversations Joyce was suggesting. *How are we going to fit in additional trips across the state to meet with the birth parents?* More questions that needed answers. I felt Nate elbow me in the side and wondered how much I had missed.

"We recommend that as you get to know the birthmother, you talk with her about the names you're considering for the baby and make her a part of the decision," Barbara said. I was initially taken aback by the suggestion that we let someone else in on this decision and was once again lost in thought, the room and the conversation fading into the background.

Choosing a name was an important, lifelong decision and I wasn't sure how I felt about conceding our child's name to another couple. I quickly felt ashamed of myself for being so selfish. *It's only a name for heaven's sake, they are the ones giving us their baby.* Nate elbowed me again. I turned and gave him an exasperated look.

"As you get to know your birthmother, talk to her about her birthing plan, and decide in advance whether or not you'll be in the room during her labor and delivery." Joyce paused and looked around the room. I was grateful for the moment of silence as it gave me a few seconds to figure out once again how much information I might have missed.

"You're welcome to be at the hospital after the baby is born, but take your cues from the birth mom." It was Barbara this time who looked around the room and made eye contact with each of us. "This is *her* time to both bond with her baby, and begin to say good-bye. You have the rest of forever with the baby." We all nodded as if we completely understood and grasped the gravity of what she was saying.

I got a lump in my throat as I thought about how opposite my experience would be from what our child's birth mom would experience. On the day our new baby was born, we would celebrate an addition to our family, a dream complete. And our birthmom would say hello and also begin saying goodbye to the baby she had nurtured for nearly a year. Our gain on the day was literally another woman's loss. My heartbreak over our journey toward a second child grew a little deeper.

"Typically you'll bring the baby home from the hospital when the birthmother is discharged. It's a good idea to agree to meet with the birthmom a couple of times over the following days to ease the transition," she continued.

My mind started to wander again. I thought about my three days in the hospital after Theo was born. How I'd felt as I got to know my new baby, how sore my body was as it began to heal from his delivery. I then thought about the first few days at home, sleep deprived and in pain as my breast milk came in. At least I had my baby to balance out the post-delivery pains. Our birthmother would not. I quickly blinked away tears as my chest started to ache.

"But what about if you live out of town? How long are we expected to stay?" the wife of a couple who lived about two hours away asked.

"You should plan to stay until after the birthmother goes to court to relinquish her parental rights." Was there an edge to Joyce's voice?

"How long will that be?" the same woman asked.

"It depends, but it's typically two to three days after she's released from the hospital. Until then, she has legal custody of the child and can change her mind at any time," Joyce explained. Her body had stiffened almost imperceptibly, I noticed she had sat up straighter and pulled her shoulders back. I wondered if the woman who had asked the question had noticed too. I wanted to ask how often it happened that the birthmother changed her mind, but the conversation quickly shifted to another topic.

"So we have to be in a hotel with a newborn for *days*?" It was clear the couple hadn't planned on spending multiple nights away from home caring for their newborn child.

"Yes. There are extended stay hotels that we can recommend which are often easier to stay in because they're slightly larger and have kitchens."

Nate and I exchanged knowing looks. We were lucky we could stay at my parents' house. We wouldn't have to worry about many of the logistics that the other out of town couples would have to address. I was also excited to share the first few days of our baby's life with my parents and siblings.

"For couples from out of town you can meet at a park, a coffee shop or restaurant for lunch for the first few visits with your birth mom," Barbara had taken over as Joyce stood up and walked toward the back of the building. "During the visits, you should let the birthmom take the lead, let her hold the baby for as long as she needs to." Barbara once again looked around the room at each of us, her eyes staying on the couple who had asked the previous questions. Satisfied she had our attention and tacit agreement she continued, "Then over the next couple of months you'll continue to get together as well. But you'll probably find after a few months, the baby no longer responds to the birthmom the same way, and then she'll begin to want to hold the baby less and less. Visits usually don't go beyond eighteen months to two years."

Nate and I weren't worried about the in-person visits. We'd begun to make the four-and-a-half-hour drive to see my family a couple times a year. It would be a good excuse to make sure our kids had an opportunity to spend time with their grandparents, aunts, uncles, and cousins. It seemed manageable.

"How are you all feeling about what you've learned so far?" Joyce asked as she walked back into the room. "We've given you a lot of information so far this weekend. In the next couple hours, as we talk about the next steps, we want you to also be thinking about whether or not you're ready to move forward."

I glanced over at Nate with my eyebrows knitted together in confusion. Leaning over I whispered, "Who would commit a weekend to this if they weren't certain?" He kissed my forehead, raised his eyebrows, and shrugged.

Overall the weekend had been pretty uncomfortable. I couldn't image sitting and listening to the birthmother and adoptive family stories if I wasn't committed to this process. There was so much emotion in the room. I could feel the sadness from the other prospective adoptive parents over their inability to conceive, the loss from the birthmothers, and the emotional impact the process had on everyone involved. Each person was trying hard to understand their role in these new family structures and finding their way forward with life. The way that Barbara and Joyce talked about it, the adoption process was both simple to understand and straightforward. But listening to the stories of the birthmothers and adoptive parents it appeared every situation was unique and complex.

Nate gently nudged me in the ribs with his elbow, "Ouch, stop doing that," I whispered. If he kept it up I was going to have a permanent dent in my side.

Once again, I wasn't sure how long Barbara had been talking, but I felt relatively confident I had been lost in thought for more than a few minutes.

"And so for the family portfolio it's important you follow the format we define in the handout that's part of your notebook. We want all of the portfolios to look similar so birthmothers can concentrate on the content. It's important that you use the folders we specify since Joyce often brings the portfolios with her on birth parent visits and these folders easily fit in her briefcase." Barbara said.

"The portfolios are the birthmother's way to get to know you, so it's also important you're honest. High quality, candid pictures help them get a sense for who you are. If you don't have pictures of certain things, like your house or your extended family, we encourage you to take some. Also, if you already have children," Barbara paused and looked first at the couple with a teenage daughter, then to Nate and me, "be sure you don't include too many pictures of your other child."

"Excuse me," I said as my arm shot into the air to get Barbara's attention.

"Yes, Kim," Barbara turned to face me as my heart began to race. I felt a sudden rise of frustration because it felt like, just as with the application, the agency was acting as if Theo didn't exist.

"Why wouldn't we put in pictures of our son? He's one of the reasons we want another child, he'll be an amazing big brother, and he's the biggest part of our life." I could hear the anger in my voice. A feeling of confusion joined the frustration and I fidgeted in my seat trying to release some of the negativity I felt.

"We want the birthmothers to get to know you as prospective parents for *their* child. And birth parents may not choose you if they feel like their child won't get your attention."

"Wow," I muttered as I shook my head slowly back and forth. I understood the birth parents' point of view, but wasn't the agency there to help them to understand what a good thing brothers or sisters were, and what that told them about who we were as parents?

Thoughts flooded my brain so quickly it was hard to make sense of them all. I was totally confused. I wasn't comfortable being asked to downplay who Theo was or what he meant to our family. Since the day I had found out I was pregnant, when faced with any big decision we had considered the impact to Theo. I put Theo's needs before my own, before Nate's, before almost everything – just as I would with any child who became part of our family. And I was confident Theo would be an amazing big brother.

Did we want a birthmother who couldn't understand that? Could we make a relationship work with a birthmother who couldn't see what an asset having a big brother would be to their child? Wouldn't the agency get to know us well enough that if the birthmother had concerns they could help her understand?

"Does that make sense, Kim?" Barbara asked, and I sensed by her tone she expected me to say yes.

"No. It really doesn't," I said as I continued to shake my head. I figured total honesty was better than pretending. To survive the stress of this process I had to remain authentic to who I was as an individual and to who we were as a family.

"These birthmothers want to know that they're selecting a couple who will love and care for *their* child. They don't care about any other children. They want what's best for their own," she looked at me again, waiting for my agreement. I understood what she was saying but I still wanted to argue. I completely related to a mother's need to know that her child was loved and cared for. And that was exactly why I was railing against the suggestion of discounting the son we had. To downplay him felt disrespectful and unloving. One of my children would never be put on the backburner at the expense of the other ... even now when I didn't know where my next child would come from.

"I hear you, but I don't agree. I think you're missing something." I held her gaze for a couple seconds. I wasn't backing down. Nate nudged me with his elbow in the ribs again; I gave him a similar look. He knew exactly what the look I'd given Barbara meant. I wasn't backing down and we would need to agree to disagree. The look was my way of saying 'just move on' and that's exactly what she did.

"Moving on," she said, dismissing me, "it's also important you represent yourselves as you truly are. Remember, these portfolios aren't a marketing brochure and you aren't in competition with anyone else. Don't take professional photos, don't worry about how you look. This is about showing your daily life." Again Barbara looked around the room hoping to meet everyone's eyes.

I looked at Nate before Barbara's eyes could meet mine. It felt like a lie to meet Barbara's eyes and tacitly agree with what she just said. I felt like she was talking out of both sides of her mouth. There was no way to represent ourselves as we truly were without including Theo throughout our portfolio. It was simply absurd.

I also didn't believe that the portfolio wasn't a marketing brochure for our family. How could it not be if they advised us not to include too much information about Theo? If the birthmoms were flipping through the stack of portfolios and made initial cuts based on pictures, how could they say we weren't trying to quickly grab their attention? Wasn't that one of the things that marketers tried to do?

Once again I was feeling dueling emotions. On the one hand, I was excited to be one step closer to meeting our baby's birthmom. On the other hand, what the agency was telling us didn't make sense. I could see no way to honestly tell potential birthmothers about our family if we did as they advised and played up certain parts of our lives and played down another. And the part of my life I was proudest of, my son, was the part they wanted me to all but ignore. I began to feel like this next phase of the process was a game and I wasn't comfortable with it.

Are we doing the right thing? Did we choose the right agency? The doubts once again began to take up space in my brain. I tried to quickly push them to the back of my mind. We had spent the last two months working our way through the process with this agency. We'd lose even more time, and money, if I decided to stop the process now.

If we decided not to pursue adoption with this agency, it would mean starting the search for an agency all over again.

I knew Barbara had continued to talk about the remaining steps of the process but I wasn't listening. I was trying to find my equilibrium in the dizzying mix of emotions the past day and a half had created. We were one step closer to adding another child to our family. And with every step we completed I felt a growing excitement and confidence that becoming a family of four was the right decision. Despite my uneasiness, however, I decided it was best to continue pushing forward with the process and turned my attention back to the group.

"So again, if you decide to continue we'd like you to write a check to the Birthmother Assistance fund today. You should also go home and begin working on your portfolios while you wait for your home visit to be scheduled. Once your home visit and portfolio are complete, you'll be placed in the adoptive family pool. Any questions?"

I felt a sense of competition growing between the couples in the room. It wasn't that one couple thought they were better than the other, rather we all wanted to get through the remaining steps of the process and into the adoptive family pool as quickly as possible. We all wanted a child and meeting him or her tomorrow wasn't soon enough. Each couple wanted to be the first of the group with a new baby.

"How quickly can you schedule the home visit?" one of the couples asked.

"Joyce will contact you to schedule, it depends on how busy she is with the birthmoms we have currently waiting and any new moms who come in to the agency in the meantime. For those of you who are out of town, it depends on when she can get a weekend free to travel."

She looked around the room, noting the silence. "Okay, if there aren't any other questions, I'll give you all a few minutes to talk to your spouse and if you're ready to move forward please come let Joyce or me know." Barbara smiled as she stood up and walked into her office.

You could hear the quiet buzz of conversation between each couple. Everyone had more questions, but nobody wanted to ask them publicly. No one wanted to tip their hand. The sense of competition between us seemed to grow.

"What do you think?" I leaned in close to Nate. His strong chest brought me a feeling of confidence and strength. He was my rock.

"We've come this far," his voice trailed off as he looked me in the eye and smiled.

"Might as well jump in with both feet," I said with more confidence than I felt. I hoped Theo would nap during our drive home the next day so I could talk to Nate about some of the things that just didn't feel right.

"Grab the checkbook," he said before standing up.

I leaned down and waded through my purse in search of the checkbook. Pen in hand, I took a deep breath, wrote the check for $500, and we stood up and walked over to Joyce who was standing by a bookshelf that held sample portfolios.

"We're anxious to move ahead," I said to Joyce with a smile. "We hope to see you over on our side of the state soon for the home study."

"Thank you, I'll call you when I have time to make it over. It'll probably be another month or two." My stomach sank in disappointment. I still wasn't used to the rollercoaster ride of emotions this crazy journey was taking us on.

"We really are anxious to move forward," I paused trying to think of something else to say so I didn't sound as desperate as I felt. "I'm sure you hear that a lot," I smiled again.

"The time will go by quickly," she said returning my smile. "Go home and work on your portfolio. There are some here you can look through for ideas before you go."

"Thanks Joyce. We glanced through some yesterday." I didn't want to spend another minute at the agency. The air was so thick with emotion it was getting hard for me to breathe.

"All of the information we covered is in the notebook we gave you," she said, "but feel free to contact us if you have questions."

"We will. Thanks again and we look forward to seeing you soon." Nate and I both shook her hand. We waved good-bye to Barbara and the other couples patiently waiting to ask their questions.

Nate and I walked hand in hand to our car. We had the afternoon and evening to spend with my family before heading home the following morning. We were quiet as we drove back to my parents' house. There were so many thoughts about what we had just experienced that I needed to try to sort out before I could talk to anyone, even Nate.

Had we chosen the right agency? Could we make our portfolio interesting and attractive to perspective birthmoms without downplaying Theo? How long would we have to wait until we were in the adoptive family pool?

I laid my head back on the headrest and closed my eyes. I wanted to try to picture our new child and imagine what it would be like to hold our new baby in my arms. The harder I tried to picture the scene the harder it was to imagine. When Nate finally pulled into my parents' driveway all I could see was the black canvas of the back of my eyelids.

For the first time in my life I couldn't visualize my dream. I had a plan, knew the next steps, but all I could recall were the risks along the way. Could it be that this time I wouldn't be able to make my dream a reality? Was

Joyce's non-committal response about the home study a sign that they'd seen something in us that they didn't like? As my anxiety returned I wondered if we had just hit the final stop on our adoption journey.

Chapter 16

A Study of Home

Memories of our weekend came flooding back as we walked through the front door and dropped our bags in a pile at the bottom of the stairs. I scanned the first floor of our house, my eyes pausing to gaze at the raw pine kitchen island that separated the kitchen from the dining room. The open bottom shelf was a jumble of Theo's shoes, toys, and a couple of kitchen strainers. Our wood veneer table sat in the middle of the dining room, my briefcase at one end and various cars and containers of PlayDoh were scattered in front of Theo's high chair that sat at the head of the table. The curtains drawn closed across the sliding glass doors blocked the view of the swing set in the backyard and the various trucks, shovels, and buckets that Theo used to help me while I gardened.

I glanced at the living room filled with soft-edged furniture, smudged with sticky fingerprints and Chinook's dog hair. In an effort to keep the toys under control there were various baskets and bins scattered around the room. There was no longer a rhyme or reason for which toys went in which container.

This was the house of parents who cherished their child. A house decorated to celebrate family, the walls covered by various art projects and family photos. The Valentine's Day decorations needed to come down so Easter decorations could go up.

This is the house where we make memories to last a lifetime, I thought. *This is the house I want to bring my babies home to.*

I'd spent hours thinking about everything we were told over the weekend. During our long drive home I had busied my mind trying to get the individual pieces of information to fit together into a coherent picture of what was to come. No picture emerged, but one thing was clear, I couldn't summarize what we had learned over the weekend. The word *learned* implied that what we were told made sense and we knew what to expect next. Instead, I found that every question I thought I could answer simply led to another question that I could not.

The truth was we had heard so much over the day and a half at the agency that it had become a jumble of words and phrases. There were facts shared, opinions provided, questions asked and answered. There were next steps and legal process, wait times and etiquette.

And there was stuff that didn't feel like it quite added up. The suggestion that we downplay Theo in our portfolio and in our conversations with birth parents. The recommendation that we have the birth parents play a role in choosing our child's name. And having the birth parents take the lead with the baby after he or she was born, giving them time to bond.

We knew the next step was the home study. Looking at our house as it was now, what would Joyce think? Would she see what I saw? Were there changes we should make to ensure she could see what great parents we were? What great parents we would be to the baby we adopted?

I knew our house was nothing fancy and would never grace the pages of *Architectural Digest*. Heck, it wasn't the house of my dreams. But it was our home, the place we'd brought our first baby home to. The place that provided us shelter and safe harbor as we healed from the ups and downs of the past several years.

The agency hadn't shared many details about the home study. Joyce only said she would conduct the visit, look at the house, and get to know us better. I had researched home studies online trying to better understand both the purpose and what to expect. There were articles, opinion pieces, and checklists. There were some who had a perfectly clean house, well child-proofed, and properly stocked with food and first aid supplies. People wrote about the home study inspector looking in medicine cabinets, closets, and even under beds. There were others that said you should simply be prepared to walk the inspector through your home and be ready to answer questions of basic first aid and child safety.

Not knowing what to expect I wondered how to prepare for the impending visit. Just like when we hosted friends, I wanted our house to be picked up and presentable. But I was realistic. I lived with a preschooler and a large dog. The definition of presentable was all relative.

Not knowing when Joyce would arrive or how much notice we'd be given left me wondering how to be prepared whenever the time came. I worried there was a "gotcha" right around the corner waiting to jump out at us like the boogeyman after dark and as a result, the agency would instantly and unceremoniously drop us from consideration.

Now even the house I loved, the home that sheltered the people I cared about most, was also a source of anxiety and worry. I wondered, not for the first time, whether I would survive the process intact. I was also concerned that the worry alone was proof I wasn't strong enough for adoption and would never become a mom again.

Chapter 17

Family Marketing & Finally Waiting

Our days continued on as normal while we waited to get the call from Joyce to schedule our home study. Each weekday I woke up at five a.m., gulped down a cup of coffee, kissed Theo's sleeping head goodbye, and was at work by six-thirty. I continued to lead my team and find solutions to the challenges that come along in the development of any large real estate development. But it was no small task as everyone seemed to want something different and we were tasked with delivering the project at breakneck speed. After ten hours of intense focus, I'd leave the office hoping to arrive home in time to eat dinner and have at least an hour to play with Theo before his bedtime.

My career was exhausting. I worked extra hard to prove myself in a field dominated by men, many of whom had a decade or two more years of experience than I had. Success meant staying one step ahead, wrangling decisions out of over a dozen people who seemed to all want something different, and managing the changes that popped up at every turn. It was emotionally taxing as I adapted my style to each group of experts and found ways to create a win-win situation out of what often looked like diametrically opposed objectives.

At the time, I didn't realize how much energy was seeping from my body as I worked to keep my thoughts and feelings about the adoption process locked away in the far recesses of my mind. I had to compartmentalize my life in order to focus on what was directly in front of me during the day. The upside was it provided me a sense of control and feelings of success as I moved the project forward and saw the fruits of my labor as the buildings began to rise from the ground.

In the evenings, after Theo was tucked into bed and I had experienced the love and contentment of our nightly bedtime routine, only then would I allow my thoughts to be consumed by the adoption.

After returning home from the workshop, I once again managed to control the wave of frustration and anxiety and find a way to move forward. To dampen my anxiety, I focused on the pride I had for the home Nate and I had created. We had built our house when I was only twenty-five and we paid for it all on our own. Those were signs of our success, signs that we had set goals and achieved them. For the first time in the adoption process I felt my confidence grow. Our house, full of imperfections, was our *home*, and I decided to trust Joyce would see that.

Feeling at peace with the uncertainty surrounding the home visit, I jumped into creating our family portfolio. The agency provided clear guidance on what to include and in what order. They had tried to drive home the notion that the portfolio was simply a means of introducing ourselves to expectant birth parents, and not some kind of marketing brochure. Both Barbara and Joyce tried to convince us throughout our time at the workshop that we weren't in competition with the other families in the waiting pool. I wanted to believe them, I wanted to be convinced that since they had decades of experience, what they said was true. But I wasn't convinced, I couldn't believe them and ultimately, I didn't trust them. *How could the portfolio not be a marketing brochure? Weren't we trying to attract someone's attention, highlighting what it was we had to offer? How was it not marketing material if we were being asked to downplay certain parts of our family?*

I decided I would call a spade a spade and accept the portfolio for what it was. It was our way of grabbing each expectant mom's attention by providing the first bits of evidence that we could give their child a great life. And that started with the main piece of evidence—our son. Nate and I talked a lot about the agency's advice to downplay Theo in the portfolio and decided not to follow it. He was our son, the center of our universe, and he would be an amazing big brother to the baby we adopted. If a potential birthmother couldn't see that, she wasn't the birthmother for us. We had discussed it at length and were in complete agreement; if we had to market our family, we would be truthful in our representation.

Our completed portfolio was 30 pages. It started with a brief introduction of Nate, Theo, and me. The cover had a photo of the three of us and the pages that followed chronicled, through pictures and short captions, how Nate and I met, our courtship, and our wedding. Nate and I both wrote a page talking about ourselves and our families growing up, followed by a page of pictures of us doing the activities we most enjoyed. We gave Theo his own two-page spread and dedicated a page to our dog, Chinook. There were a couple of pages showing our house and what we did when we hung out at home. There were several pages covering the way we celebrated holidays and birthdays. We dedicated space to how we spent time with our extended family.

With our lives summarized in pictures and captions, we came to the final page of the portfolio, the birthmother letter. In a single page, we had to find the words to introduce ourselves and reassure the birthmother we were the best family for her child. It was the most daunting and potentially most important part of the portfolio, not to mention the most important letter I may ever write. How do you put into words why you should be trusted to raise another woman's child? I truly didn't know the answer and after several attempts, I realized I couldn't even figure out how to begin.

Each time I tried, my mind would go blank. My fingers would rest lightly on the computer keyboard, my index fingers resting on the letters j and f, but I was unable to type a single letter. My fingers wouldn't move, my mind unable to form a coherent sentence through the speeding traffic of random thoughts competing for my attention.

After my seventh or eighth try, I was able to convince my fingers to move enough to open a web browser and type a search into Google. I needed guidance and the Internet was at my fingertips. I knew I would get wildly varying advice but at least it was something. Among the thousands of search results, I had faith I would find the inspiration I needed to untangle my own thoughts and figure out where to begin.

Typing 'birthmother letter' into Google, the search came up with over half a million results. Just as my experience of researching adoption had taught me early on, there is nearly no end to the amount of information on the Internet. I quickly scanned the descriptions beneath the headlines for the first page of results and settled on two. One included a checklist of things to cover, along with phrasing to avoid because it could be easily misinterpreted by the birthmother. The second was an article, written by a father, on the letter he had written. His letter was touching and genuine. And most importantly, it sparked my imagination.

I opened a new document on my computer and my fingers flew across the keyboard. The words appeared on the screen even before I consciously acknowledged them. The page was filled in less than five minutes. I read over what I wrote a couple of times, made a few changes, then went in search of Nate to get his feedback. With only a couple minor changes at Nate's suggestion, the letter was complete. Here's what we wrote:

Dear Birth Parents,

Thank you for choosing to get to know us through our portfolio. Over three years ago we were blessed with the birth of our son. When we discovered we couldn't have another biological child we thought for a long time about our options. We decided open adoption is the right choice for us. All three of us are looking forward to welcoming our new baby.

We have seen the success of open adoption. A few years ago one of Kim's childhood friends had a child who was adopted by a wonderful couple. Her family got to know her baby's adoptive parents through email, phone calls, and exchanging pictures over the Internet. The baby's parents are amazing and Kim's friend is glad that they chose open adoption to start their family. This experience allowed us to see, just a little bit, what the adoption experience is like for you, the birth parents. We understand what a big decision this is and how difficult it may be.

We have a strong marriage filled with love, respect, and support for each other. We have created a home where family and friends feel welcome and appreciated. We enjoy raising our son, watching him grow and learn. We look forward to another child joining our family, watching him or her learn and grow. We are excited about the additional love that our next child will receive from not just us, but his or her big brother. Theo, in his 3-year-old way, is also getting ready to be a big brother. He is excited to make sure our home is ready for his brother or sister and talks about how he can help and teach "his baby."

We look forward to seeing our children attend preschool, elementary school, graduate high school, go to college, and enter the working world. We will support our children in exploring their interests, whatever they may be.

We create opportunities for our family to experience nature, music, the arts, and sports. We take hikes, cook together, garden, play outside, go to the zoo and museums, listen to music, read books, and just hang out. We look forward to a life filled with decorating our home with kid-made crafts, attending school plays, coaching sports, and listening to music recitals.

We strive to raise healthy, happy, confident, creative children who dream big and work to realize their dreams.

Our very best wishes are with you as you travel through this life journey.

Yours truly,
Kim and Nate

When the letter was finally done and printed I felt a weight lift from my shoulders I hadn't realized was there. Reading the letter one final time I prepared to print the dozen copies of our portfolio we needed to send to the agency. The letter also made me realize how much we had been through since our marriage began twelve years earlier. I thought of how much we had accomplished together, how many times we chose to pick ourselves up, dust ourselves off, and find a way forward. I felt proud of who we were and what we had accomplished. The mistakes we had made felt less punishing and our choices to move forward more rewarding. In the midst of the anxiety, worry, and unknowns came an unexpected blessing. A moment of clarity was created that would carry me through some dark months to come.

* * *

When I was pregnant, I had to patiently wait for Theo to be born, but I knew there was a deadline. With adoption, there was no set gestation. The waiting could be years, and I prayed that wouldn't happen to us. But it felt like it might. With our portfolio submitted, there was nothing more we could do but wait for the home visit, whenever that might happen.

A week later it appeared that sending the portfolios before our home study was completed had been enough to motivate the agency to schedule the visit. It was a sunny morning in early April when my phone began to buzz on my desk. I looked down and saw the agency's number.

"Hi Kim, this is Joyce from Alto," she said in her business-like manner. "I'm headed over to your side of the state to meet a birthmother who just had her baby. If you and Nate will be home tonight, I'd like to come for your home visit."

"Um, wow," I felt my face flush with excitement as my heart began to race. "That's great. What time do you think you'll arrive?"

"I'm not sure, it all depends on when I get out of town and how the birthmother is doing when I get to the hospital."

"Okay, well I'll be home about six. Do you need directions to our house?" It took a tremendous amount of self-control not to start jumping up and down to release the excitement I was trying hard to hold in.

My hands shook as I hung up. I had to call Nate and let him know. As the reality of the plans I'd just made sank in, my stomach dropped. How clean was the house? Would I have time to vacuum? Was the pile of laundry still on the couch waiting to be folded?

I quickly checked the calendar on my phone before calling Nate and giving him the good news. Luckily my last meeting ended at two-thirty and I could likely leave by three. That would give me at least a couple of hours to quickly straighten up the house and calm my nerves.

"Hey babe, it's me," I said slightly out of breath even before he said hello. "Joyce just called and she'll be at our house tonight for the home visit!"

"Anything I can do to help get things ready?"

I was touched he had asked. In the months since we'd decided to move forward with adoption I'd done most of the heavy lifting and it had felt like Nate was just along for the ride. I suddenly felt like I had a co-pilot and it was a huge relief.

Arriving home just after four o'clock I wondered how much Nate had gotten done at the house. He was substitute teaching and working part-time at a graphic design shop. Luckily that day he was doing neither. With Theo at daycare, chances were he'd had time to pick up a bit.

Walking into the kitchen I quickly saw he had done a wonderful job cleaning the entire first floor of our house. The kitchen sparkled, the dining room table was free of the clutter that always seemed to accumulate there, and the toys that were usually scattered throughout the living room had been put into bins. On my way to the closet to hang up my coat, I even noticed he'd dusted the end tables. *He wants this, too!*

That thought nearly took my breath away. *He's really bought in and invested.* Until that moment, I hadn't realized how fearful I was that I was the only one who wanted another baby and that he really was only going along with it to keep me happy. Now I knew that was not the case. I felt more weight lift from my shoulders and I stood up a little taller. *We can do this!*

* * *

Theo sat happily playing in the living room as Nate and I cleaned up after dinner. Joyce still hadn't called and we tried not to worry that she would cancel. To distract ourselves, we decided to take advantage of the warm spring day and took Theo outside to play.

While Theo ran around in the front yard and drew on the driveway with sidewalk chalk I began pulling weeds from the flowerbed leading to the front door.

"Do you really think you need to do that?" Nate asked sitting down on the step next to me and grabbing a piece of chalk to draw with Theo.

"Well, this *is* the first impression she'll have of the house," I said with a half-smile. I knew I was being a bit neurotic, but at least I was putting my nervous energy to work doing something that I'd have to tackle sooner or later anyway.

"Whatever makes you feel better," he said kissing the top of my head.

Finally, around seven thirty, with only half an hour before Theo's bedtime, we recognized Joyce's car coming down our street. My heart began to pound as she parked in front of the house. I stood up and dusted off my hands the best I could. There was no time to run inside and wash up before greeting her.

"Hi Joyce," I said as she walked up the driveway. "Did you have trouble finding the house?"

"Hi you two, sorry I'm late," turning to Theo, "You must be Theo."

"Hi," Theo said shyly before melting into my leg. I put my arm around him and patted his back, the motion comforted both of us.

"Why don't we head inside," I suggested extending my hand to indicate that Joyce should go first."

Here goes nothing!

With Joyce seated in Nate's leather recliner, Nate and I sat down on the couch, and Theo crawled up on my lap. Joyce spoke first. "I'm just here to get to know the two of you better and answer any questions you have. It's my way of getting to know more about you so I can talk to birthmothers about you when they're looking at portfolios." She paused before continuing. "I had a chance to look through the portfolios you mailed in. You did a nice job."

We chatted for the next twenty minutes expanding on the information in our portfolios, while Theo busied himself building a block tower in the middle of the living room floor. Joyce asked us more about each of our families, what it was like growing up with our siblings, and how our parents had influenced us.

As we finished our conversation about the portfolios, as if on cue, Theo began to squirm, yawn, and rub his eyes. He was tired and it was a few minutes past his bedtime.

"Kim, why don't you go ahead and put Theo to bed? Nate and I can talk a little while you're gone," Joyce said.

Was I just dismissed in my own home? Did she just tell me it was time to put my child to bed? I also wondered why she assumed it was my job to put Theo to bed. It was true I did the bulk of the bedtime routine, but Nate and I worked as a team to help Theo get his pajamas on and brush his teeth.

"Well, we usually ...." Nate said sensing my irritation.

"Don't worry, babe, I got this. I'll be back down in twenty minutes or so," I patted Nate's leg and turned my attention to Theo. "Let's go buddy. Tell Miss Joyce nice to meet you and give Daddy kisses. Let's get you up to bed."

"Night Daddy," Theo said as he leaned over to give Nate a kiss on the cheek. "Nice to meet you Miss Joyce," he said as I picked him up and headed toward the stairs.

Joyce smiled. "It was nice to meet you Theo. Good night."

Twenty minutes later, our nightly bedtime ritual complete, I quietly closed Theo's door and walked down the stairs.

"Sorry for the interruption," I said as I joined them in the living room.

"It was no problem, Kim." Joyce said. "It gave Nate and me a chance to get to know each other."

"Oh good," I said looking over at Nate for any hint of what they'd talked about.

"Well, it's getting late and I think I have what I need," Joyce said as she reached for her purse that sat on the floor next to her.

"Is there anything else you need? Did you want to see the rest of the house?" I asked. It felt strange that she was ending the visit so quickly after I returned. *What about the inspection portion of the home study I had read so much about?*

"No, I have what I need," she said as she made her way to the front door.

"Okay," I paused to quickly gather my thoughts. "Can you tell us what to expect next?" I wanted to know whether we had successfully passed this final step in the approval process.

"I'll go back to the office, write up my notes and if we have everything else in order, we'll get your portfolios into the pool," Joyce said as she stopped in front of the door.

I let out my breath very slowly as I walked past her to open the door. "That's wonderful to hear. We're very excited."

"Thanks for your time tonight. It was nice to meet Theo and get to know you both a little better. We'll be in touch."

And with that, Joyce left our house. Nate and I stood at the front door until she drove away.

I slowly closed the front door and turned to Nate. "We passed," I said, suddenly crying. "We're finally in. And why in the heck am I crying?" I started to laugh at the ridiculousness of it all.

Nate reached out and wrapped me in a tight hug as we stood in the entryway, Chinook dancing around our feet wanting attention as I cried tears of relief, finally releasing the frustration, anxiety, and self-criticism I'd carried for the last several months.

Now we waited. Would it be weeks or months until we were chosen? Would we have a son or a daughter? Would there be any more surprises in store on this wild journey? I wasn't sure what to expect, but I hoped I'd be strong enough to handle whatever came next.

Chapter 18

Time for a Little Dreaming

I rolled over and hit the snooze button; I was tired and didn't want my dream to end. I quickly fell back to sleep and rejoined my dream right where I'd left off.

Nate and I were standing in the reception area of the adoption agency. Our backs were to the receptionist as we stared at a bulletin board filled with pictures of loving couples with arms around each other, wide smiles on their faces. Dozens of portfolios lined up one next to another on the top shelf of a bookcase.

"There's our picture," Nate said pointing to a photo in the upper right-hand corner of the bulletin board and as he put his arm around my waist.

"We're finally on the board," I said, looking up at him as he pulled me closer. "I didn't think it'd happen."

We stood there looking back and forth between our photo and the bookshelf, checking to see if our portfolio had been chosen. But the room we stood in seemed to float amongst the clouds, only the bulletin board and bookcase were connected to the ground. The only thing that seemed real was the paper our family marketing brochure was printed on.

I fought to stay asleep, surrounded by the peace and pleasure of the moment. I didn't want to wake up and face the unknowns that came with waiting to be chosen.

"Kim, aren't you going into work today?" Nate asked as he rolled over and draped his arm over my shoulders.

"I don't wanna," I whined as I opened my eyes and saw it was nearly six, the time I usually left for work. "Ugh, I'm so *tired*! And I was having a good dream." I gently removed Nate's arm, sat up, and swung my legs over the side of the bed. "I never remember my dreams." I wanted to believe that this one was the sign I needed that we were just weeks away from being chosen by a birthmother.

* * *

The days went by more quickly as the weather warmed and the sun set later in the evening. On weeknights I managed to get home in time to have dinner with Nate and Theo and whenever the weather allowed, we spent an hour outside running around in the yard together.

"Push me mommy!" Theo squealed as he climbed into the swing of our backyard playset. "I know how to pump my legs now," he said with a smile that filled his entire face.

"You can? That's so cool buddy," I replied as I grabbed hold of the swing and pulled it toward my chest. "Are you ready?" I asked over his giggles.

"Yes!"

"Are you *sure*?" I asked again, resting my chin on his shoulder and gave him a peck on the cheek.

"*Yes!*"

"Okay. Ready, set, *Go!*" I shouted as I released the swing. Theo's laughter filled my ears and I saw he was indeed moving his legs out and in as he swung forward and back.

"See Mommy! Do you see me? I'm doing it!"

"Wow buddy, you *are* doing it!" I walked to the front of the swing set so I could see his face. "Whoa, you're going really high!" I looked over at Nate. "I sure hope Daddy did a good job building your swing set. You're like a rocket and might take it to the moon!"

"Swings can't fly Mommy, you're just silly."

There was our boy, three and a half, growing up so fast. He had mastered swinging by himself; another childhood achievement unlocked. I remembered swinging on the metal swing set in our backyard as a kid. We could swing so high the entire swing set jumped off the ground. It was thrilling! But I wasn't sure I was ready to watch Theo recreate my childhood experience so I walked over to one of the legs of the swing set to make sure it wouldn't leave terra firma.

Without the stress of working our way through the application process my energy gradually returned. I hadn't realized the toll the application process had taken. My body began to feel lighter, I wasn't constantly on edge, and my creativity slowly returned.

I'm not an artistically creative person. I experience creativity in my ability to develop multiple solutions to a problem, figure out how to get a new project started, or how to get people to buy in to a plan. At home, I expressed my creativity in my growing garden, picking and placing plants with a variety of colors, textures, and seasonal interest.

Bored during my hour-long commute each way to and from work, I would daydream about what I wanted for my life. Where did I want to take my career? How did we need to improve our marriage? What should I be doing to help Theo learn and grow? Driving home on an otherwise normal Wednesday evening my mind wandered into new territory as I began to wonder what our child's birthmother would be like.

I wondered what Barbara would share about the woman who chose us to parent her baby. As I imagined what Barbara would say, I remembered the moment, over four years before, when I first discovered I was pregnant.

Sitting in bumper to bumper traffic, after months of effort, I felt like our baby's gestation had finally begun.

"We're having a baby!" I cried out to the universe. "We're gonna have another baby!" I felt hot, salty tears tumble down my cheeks and pool between my closed lips as relief washed over me. "It's safe for me to think about you," I whispered to my future child as I looked through the windshield into the clear blue sky.

It finally felt safe to think about the woman who would trust me to become the mother of her baby. I gave myself permission to wonder about the baby who would become our child. Would we have another son or our first daughter? What color eyes and hair would our baby have? Would he or she be easy-going or demanding? I wondered how much their personality would be shaped by our nurturing, and how much by nature? The familiar feeling of wonder about an unborn child comforted me. It was exciting to dream about the baby I wanted so desperately. The devastation of infertility was no longer a permanent shade over the light illuminating our future.

I spent the majority of my drive to and from work thinking about who our child's birthmother might be, the circumstances of her pregnancy that would lead her to choose adoption, and what role she would have in our family. The profile formed with such detail I had to remind myself I had not yet met our future child's birthmother.

I imagined she would be a university student and that even though she and her boyfriend were careful, one determined sperm had survived the journey. Wanting to finish college and begin a career, she chose adoption for her child.

Our child's birthmother would be intelligent, confident, determined, and kind. She would be well-spoken and clearly communicate to the agency, and later to us, her dreams for her child. We would bond over her dreams and desires for the baby. We would become friends, our relationship a mixture of sisterhood and mentorship. She would have an aunt-like relationship with both our children, like the information about the benefits of open adoption had promised.

With the risks and uncertainties surrounding the adoption process and my questions about how to build a successful relationship with our child's birthmother, I found comfort in the profile of the birthmother I created in my mind. She was a woman I was comfortable getting to know and letting into our life. She was someone I felt confident I knew how to develop a healthy relationship with.

As weeks of waiting turned into months I started to think more about our new baby. I was always on guard when I let my mind wander into the wilderness of wonder about our second child. At times it was a joyous discovery and that brought feelings of excitement similar to those I experienced while pregnant with Theo. And then there were times when I would stumble onto the hurt of not being able to experience pregnancy a second time. I would feel a stab of pain in my chest at the reminder that I would never again feel the first gentle flickers of movement that left me breathless and waiting for the next flurry to confirm I had indeed felt my baby move in my belly. I would never again feel and see the rolling wave across my belly as the baby turned. Never again gently press my hand against the little foot that kicked me in the ribs making me call out in discomfort and surprise.

There was comfort and delight dreaming about the baby I yearned for and knew deep in my soul would someday join our family. But at the same time I was heartbroken. Experiencing the development of a baby in my womb only once still didn't feel like enough.

To buoy my spirits, I thought about whether our next child would be a boy or a girl. It didn't really matter; we wanted a healthy baby more than we wanted to wait for a specific gender. Secretly, though, I hoped for a daughter. I wanted to buy pink frilly clothes and put my daughter's hair in ponytails. And as our children grew up, I didn't want to be the only one in the house who wanted the toilet seat left down.

* * *

Nearly six months had passed without hearing anything from the agency. Finally, on a sunny Friday afternoon in mid-August I decided to call and check-in.

The sky was bright blue and temperatures were set to hit the upper 80s. I left work early and drove home through the winding backroads that cut through tree-covered hills. I wanted a break from the frantic pace of work and the bustling city. And I figured I would use the extra time to absorb whatever news the agency had for us.

Worried I would sound too anxious about how the process was going, I thought I'd use the call to let the agency know I was considering a job change. One of my client's executives had asked me to interview for a position with their company and I had decided to go for it. It was a great opportunity that would take my career in an entirely new direction.

With the earbuds firmly in place and one hand solidly on the wheel, I dialed the agency's number. I was surprised when Joyce answered on the third ring. "Oh hi Joyce, it's Kim Severn calling," I said, suddenly feeling flustered.

"Good afternoon, Kim. You were actually on my list of people to call," she said causally.

My curiosity was piqued as my heart began to race. I gripped the steering wheel a little tighter making sure to focus on the road. "We hadn't heard from you in several months, so I wanted to give you a call, check-in, and give you some news."

"Sounds good, why don't you go first," she said. *Why hadn't I asked her what she wanted to call us about?*

I gave her the update on my pending job change and she assured me they'd update my file. Then she paused and I heard her shuffle papers on her desk.

After a couple seconds of silence that felt like a millennia, I said, "You said you were going to give us a call?"

"Yes, I was just pulling out the file," she paused again and I could hear her chair squeak as she moved. "Here it is. We have a couple who've used our agency twice before. They're a nice couple and have had two baby boys together. We've placed both of their sons with adoptive families."

Is she saying we've been chosen? I wondered. *Wow, already placed two babies for adoption?* My heart ached for the birth parents and I wondered how they could bare the strain of going through adoption multiple times. I brought myself back to the present, as Joyce continued to talk, unaware she'd momentarily lost me.

"The birth parents are both deaf," I heard her say as I wondered how much I had missed. "She had healthy full-term pregnancies with both boys and one of the boys is deaf."

Did she just say both were born healthy but one of the boys is deaf? I couldn't have understood her correctly. She still hadn't stopped talking so I pushed my question aside and continued to listen.

"They've been together for several years and are in their mid-twenties. The state won't allow them to keep the children because they struggle in their decision making." She paused, and I assumed she was waiting for me to respond.

"Oh wow," I said unsure what to say. *What does it mean that they 'struggle in their decision-making'? Was it okay to ask for more details? What do I want to know?*

"And they picked us?" I said feeling bewildered.

"Yes, they're interested in meeting you. But its early in her pregnancy; she's less than three months along. Normally I wouldn't contact prospective adoptive parents this early, but we have a solid history with this couple. But, I wanted to let you know in case you're planning a visit soon."

"I see," I said as I took a deep breath and tried to understand the ramifications of what I was just told. "Well, we typically come for a visit in early fall to celebrate Theo's birthday with my family. We could

162

arrange to meet them then if a couple months isn't too long to wait."

"That timing works great. I'll contact the birth parents to let them know you're open to meeting."

"Sounds good, but I need to talk to Nate. We hadn't considered adopting a baby with any kind of special needs." I hoped my honesty wouldn't hurt us, but it was true. We never thought about the possibility of having a child who was deaf. We didn't know anything about raising children with hearing loss. What did we need to know? What did we need to do to prepare? What resources would we need? My mind went straight to where it was comfortable, identify the challenge and begin building a plan to address it.

"Okay, let me know what he says and in the meantime we'll set your portfolio aside for this couple."

I thanked her and hung up. I was glad I chose the long way home. There was suddenly so much to think about. *How would the birth parents' hearing loss impact building a relationship with them? What would it be like raising a deaf child?* I wondered if we had time to do research and find out what resources we would need for our child. *How quickly could we learn sign language?*

We can do this! I thought, as the idea of raising this baby took hold. Besides, it wasn't even a sure thing that the baby would be unable to hear, I reasoned. The couple had had one hearing child.

As I continued to drive through the winding backroads, sunlight filtered through the leaves of maples and thick branches of evergreen trees, I thought about what we would have done had Theo been born unable to hear. It wouldn't have changed the fact we were his parents. We would have loved him and figured it out as we went along. Following this logic, rejecting a child with special needs seemed as unacceptable with adoption as it did had I given birth to the child. *Wouldn't we love whatever children we were blessed with?* Still, I wondered what Nate would say about it. I decided to call and find out.

"Hey babe, I'm on my way home and I just got off the phone with the agency."

"Hey sweetheart, you're on the way already?" He sounded surprised. "What's up?"

I took a deep breath. I realized I wasn't feeling as excited as I thought I would. It felt like delivering fantastic news with a catch. "I called the agency to ask if there was any news. Turns out Joyce was going to call us. We've been chosen by a birthmother, but she's early in her pregnancy," I paused, "and there might be an issue with the baby."

"Okay ...." drawing out the word longer than necessary to signal his concern.

"There's a chance the baby could be born deaf," I said and held my breath as I waited for him to respond. After a couple seconds of silence I continued, "They've already used the agency to place two other baby boys for adoption. One was deaf and one wasn't."

"Sounds like we have something to talk about."

"Do we?" There was an unexpected edge to my voice. I knew what he meant. But in the few minutes I had taken to think things through, I thought I had made my decision about what we should do based on solid logic. "I'm sorry Nate, I didn't mean that. Let's talk about it tonight after Theo's asleep."

"We'll talk about it then." I could hear the irritation in his voice and I knew I deserved it.

"I'll see you guys soon," I hoped the smile I'd put on my face came through in my voice.

There was clearly more for Nate and me to talk about when it came to having our next child. There were questions we didn't know we needed to answer, situations we hadn't thought to think through, complications we hadn't known we'd need to be on the same page about.

I was just beginning to stumble upon something important in the way I approached life. And the impacts my choices had on other people. In our marriage, I was the one to take charge and make a decision. I found comfort in making decisions, solving problems, and then moving forward. It made me feel like I had a firm grasp on control and created a sense of safety. My automatic response was to make a decision, communicate it to others, and take action. This approach had enabled me to excel professionally. But in interpersonal relationships, it was problematic.

In the past several months Nate and I had felt closer and more connected than we ever had in our 14-year marriage. Were we headed toward the beginning of a new chapter of stress? Were Nate and I worlds apart on something we didn't even know we had to address?

My stomach churned and my heart felt heavy. The sun that lit the way to a happy future just a moment before had turned to pure heat on my face as it blinded my eyes. I hoped Nate and I could agree on how to move forward before we experienced a detour, or even worse, a dead end. As I continued to mull it over, I began to realize that the adoption wasn't just about making room in our family for another child. It was also about making room for the possibility of another way to successfully live my life.

Chapter 19

Dumped. Declined. Recovered?

Over the next several nights Nate and I discussed whether to move forward with meeting the birth parents who had selected us. My opinion didn't change; I felt strongly we should meet them even though there was a risk the baby would be born deaf.

Life wouldn't be as we had expected, but I knew had Theo been born with a disability we would have loved him unconditionally. And that fact seemed to be the only one that mattered. *Didn't the same logic have to apply with adoption?* When you have a baby there are no guarantees.

There were two factors that cemented my point of view. First, when we decided to have a baby, we never thought about our odds of having a healthy child. We just assumed we would have one and if we didn't we would figure it out. And second, of all the disabilities a person could have, deafness was one we could learn about, prepare for, and locate the services our child would need to live a happy and successful life. It was scary, but we could do it.

I had spent countless hours thinking about the differences between having a biological child and adopting a child. There were aspects of adoption I still wasn't completely comfortable with, choices that existed with adoption that we didn't have with a biological child.

For instance, when applying to adopt we had to make a decision about the age, race, and sex of the child we wanted for our family. There was part of me, some days a big part of me, that wanted to be very selective. Being selective provided a false sense of control over the situation and helped me feel protected against the fear and uncertainty.

The family I had dreamt of having included two children, a son and a daughter. Both of our children would be independent, kind, and talented. We would all get along and enjoy spending time together. If I wanted this dream to become reality, we would wait for a daughter. And if I took it a step farther, we would wait for birth parents with similar physical features so our daughter would look like us. That would mean we would wait for birth parents of northern European descent with brown hair and brown eyes. My desire to be so selective was strongest when I was tired, anxious, and sad about our inability to conceive a second time.

But no matter how much comfort the thought of being selective brought, there was the reality that the more rigid our criteria were, the longer we would have to wait for a child. This practical reality didn't really matter either.

What I wanted most of all was a healthy baby. That was, after all, the reason we began this crazy journey. Race didn't matter, sex didn't matter, physical characteristics didn't matter; having a baby to complete our family is why we had chosen adoption. I had love to give and every child is worthy of my love.

When we were presented with the possibility of a child with hearing loss I was no longer presented with a black and white decision; shades of gray suddenly appeared. For example, in mere minutes, my definition of healthy changed. Children who grew up to become independent, successful members of society became the new definition of healthy.

No matter how comfortable I was with my reasoning or my new definition of healthy, in the end I knew Nate and I had to come to an agreement we could both live with. I had to decide if I was willing to decline these birth parents if Nate wasn't comfortable moving forward. In order to find peace with whatever decision we made, I wanted to feel confident that I had clearly communicated my feelings and point of view. If I was able to do that and Nate still wasn't comfortable with the decision, I'd let it go.

We had several conversations over the next few days and ultimately we decided to move forward. We had waited months to be chosen and if these birth parents selected us it must have been meant to be. Based on the birthmother's previous pregnancies, it seemed there was a 50/50 chance the baby would be born without hearing loss. Just like we assumed I'd deliver a healthy baby when Theo was born, we would approach this birth the same way.

I sent Joyce a short email letting her know Nate and I had agreed to move forward and confirmed the dates we would be in town six weeks later. Our decision meant we were no longer part of the prospective parent pool and we could begin to make plans around a due date. In a little over a month we would meet the birth parents of our next child. And if all went well we'd be a family of four the following spring.

A couple of weeks passed before Joyce replied and asked me to follow-up a few days before our trip to arrange a time and a place to meet. She said the delay in her response was because she wanted to confirm with the birth parents that a meeting in early October would work for them. The delay seemed strange, but I put my worry aside. We didn't hear anything more.

Dressed in shorts and a t-shirt, a towel still wrapped around my wet hair, I sat down on the edge of my bed to begin a journal for our new baby. I had started a journal during my pregnancy with Theo and I saw no reason not to do the same thing for our next child. Running errands after work the night before I had found a five-inch square spiral bound journal with a blue on blue paisley pattern. I flipped to the first page, maneuvered myself so I could lean back against the headboard, rested the journal on my bent knees and began to write.

Do I know of you yet? About a month ago I called Joyce at the adoption agency and a couple had just left. They had preliminarily chosen your dad and me. Your birthmom is early in her pregnancy so if this is you, our child, you are newly created.

Early last week we set a date to meet your birth parents on Friday, October 10th. I am excited to meet your birthmom, excited to know if she will like us. If you are the baby growing inside her body, I am excited to know that you will be with us in less than a year.

There are so many questions. When will you arrive, will you be a boy or a girl? What will you look like? Will you be a good sleeper? Will you like to be cuddled? Will you be laid back or want to be entertained? Oh so many questions we are so excited to meet you and learn the answers.

Your big brother is excited to have you too. He really wants a sister. We are not sure why. However, if you are a boy, he'll be excited about having a brother too. Theo told me this morning that he needs to stop wearing diapers before you arrive. I sure hope he does.

We are so excited to have you join our family. I am glad you will have your great big brother Theo to grow up with. Oh what a journey we are on.

I closed the journal and placed it on top of my nightstand so I would remember to continue writing in it from time to time. It felt wonderful to take this next step in preparing for our child.

A week before our trip, I called Joyce to make arrangements for the meeting with the birth parents. I sat in a conference room and tapped a pen nervously on the table while I impatiently waited on hold for several minutes.

"Hi Kim, thanks for waiting," I heard the familiar squeak of Joyce's chair as she moved. "I've been trying to reach the birth parents for a few weeks and I've been unsuccessful."

"Um hum," my stomach sank as my heart beat quickened. *What did she mean trying to reach them? For a few weeks?*

"I finally reached one of the birthmother's friends and she said the birthmother has moved out of the state." Joyce's tone was all business and made my blood run cold. *What is she talking about?* I said nothing, not trusting myself to speak as my anger grew. *Why hadn't she told us they'd disappeared weeks ago? All this time I've been thinking of raising their child and they've disappeared?*

"She didn't want to give up another baby, so she moved away. That way the State won't step in and take away this baby too."

I could barely hear what she was saying over the pounding of my heartbeat. I wasn't angry with the birthmother, I understood her decision. I was furious with Joyce. *How long had she truly known? Had she strung us along for weeks?*

"So there are no birth parents for us to meet when we're in town next weekend?" I could barely get the question out. All I wanted to do was yell.

From the moment Joyce told me the birthmother had moved away I knew she had withheld information from us. When she first told us about this couple nearly two months before, she had assured me that they had reached out to her and had chosen adoption for this baby. *How naive had I been to trust her.*

And it suddenly dawned on me, this meant we had gone for weeks without our portfolio being available for other birth parents to choose from. I wanted to throw the phone across the room in frustration. I couldn't keep my anger and disappointment inside for another second.

"So we've been out of the prospective parent pool for two months and now we're back to square one?" My voice cracked in the middle of the question.

"Yes," she said simply. When I didn't say anything she continued, "I'm sure there will be more birthmothers coming in soon and your portfolio will be on the top of the stack."

"*Soon? At the top of the stack?* Wow, Joyce, you really think that makes us feel better? You really think that makes this situation okay?" My questions were filled with sarcasm. "And what do you mean top of the stack? We never knew there was a priority given to the portfolios." She said nothing and I decided to fill the silence. "This is *beyond* disappointing!" I couldn't seem to catch enough air to say another word. I knew there were no guarantees, but I couldn't help feeling like we'd lost a baby.

"Kim, this is how these things go sometimes. We'll contact you as soon as there's interest in your portfolio." She was all business, without a trace of empathy. *Were we nothing but a payday?*

A silent sob filled my chest. We were over ten months and nearly ten thousand dollars into the process. Turning back would cost the agency nothing, and us a great deal. If we cut ties, we would have to start from scratch with another agency. I felt completely powerless. "I need to go." I hung up the phone before she could say another word.

I sat with the fluorescent lights humming softly above me, too stunned to move. A paralyzing mix of anger and disappointment pulsed through my veins. *What in the hell just happened?*

It took all my self-control not to throw my phone across the room, not to stand up and punch the wall. I wanted to throw my head back and scream in fury. I wanted the freedom to act like a wronged toddler, to throw myself on the ground kicking and screaming until I got my way. I wanted my feelings acknowledged and my needs met.

I'm not a violent person and under normal circumstances have nearly endless amounts of patience. Combined with my dislike of conflict, it was very unusual for me to show my emotions or confront someone. But this was no ordinary situation.

As the anger slowly subsided and the disappointment settled in, I dropped my head onto my arms and sobbed. I didn't care if one of my coworkers walked in on me. It was as if a thunderstorm had appeared out of nowhere and lightening had struck me in the heart, bringing with it a powerful loss—the loss of a baby that was never mine. The loss of a child I had never met. The loss of the time and turmoil that I had devoted to preparing for that child.

I cried so hard I nearly threw up. The ache came from deep within me, a twisting, tugging, pressure-filled pain that I felt would take residence and never leave.

* * *

Nate took the news in stride. I don't think the possibility of this baby had felt as real to him as it had for me. He was contented with being Theo's dad and living in the moment. For him, it simply wasn't meant to be and our turn would come. For me, our family was still incomplete, and that meant I was incomplete. That was something I knew Nate couldn't understand, perhaps because I didn't understand it all myself.

* * *

I started my new job at the end of September and was busy figuring out both the work and the new team. Thank God for that job and the distractions it brought. I thrived in the distractions that work brought and only allowed my feelings about the adoption to occupy my mind at night when Theo and Nate were fast asleep.

Halloween, Thanksgiving, Christmas, and New Year's all came and went without a word from the agency. I called once just to make sure what I said on the phone with Joyce the previous fall hadn't disqualified us and to make sure our portfolio was still on the shelf. Barbara said it was, although I doubted it was at the top of the stack.

After that heart-wrenching call we would wait another four months before hearing from the agency again. I was sitting at my desk when my cell phone rang. Recognizing the number on the caller ID, I quickly stood and walked to one of the glass-fronted conference rooms to take the call so I wouldn't disturb my coworkers.

"Kim, it's Joyce," her voice was clipped as she spoke more quickly than usual. "I'm headed over to your side of the state right now." Clearly something was going on, but I was finding it hard to care. I was still hurt by the way she had handled the situation months before.

"What can I do for you, Joyce?" I had no interest in pleasantries. I needed to protect myself by keeping my guard up.

"We placed a child with a couple living near you a few months ago. The adoptive mother is having a hard time since we placed the baby. The adoptive father just called and said they can't move forward with the adoption. I need to come and take custody of the baby. If you and Nate are interested, you can meet him tonight."

She went on to tell me more about the circumstances. His birthmother, who had schizophrenia, had tried and was unable to keep him. He was less than six months old and had already been in the custody of multiple adults. By the end of the call I was feeling seriously uneasy, but I agreed to talk to Nate about the situation. She would call again after she arrived in town.

As I said I would, I talked it over with Nate. This time it didn't take days or even hours to make a decision. It took less than five minutes. We would say no. It didn't feel right. It was too rushed. And we knew we couldn't meet the baby, the chance that one of us would lose our resolve was too great and we didn't want that to happen. I couldn't imagine holding a baby who needed love and safety and hand him back without knowing for sure who would be there to give him what he needed.

I was packing my briefcase for the night when Joyce called again. I kept it brief and told her of our decision. She tried one more time, offering to drive down with the baby for us to meet him. "I'm sorry Joyce, we just can't."

I knew it was the right decision, but it hurt. I felt the loss of another child. I had never in my wildest dreams thought the adoption process would be filled with such heartbreaking choices. I never imagined I would feel the loss of a baby I had only known existed for a matter of hours. But each loss, however short the dream, cut deeper into my heart until soon I feared I'd lose hope altogether.

The next night, with our decision still occupying my thoughts, I sat down to write in my journal. Writing seemed to be the one thing that eased the pain of my aching heart.

Yesterday morning, I received an unexpected call from the birth parent counselor, Joyce. There was a 5-month old baby boy, Ashton, that needs immediate placement. His next home, hopefully the last, will be his 3rd in just 5 months! Ashton's biological mom has schizophrenia. I say that, because ultimately that fact, above all our other concerns, was what swayed us to say no.

Whoever thought that a life's worth of decisions would include saying no to a baby? Admittedly my dreams do not include having one of my children in our home forever. Our dreams include children who are on their own after college.

The struggles and philosophical questions this adoption process has raised are way beyond any I could have imagined. Crazy as it may seem, when I look at the journey I consciously started over a year ago I am so thankful for it. It has finally dawned on me that part of this journey is about trust; trusting myself.

Making this decision I have to trust I did the right thing. That the right baby is out there for our family. That if the right baby doesn't come our way, our family of three is what's right. Another lesson learned is that I need to write to find solace, to process, to find the freedom to let go.

More weeks passed. It had been more than a year since we had attended the weekend workshop at the agency. I tried not to wonder what it was about our family that birthmothers didn't appear drawn to. I tried not to imagine all the birth families who must have seen our portfolio, looked at our pictures and read about our life, and closed the book having decided we weren't the ones to raise their child. And when those thoughts entered my head, I remembered how much I loved our family that Nate and I had created together. The longer it took to be selected the more protective I was of who we were and what we had achieved. It was not that I wasn't already committed to my family, but the waiting further solidified my love for, and dedication to, Nate and Theo.

And if including so much information about Theo was the reason we hadn't been chosen again, I was okay with that too. Of all my achievements, he was by far what I was most proud of.

I reminded myself to have faith that the right birth parents would come along sooner or later and if they didn't, I would find a way to be at peace with that too.

I had struggled with what felt like the loss of two children in the past six months. *Third time's a charm, right?* Maybe, just maybe, the third time we were chosen it would be by that birthmother whose profile I created while daydreaming during my commute. It just had to be, because I didn't think I could survive a third blow.

Chapter 20

Could This Finally Be It?

The tug of emotions was intense. When we declined to meet baby Ashton I knew we had made the right decision for our family. But I was once again concerned about the consequences.

Had we taken the easy way out? Had we chosen the smooth road? I was confident in the logic I had used to find comfort in moving forward with the risk of possibly having a child with hearing loss. But the possibility of having a child with a serious mental illness felt different than a physical malady. The same logic didn't seem to apply. The potential impact to our family, and especially to Theo felt more severe. And I knew that schizophrenia didn't appear until early adulthood. The thought of raising a healthy child, only to discover they'd need lifelong care just when they reached adulthood, was a stress I didn't think I could take on. Deafness I felt I could handle; schizophrenia I felt I could not.

The other difference in the two decisions was how I felt when presented with each of the situations. I had learned years before to listen to my gut. And my gut said meeting baby Ashton wasn't right. The timing was too rushed, he had been through too much in his short life, and we just weren't prepared.

But while I was able to come to terms with the impact saying no to baby Ashton had on my personal morality, I remained concerned about how it would impact our relationship with the agency.

I appreciated the fact that Joyce thought of us when she needed to place him quickly, but the way she approached the situation had set off alarm bells. When I tried to pinpoint exactly what hadn't set right, it was just another amorphous concern that nagged at the edges of my thoughts and sat, unsettled in my gut.

I had spent months looking for an agency and the one we chose seemed to be the best option. They had successfully placed my friend's baby with a loving couple, they had been in business for decades, and their record of placements appeared strong. The other agencies I'd investigated had all been bad fits for a variety of reasons: one had a multiple year waiting list, one primarily focused on foster to adopt, one required the child be raised Christian. Many of the agencies were out of state and required significant amounts of travel or unknown financial commitments based on the requests of the birthmother. From all the information we'd been able to gather in advance, the agency we had chosen was the right one for us. Without any real-life experience to compare our situation to, I thought maybe what we experienced was simply what it was like for a domestic open adoption.

We'd made too many heart-wrenching decisions, experienced too much heartache, waited too long to stop and change course. I felt like we had to be on the edge of success and I was committed to stick with our decision and wait for our baby. We had to be close.

The first few weeks of February passed without a word from the agency and I unexpectedly found comfort in that. I figured no news was good news. Life continued on as normal. Work was busy and my evenings were filled with entertaining Theo as we all fought off the cabin fever that had settled in after a long, wet winter. On the weekends, whenever it wasn't raining, we were outside running around the yard and cleaning up the garden. I pruned the dead blooms off the bushes and trees, filling the back of Theo's Tonka truck that he dumped next to the yard waste bin for me. We had a great routine that kept us busy for hours at a time.

* * *

It was an otherwise ordinary Tuesday morning as I sat at work answering email and getting organized for the day. Still deciding what task on my long to-do list to tackle first, I checked my personal email and for some reason clicked on my junk mail folder which I usually only checked when suffering from insomnia. But on that rainy morning, I leaned toward my monitor and slowly read down the list of emails. My eyes scanned the list of sales offers from a variety of websites, blogs, and online retailers. Just before I clicked the box to select and delete them all, my eyes stopped. There, in between an offer for 25% off my next purchase at Lands End and a donation request from the American Cancer Society, was an email from Joyce.

Hi Kim,

I have a birth mom due in about a month. She and her boyfriend both have learning disabilities due to brain injury. Hers a result of seizure, his of unknown origin.

She's in her early twenties, he's in his mid-twenties. They're a cute couple and he's attending classes at a community college.

They're both nice people and she has received great prenatal care. They've had two ultrasounds; the baby is a girl.

Are you interested in having your portfolio presented to them? They had another couple selected, but things have changed.

Let me know,
Joyce

I leaned back in my chair, slouching low in an attempt to relax as my heart pounded. A baby girl! I really wanted a daughter. Without thinking, I replied to Joyce thanking her for her email and promising to talk to Nate and get back to her.

I clicked to Google and did a search on seizures wondering whether they were hereditary. I knew little about them and was curious to learn more about the risks we might be facing. I moved into investigation mode so fast that it didn't even occur to me that we were facing another decision about whether or not to take a chance on the health of our child. As expected, the search yielded thousands of results. There were several types of seizures, caused by dozens of conditions. I didn't have enough information to narrow my search.

In mild forms, seizures seemed manageable. As they increase in severity, however, the impact could be devastating. There was no way for me to understand the risks without knowing more about the birth parents' health history. I wasn't sure how to think about the chance we were being asked to take.

Wanting more information, my next step was to email our family doctor. I was sure she could at least give me some questions to ask the agency about the birth parents' health.

I needed to get to work, so I quickly forwarded Joyce's email to Nate and asked what he thought. I knew we'd have to wait to talk things over after Theo was in bed that night. What other time is there for parents of preschool aged children to talk?

I struggled to concentrate for the rest of the day. I forced myself to pay attention in meetings by taking meticulous notes. In the late afternoon, as a reward for my hours of focus, I took a break to do a little more research. I kept coming up with the same information and no matter how I changed my search terms, I couldn't get around the fact that I simply didn't have enough information.

As I walked to my car after work I checked my email. I was surprised to see Nate had responded.

Sounds promising... would like to know more about the seizures... let me know what you find out. See you tonight. Love you – Nate

When I sent the email to Nate I wasn't sure he would be open to the discussion. I had to do quite a bit of convincing to get him onboard when we considered the first baby and we had both quickly agreed not to meet baby Ashton. The facts we had about these birth parents landed us somewhere in the middle of those two situations.

If we moved forward, agreeing to be considered by these birth parents, there was a good chance the baby would be healthy. And if she wasn't, there was still a chance everything could turn out okay. But there was also a chance the child's life - and ours - would be significantly impacted if the seizures were frequent or severe. The resources we might need in either case were unknown. There was no way to get a handle on the odds.

That night Nate and I only had a brief conversation about this newest possibility of a baby. We both wanted more information before making a decision and felt confident that our doctor would be able to give us guidance on what questions we could ask that would help us decide.

The next day we heard from Joyce again and she told us that the couple the birth parents originally had chosen had gotten cold feet but they were once again committed to moving forward with the adoption. She went on to tell us not to worry, she was meeting a few new birthmothers in the coming days and we were sure to be picked soon.

I tried to take the news in stride. My heart and mind had become calloused by the ups and downs of the process. I told myself it wasn't meant to be so we would continue to wait. On the upside it appeared maybe Joyce had begun to advocate for us with new birthmothers. While I didn't know if that was the case, it comforted me to think so. Still, I couldn't get them out of my mind. I kept thinking about that baby girl and wondering what would have happened if the original adoptive parents hadn't decided to go through with it after all. Something about it lingered at the back of my mind and I did my best to push it away and kept my mind focused on my work and taking care of Theo.

A little over a week later, I received another email from Joyce:

Kim,

We might be looking again for a family for the baby girl, due in about a month.

Birthmom has a seizure disorder that may be genetically linked, but there's no way to know for sure. I've talked to her mom, there's no family history. If it's genetic there's a 50/50 chance the baby could also experience seizures.

The couple the birthmom originally picked have backed out. Need to know if you're willing to meet the birth parents to see if this is a potential match. Baby is due in less than a month and I need to find a family before presenting the birth parents with the change.

Let me know if you're interested or have questions,
Joyce

It was as if Joyce didn't remember talking to us about these same birth parents only a week before. The rollercoaster seemed to be getting stranger with every twist and turn.

After calling Nate and discussing Joyce's email, we agreed that I'd call her and see what was going on. The entire thing was so confusing that my mind raced between logical questions and churning emotions. By the time I reached Joyce, I was frowning and my shoulders reflexively slouched forward to protect my aching heart. I watched as rain drops bounced off the granite sill outside and sent tiny droplets of water onto the bottom of the window. I got straight to the point. "I'm hoping you have time to tell me about these birth parents. The situation seems to be changing and I'd really like to understand what we're dealing with."

Joyce explained that if we said yes, she would present only our portfolio to the birth parents and she'd like us to come over to meet with them the following weekend, only four days away. She was in a rush to get an adoptive family identified because the baby was due so soon. She also wasn't sure how the birth parents would take the news with so little time to get used to the change.

I asked about what she knew about the birthmother's seizures and the possibility the baby would be affected. She told me she had talked to a genetic counselor about it and learned it was a rare disorder that usually appeared by 18 months. But seizures could start any time in the first two years. The only way to know was to wait and see.

I thanked Joyce for her time and told her I would call her the next day after Nate and I had a chance to talk it over.

I had managed to get us 24 hours to make a decision about whether or not to move forward. I was still unclear about what we should do. If we said yes, we would have a baby girl and the waiting would be over in about a month. But we would then be spending the next couple of years waiting to see whether or not our daughter was healthy. The risk felt like a big one.

Even though I wanted to let Nate know what Joyce said, I just couldn't bring myself to talk about it anymore. I decided to send him an email, recapping the call and asking if he could ask his mom to watch Theo so we could go to dinner and talk about it. I hoped writing out my thoughts would help me gain the perspective to make a decision.

Writing it out didn't work. By the end of the email I was 50/50 about whether I wanted to move forward.

Arguing each side from an emotional and logical point of view I had equally strong positions supporting both the move forward and pass positions. I hadn't thought that the adoption process could get any more tortuous. I was wrong.

For the first time in months I was scared. I couldn't predict what would happen and I didn't know if Nate and I were on the same page. Would we be able to come to agreement? Would we be one step closer to meeting our new baby? Based on my growing uneasiness, I was afraid I was about to fall farther from my dream.

Chapter 21

No Risk, No Reward

By the time I arrived home Nate had already dropped Theo off with his mom. I quickly changed out of my work clothes and five minutes later was ready to go. I still wasn't sure how I felt about moving forward with the new birth parents. The birthmother was definitely different than the one I assumed we were waiting for. She wasn't a successful college student with the ill-timed pregnancy. Nor was she a woman I shared common life experiences with and could easily relate to. But Joyce had described her as a thoughtful young woman who was taking her prenatal care seriously. I respected that and felt that was enough to begin building a relationship on.

Still, the risk of a child with a seizure disorder scared me. Add the fact that we wouldn't know for two years whether or not she was healthy and a part of me wanted to turn and run.

I was confused. For all the fear and uncertainty I felt, I couldn't stop thinking about the baby girl. Despite all my anxieties over the circumstances and the seizure disorder, the more I thought about her, the more certain I was that I wanted to be her mother. Why did I feel so strongly about this child? Why wasn't the uncertainty of her health enough to make me walk away? Did I want to say yes only because I was anxious for the wait to end? I wanted to find solid footing somewhere and no matter how I approached the situation there was none to be found.

We drove to the restaurant in relative silence. I continued to try to figure out how to start the conversation we needed to have. Nate hadn't given the slightest hint where he stood. It could have been just another ordinary date night.

Nate exited the freeway and as we sat waiting for the light to change I began to cry. He looked over at me, his eyebrows knitted together, looking as surprised as I felt. I had no idea where the tears had come from or why they had begun to stream down my cheeks so unexpectedly.

I looked over at him, tears falling off my chin and onto my chest leaving two growing spots on my white cotton shirt. "I can't let her go," I sobbed. My shoulders suddenly shuddered as my chest tightened and I heaved for breath. "I'm sorry, babe, but we have to take the chance. I just can't let this baby go." I looked straight ahead and couldn't see anything with fat tears obscuring my view. Certainty and clarity arrived in that moment. I wanted this baby more than I'd wanted anything in my life. The pull, the need, the raw desire. This was my baby and I needed to fight for her. I had to make her mine.

"Let's wait and talk about it at the restaurant," Nate said, looking at me briefly before the light turned green and he pulled into the intersection.

"There's nothing for me to talk about Nate," I was trying to stop the tears and regain my composure but my feelings were too strong. "I don't know why I'm so emotional about it, but you just have to say yes, too." I was suddenly pleading with him. I knew my tone was making him uncomfortable and I was potentially being terribly unfair. But the words just kept coming. "There's never a guarantee in life. In this case we know there's a risk, but there's no reason to think it's any greater than an ordinary pregnancy. No science, Nate."

"Kim, I know you want a baby and I know you want a girl. Can we please wait to have this conversation until I've at least parked the car?" I sensed his growing impatience as he tried to pay attention to heavy traffic on the five-lane arterial.

"I'm sorry, Nate." I wiped my cheeks with the back of my hand and pulled my jacket closed over the wet spots on my shirt. "I'm going to look amazing by the time we get to the restaurant." I laughed and reached over to grab his hand that rested on the gear shift. "Nothing says hot date like a girl with bloodshot eyes and tear stained cheeks."

"You look amazing babe," he said as he laced his fingers in mine and squeezed my hand.

I was truly as shocked as he was by my reaction. Until the moment the first tear fell I was uncertain what I wanted. Until that very instant, I was leaning toward taking the safe road and letting these birth parents pass as well. There were so many reasons why life would be seemingly easier if we just held out a little longer. I would feel more prepared if we continued to wait for a woman that fit the profile of a birthmother I had dreamed up months before. She was out there; she just hadn't found us yet.

At the same time, I'm a person of faith. I had continued to think about the birth parents, even after Joyce said she was no longer looking for an adoptive family, and thought about what we would have done if we had remained an option for them. *Why had I continued to care about the decision? Why had I, for a week in between Joyce's emails, still tried to sort out my feelings about this baby?*

Sitting in the passenger seat, I leaned my head against the headrest and realized I had unwittingly let my guard down. With nowhere to go and my partner by my side, my body had relaxed enough to allow my brain to listen to my heart. That is when the decision was clear and the unexpected tears had communicated the message my heart was sending so clearly I couldn't ignore it. I couldn't "logic it" away.

Realizing how certain I was of my decision, I was able to pull myself together in the remaining few minutes of our drive. By the time we walked into the restaurant and the hostess greeted us, the red eyes and makeup smears were gone.

Seated in a private corner of the restaurant I busied myself looking over the menu while the busboy filled our water glasses. After he was out of earshot I glanced at Nate over my menu and asked, "Do you know what you want?"

The double meaning of the question wasn't lost on me. "Are you going for your usual?"

"Yep, and you?" Nate asked setting his menu down on the table and reaching for his water glass.

"Of course," I smiled and willed myself to be quiet and trust that he'd talk when he was ready. I didn't want to start our conversation only to be interrupted a minute or two later when the server arrived. What we needed to discuss would take time. I had laid my cards on the table during our drive and it was now time for me to wait for Nate to share what he was thinking.

I held his hand, rubbing my thumb up and down across his fingers, as we waited for our order to be taken. His strong, warm hand helped me regain some perspective on what had happened over the last week. After what felt like an hour, the waiter arrived and we placed our orders.

"Sorry about what happened in the car," I said squeezing his hand. "Honest to God until that moment I wasn't sure how I felt about moving forward. I thought I wanted a sure thing and would wait for circumstances I'm comfortable with." A single tear leaked out and I quickly wiped it away.

"We don't have much information, Kim. And we're potentially taking a huge risk." He looked me straight in the eyes with an intensity I wasn't expecting. I knew he was serious and wasn't feeling good about moving ahead. "Our dreams have *never* included a child who doesn't leave our home at some point. I don't know if we're prepared to parent a child with serious special needs."

"You're right," I said quietly looking down. The intensity of his gaze was too unsettling. I agreed with him. I didn't think we were prepared to parent a child with serious disabilities.

"We're taking the chance that we could be actively parenting one of our children for the rest of our lives. I don't want that."

"I don't want that either," I could feel the heat rising in my cheeks. It felt like I was arguing with myself. I couldn't disagree with anything he was saying. But I knew I wanted this baby. I couldn't explain it, no matter how hard I tried. She wasn't just any baby. She was my baby.

Was he asking me to convince myself that my feelings and opinions were wrong? Did he believe I was wrong to feel so strongly about moving forward? Did he think I was just being emotional?

I knew he wanted us to make the right decision for our family and neither of us knew how to guarantee that we did. I also knew the decision we faced had nothing to do with right or wrong. We were venturing into territory neither of us knew existed.

"And there is no way for us to know what the chances are?" he asked again. We both wanted someone to give us the odds, to know how likely it was we were saying yes to a potential disaster.

"There's just no way to know. The science isn't there yet," I stopped and took a drink of water. "What we do know is that the birthmother comes from a large family and she's the only one with medical issues. And that even with her history of seizures, she's able to live on her own. Those must be good signs, right?" I knew I was grasping at straws because I only felt partial comfort in what I said.

"I realize what I'm asking," I paused and looked him in the eye once again. "And I know we can't move forward unless we both agree. As crazy as it may be, I clearly want to say yes. I feel like this is our baby. That she was meant to be our daughter." I paused and then whispered, "I know it sounds crazy."

"I need to think about it Kim."

I prepared myself for another loss. This was a decision we had to make together and if Nate said no, the answer was no.

As we settled into bed that night, I leaned over and tenderly kissed him on the cheek. "Thanks for dinner tonight. I appreciate your willingness to hear me out."

"It's a tough decision, sweetheart," he said as he pulled me close to him. I rested my head on his bare chest and listened to his heart beat. "I need more time."

"I understand," I closed my eyes and began to pray silently.

I don't know your plan Lord. But I really want this baby. I'm scared and I don't know why I want her so badly, but I do. Please help us make a decision, Lord. Please help us decide. Thank you for all that we have. Keep us healthy and safe ... and please help us make a decision.

The next morning, I woke up with a throbbing headache, feeling hungover even though I hadn't drunk a drop of alcohol. I drug myself out of bed and into the shower. Nate hadn't given me an answer and I vowed not to ask him. If he didn't say anything before Joyce called, I would tell her no.

I woke him to say goodbye before I left for work. "I'm headed out. Theo's still asleep. Have a good day," I said and kissed him lightly.

"Have a good day, call me later," he said his voice still deep with sleep. I turned and left our room.

Before walking down the stairs I looked at the door to our third bedroom, the room we planned to be the nursery. I took a deep breath, exhaled and whispered, "Not yet," then walked down the stairs.

I didn't expect to hear from Joyce until later in the day; there was still a chance that Nate might say yes, but my hope was fading. I wouldn't push him into something this important. I had to continue to be patient and wait for our baby. I hoped I was strong enough, but I wasn't sure that I was.

Chapter 22

Moving Forward

During the drive to work I fought the urge to replay the events of the last 24 hours over in my head. I wanted to analyze every moment to figure out if there was anything I should have done differently to feel more certain about the decisions I had made. I searched for clues to help me figure out what Nate was thinking and whether or not his lack of an answer was his way of saying no.

I knew there was little to be gained from the mental gymnastics I was attempting. But at the same time, I yearned for a sanctuary from the turmoil of the difficult decisions we'd faced over the past year and a half. I wanted the peace and comfort that I thought would come when our family was complete. And as much as I knew my family was perfect just as it was, I still felt our family wouldn't be complete until we had two kids. I wanted my son to have a brother or a sister. And I wanted the joy of their fights and laughter and the wonders of raising two different personalities and people. Nate and I had both grown up with siblings, and that experience had defined family for me. Children, not child.

A few hours later, my phone chimed while I was busy reviewing contracts. I debated whether to ignore it. I had a lot to get done before a major deadline on my project and it was my first chance to make a big impact with my new team. But after a few minutes my curiosity got the better of me. I turned my phone over and saw a text from Nate.

Hey babe, hope you're having a good day. Heard from Joyce?

I sighed, annoyed at the distraction, but felt obligated to reply. I was tired, physically and emotionally, and just wanted to forget about my personal life for a while. I wanted to dive into the protection of my professional life where I felt confident, competent, and secure. Professionally it all came down to defining the work, identifying the talent, and obtaining adequate resources. Once that was done, communication was the key to making sure everything stayed on track and leadership remained supportive. Work was so much simpler. When there didn't seem to be a right answer, I could always fall back on dollars and cents to decide. Unfortunately, the same didn't apply to my personal life.

Work's really busy, I've got a lot to get done. Probably won't hear from her until later, I replied.

After hitting send I put my phone face down once again and dove back into my work. A few seconds later it chimed again.

"Seriously?!" I said out loud and a couple of my coworkers looked at me in surprise. "Sorry," I said giving them an apologetic wave.

I grabbed my phone to switch it to silent and saw the text from Nate. *Tell her yes.*

I jumped out of my chair and dialed his number. "Are you serious?" I asked, giddy with excitement and surprise.

"You clearly feel strongly about it. I'm in." I heard the nervousness in his voice.

Relief flooded over me and my legs suddenly felt weak. I looked for the nearest place to sit down and took a deep breath. *We're doing this!* "I love you, Nate."

I had never meant it as much as I did in that moment. I knew he was stepping outside his comfort zone. I knew he had decided to trust my judgment. And I knew he was willing to be uncomfortable so I could find happiness. I was deeply moved by his willingness to re-envision his future so I could fulfill my dreams.

I floated back to my desk with a smile spread widely across my face. I realized how silly I must look and I tried to pull myself together. I didn't want to explain to my coworkers what was happening. I had gotten my hopes up before and I was trying not to get fooled again. As I willed myself to complete a detailed review of contracts, all I could think about was how close we were to holding our baby girl!

Hours later, as I began to think about packing up for the day, Joyce called.

She told me if we agreed to move forward, she'd ask the birth parents to meet with her the next day to present our portfolio, and she'd let them know we'd be there on Saturday to meet them.

"You mean you want us there *this* weekend? As in three days from now?" I asked, my head spinning as I tried to figure out how we could make it work. I tried to picture our calendar, struggling to remember if we had any plans. If she wanted us to meet Saturday morning, we had to travel on Friday. I didn't want to take a day off, hoping to save as much time as possible for my upcoming maternity leave. But if we were going to make it there by Saturday morning, it would mean missing at least a half day of work.

"Yes, that's right. I'm confident I can get them comfortable with the change if they know they'll meet you Saturday."

While I appreciated she was trying to manage the change for the birth parents, my excitement was slowly replaced by frustration. It seemed like we were constantly asked to bend over backwards for the agency while they gave no thought to how things impacted us. I felt guilty for feeling frustrated; we were talking about meeting the birth parents of our future child. However, the reality was, we had a life that included responsibilities that couldn't just be dropped at a moment's notice, even if it was a part of the adoption process. We lived hours away and had a child, yet Joyce was consistently acting as if we had to do what she wanted, when she wanted it, or we could forget about adopting.

But what could we do? Did we want another baby or not? *I guess this is what we signed up for*, I thought as I shrugged my shoulders. We were the ones getting the baby we wanted, so I supposed we were therefore expected to put our needs at the bottom of the list.

I told her I'd talk to Nate and look into getting plane tickets.

"Sounds great, we'll make arrangements over email. Why don't you plan on meeting Danielle and Mark for breakfast, say ten-ish on Saturday?"

"Okay, I'll confirm with you when we have our travel plans and we can decide where to meet." I sat in stunned silence for a few minutes, staring blankly at my reflection in the black screen of my cell phone. *What did I just agree to?*

Danielle and Mark. Hearing their names made what was once an abstract concept of birth parents real in a way I wasn't expecting. My mind was suddenly filled with curiosity about what they were thinking and feeling as they heard about our family. My heart felt heavy and my chest tightened. I began to sweat. Unconsciously, I put myself in their shoes and the experience was nearly overwhelming. I imagined the mixed emotions Danielle must be experiencing - the excitement over the child growing inside her womb, held alongside the anguish of her decision to give up the baby for adoption. It must be overwhelming. I wondered how much emotional pain she was experiencing and felt suddenly guilty for wanting her baby.

In the next moment my guilt morphed into feelings of responsibility for whatever hurt Danielle was feeling over giving her child to us. My chest continued to tighten and numbness spread across my chest and down my arms. I began to feel lightheaded. I realized I was holding my breath as the panic continued to rise. The reality of everything I had just agreed to hit me hard, like a prizefighter's punch to the gut.

The list of everything we had to get done to prepare for our new family member ran through my mind. We could have a baby in less than a month, and we hadn't even started to get the nursery ready. *Forget about that,* I thought, *the baby won't care where she sleeps.* The real question was, how were we going to get Theo prepared for the big change coming for him?

We had included Theo as much a part of the adoption process as we could. He was a little over three when the process started and he helped us pick out the pictures we used in our portfolio. But we didn't talk a lot with him about it after that. How do you prepare a preschooler for something without knowing when it would happen? At almost four and a half, he was just beginning to learn the days of the week, and most of the time a day was simply defined by a workday or a family day. If I was pregnant and expecting a baby, he would have seen my stomach growing, would have been able to feel the baby move, and we could have marked the days off on the calendar. With adoption there was no knowing when the baby would arrive, no way to count down the days.

Instead of having nine months to prepare for a new baby, if everything went smoothly, we had less than four weeks. I knew we could get the essentials pulled together in time to be physically prepared, but I wasn't sure how to get Theo ready for the new arrival in such a short period of time.

Thinking about Theo's needs helped me settle the rising panic and gave me something to focus on. But before I could figure out how we were going to prepare Theo, I needed to tell Nate that Joyce wanted us there in less than 72 hours.

I went back to my desk and quickly checked the flights. Flying to meet the birth parents would be more expensive but would save us a lot of time. Instead of a minimum of 12 hours in the car round trip, we would have an hour flight each way. And it would be Theo's first time on an airplane. I hoped the excitement of a first plane ride would provide a fun distraction from all the unknowns the weekend brought with it.

Then I called Nate and filled him in on the news that we would all be flying across the state in three days' time to meet the birth parents of our new daughter, assuming everything went smoothly. He was as stunned as I was at how suddenly everything had shifted from adoption limbo to adoption reality, but by the time I got home and we were all cuddled together on the couch, the three of us couldn't have been more excited to talk about the new baby girl on her way.

No life experience had been so fraught with emotion for as long as our adoption process had, nor had I initiated an endeavor so unpredictable and surprising. There was truly no way to be prepared for what happened next. All I could rely on was the use of common sense and the healing power of deep breathing.

* * *

With everything packed and boarding passes in hand, we made our way through the airport to our gate. It was post 9/11, the airport security lines were long, but thankfully we had left ourselves plenty of time.

Nate and I were excited to share Theo's first plane ride, and as expected, it helped distract us from our worries about meeting Danielle and Mark. Neither of us was sure what to expect the next morning. We had made plans to meet Joyce, Danielle and Mark for breakfast at a 24-hour diner the next morning at ten. Theo would hang out with my parents while we were at breakfast.

When I made the final arrangements with Joyce, she had reminded me it was customary for us to bring the birthmother a small gift.

I had mixed feelings about the recommendation. We were supposed to get a meaningful gift for a woman we had never met, which conveyed our thanks for her decision to give us her baby. The absurdity of the situation was almost too much to wrap my mind around. *Even if I knew the woman well, was there ever a gift that conveyed the deep gratitude we felt?*

* * *

After getting Theo down to bed in my parents' guest room, I helped my mom put away the dinner dishes.

"So, I totally forgot until Joyce reminded me that we're supposed to bring a gift to the birthmom tomorrow," I said as I placed a plate into the cupboard and reached for another.

"You need to bring a gift?" Her bewilderment mirrored my own feelings.

"Do you know what the adoptive couple gave to Amy when she met them?" Amy was my childhood friend who had used the agency.

"I have no idea. I don't know that she received anything at all." I knew my question was a long shot and hadn't expected her to know.

I stopped drying the dishes and sidled up against her, leaning my head on her shoulder as I felt tears begin to form behind my eyes. I was ill prepared for this phase of the process.

Mom dried her hands on a towel hanging below the sink and wrapped her arms around me. I felt safer than I had in months. We had reached a new phase in our mother/daughter relationship. I not only felt her motherly love and protection, but something had shifted inside me – in becoming a mother myself, I felt a deep compassion for her; we not only shared the experiences of our lives together, but we now shared the experience of motherhood. I wanted to package the feelings of protection and compassion and take them with me so I could pull them out whenever I needed to in the weeks to come.

After a minute we continued with the dish washing. I told her everything I knew about the birth parents, hoping it would generate an idea for the gift we were supposed to bring with us. I couldn't think of anything that would be appropriate.

After the dishes were washed and put away, my mom walked to the hallway closet. She pulled out a basket, some scented soap, lotion, and fancy notepaper.

"What's that?" I asked her.

"I picked these up last week when I was shopping. I thought they'd be good to have around, just in case. After all, you never know when you need a last-minute gift."

I looked down at the colorful collection of feminine gifts. *How had she known?*

"Mom, how do you do it?"

"Do what?" she asked, giving me a quizzical look. "I haven't done anything."

"Haven't done anything? Are you serious?" I raised my eyebrows and laughed. *Was she kidding?* "I figured you'd have the answer but I never expected you'd have the actual gifts!" With some tissue paper and ribbon, we put together a delightful gift we hoped Danielle would enjoy.

I was filled with love and gratitude for my mom. Not only was she there for us at every crazy turn of the adoption process, she had once again come through in a crunch and helped save the day. How was it that she could find the energy to be so giving of her time and always prepared for any situation? I was in awe of my mom and her seemingly countless abilities. She was my personal super hero.

Nate and I both woke up the next morning feeling nervous and restless. In contrast, Theo woke up energized and excited to spend time with his grandparents, aunts, and cousins. It was like a day at Disneyland for him. For Nate and me, it felt like a trip to the dentist.

As I showered, I tried to picture the meeting in my mind as if rehearsing for a job interview. *What would they want to know? What questions did we have for them? What were we told to avoid?*

We arrived at the restaurant ten minutes early and sat in the car, listening to the radio, and attempting to keep our nerves in check. We were both trying to wrap our minds around the fact that if everything went well, we were about to meet the couple who would bring us our child.

"You keepin' an eye out for Joyce's car?" I asked, scanning the parking lot for the third time in 60 seconds.

"I think you have that covered," Nate reached over and squeezed my hand.

"Don't make fun of me," I said, feeling both comforted and annoyed by his response.

"Sorry babe," he looked over at me, and as I turned to face him, I saw Joyce's car pull up in front of the restaurant.

"There they are," I said pointing to where Joyce had stopped, directly in front of the entrance. "Here goes nothin'!" I gave him a half smile before opening the car door. That's odd, why isn't she parking her car, I wondered.

We watched as Joyce got out of the car and opened the door for a young, visibly pregnant woman. A man walked around the back of the car. The woman was short, maybe five feet tall, her dark blond hair pulled back in a low pony tail. The man was tall, well over six feet, his head covered in dark unruly curls. When the man stepped next to the woman the difference in their height was so stark, it reminded me of a lamppost next to a newspaper box.

We were parked near the back of the lot, so by the time we reached the door Joyce, Mark, and Danielle were standing just inside the entrance of the restaurant.

We exchanged pleasant, but nervous, greetings, then not knowing what to do next, I held out the basket my mom and I had assembled the night before. "This is for you, Danielle," I said. Then I turned toward Joyce and added, "I assume you're joining us for brunch?"

"No, I have some other business. Just give me a call when you're done getting to know each other, and I'll come back to pick up Danielle and Mark."

I was completely surprised. That was not what she had led me to believe. We didn't feel prepared for this meeting and we assumed she would be there to help us through it. *Time to put your big girl panties on and go for it,* I told myself. But I couldn't help feeling like we'd just been pushed off the high dive.

"Oh, it's okay, they can drive us where we want to go next," Mark replied. I turned and smiled at Nate, raising my eyebrows. *Were we supposed to spend the day with them?*

"No, Mark. Nate and Kim are here to meet you for brunch. Take the time you need to get to know each other, and then I'll come back and drive you both home." She smiled at them before turning towards us. "Have a good meeting and we'll talk soon." She turned and headed back to her car.

The hostess smiled as Nate approached. By the look in her eyes, I suspected she had been eavesdropping on our conversation trying to figure out the circumstances of our meeting. I doubted it was every day that people met at the restaurant to get to know each other prior to an adoption.

"Table for four please," Nate said.

"Yes, follow me," she said. I gestured for Mark and Danielle to go first and grabbed Nate's hand as I walked beside him on my tiptoes so I could whisper in his ear.

"Ready or not ..." I let the sentence hang as we reached a booth by the window. There was an older couple sitting in the booth behind me and Nate and a family of four sitting behind Mark and Danielle. *Those people have no idea what they're in for*, I thought as Mark dove right in at a volume loud enough for half the restaurant to hear.

"So, what are we eating?" he asked as he flipped through the laminated pages of the spiral bound menu.

"Order whatever you like," Nate said. "Brunch is on us."

While Mark and Danielle looked over the menu and discussed whether they wanted breakfast or lunch food, I had a few minutes to take them both in.

Danielle sat next to the window with her dark winter coat now rumpled behind her back. She was fair skinned, with blue eyes, framed by dark oval rimmed glasses. Her peasant-style maternity shirt was draped over her swollen belly.

Mark had a slim face and square, metal-rimmed glasses that kept sliding down his narrow nose. He had several days' growth of facial hair covering the lower half of his face. He had kept on his well-worn wool coat that covered a green and blue crew neck sweater.

The waiter finally arrived and as soon as he took our order, the questions began.

"So, we saw you have a dog. How will you keep it away from our baby?" Mark asked, his voice full of authority.

I looked over at Nate before replying. "Yes, we have a husky named Chinook. He's a very good dog and he's great with kids." I paused, realizing I hadn't answered their question. Both the question and its phrasing had caught me off guard. I hadn't imagined their first question would be about the dog. And the "our baby" had me on alert.

Even though I had never thought about it, I realized my assumption was that once birth parents made the decision to give up a child for adoption they mentally prepared themselves by thinking about the baby as someone else's. I was ashamed at my naiveté and unintentional thoughtlessness. *Of course it was their baby.*

"It's important the dog stays away from our baby. They're dangerous," Danielle said.

"Our dog is very nice. We've had Chinook since before our son was born. He's very good with him. He's a nice dog and not dangerous, but of course we wouldn't leave the baby alone with him."

I tried to remember that although I was comfortable our dog wouldn't harm our children, they had no way of knowing that. I also reminded myself that while this wasn't our first baby, it was theirs, and they had every right to be concerned about the baby's care and wellbeing.

"We've learned a lot about how to keep babies safe in our child safety classes," Danielle said looking directly at me. "Have you taken safety classes?"

"We did before our son was born," I said with a smile. "What information was covered in your class?" I hoped my question would help us develop some common ground we could build upon.

"How to keep our baby safe," Mark said before Danielle could respond.

"That sounds like good information to have," Nate said.

Thankfully the waiter arrived with our food. Mark and Danielle quickly dug in as I pushed a pile of hash browns around my plate. I was too nervous to eat so I focused on thinking about what to say next.

After taking a few bites Mark began to tell us about himself. He had his own room in his parents' basement, enjoyed playing video games on his computer, but didn't like the ones that were a bad value.

"A game is a bad value when you can finish it really quickly. That makes it a waste of money," he explained.

He told us about building a computer with his dad and working on his sign language certification at the local community college. He took the bus to school every morning and after school met up with Danielle. They rode the bus to the mall to visit the video game store or hung out at the bus plaza downtown with their friends.

When he finally paused to take a few more bites of food, Danielle took the opportunity to tell us about herself. She explained that she didn't go to school because she didn't have the money, so she spent the morning hanging out in her new apartment before meeting up with Mark. She told us about the agency that helped her find her new apartment, what she liked about it, and what she didn't like as much as her old apartment.

"And there is someone who comes to help me run errands a couple days a week. Her name is Meredith. She also teaches me stuff, like how to cook. But she can be really bossy, and I don't like that."

"Yeah, I don't like feeling bossed around either," I said. "But that's pretty cool that she teaches you how to cook."

"I was taught how to make stuff in high school when they taught us how to live by ourselves," she said with an edge to her voice that hadn't been there before. I had clearly said something wrong but I wasn't sure what.

"We spend most of our nights at my apartment watching TV and listening to music." She continued, glancing in Mark's direction as if waiting for him to agree. "The baby really likes the Insane Clown Posse. Do you like them?"

I looked at Nate, hoping he would catch the signal to respond. I had no idea who the Insane Clown Posse was.

"Wow, that's heavy metal," he said.

"We love them," Mark replied for both of them. "What music do you listen to?"

Nate and I rattled off the bands we enjoyed listening to, a mix of pop, classic rock, and classical music. Nate took the opportunity to mention that he played classical piano.

"Well, we want you to play Insane Clown Posse for the baby. She likes it," Mark said.

"We'll see," I said, knowing our kids wouldn't be listening to heavy metal any time soon. "Do you listen to any other music with the baby?"

"Her name's Sara Claire Hannah," Danielle replied, her pride evidenced by the way she sat up taller as she said the names which ran together as if one name, Saraclairehannah.

"How did you decide on those names?" I asked, curious to learn more. All three were nice names, but none sounded right to my ear. None reflected the strength, courage, or originality that I wanted in a name for our baby.

"One is my best friend, one is my brother's girlfriend's sister's name, and one is Mark's sister's best friend's name."

"And we like them," Mark added.

After the conversation about the baby's name, we answered questions about where we worked, what we liked to do, and took the opportunity to tell them about Theo.

They hadn't asked about him, but we felt it was important they knew the baby would have an excellent big brother. Chinook was only mentioned on a single page of the portfolio, while Theo graced many of the pages. It struck me as curious that they had shown more interest and concern about the dog's involvement in the baby's life and hadn't mentioned Theo at all. *Maybe that's what the agency meant when they said that birth parents only want to know how their child will be cared for by the adoptive couple.*

As our meal wound down, Mark reached into his pocket, pulled out a brochure and handed it across the table to us. "Here's a map of the hospital. You need to have it with you when the baby's born so you know how to get to the maternity floor."

"Thank you, Mark, that's thoughtful," I said, glancing at the brochure. Danielle would deliver at the medical center where I had volunteered as a candy striper the summer before my freshman year of high school. "Oh, I'm very familiar with the hospital. I actually volunteered there for a summer."

"Well, it's big and confusing. You need to keep the map with you," Mark said with a severe tone.

"Thanks. We'll be sure to bring it home with us," I said, taken aback. I could tell he was taking his responsibility as an expectant father very seriously and I appreciated that. However, I bristled at his tone and didn't appreciate being told what to do. Picking up on my reaction, Nate reached under the table and gently squeezed my leg.

While Nate paid the bill, I took the opportunity to get up and go to the ladies' room. Danielle followed me. As we walked toward the restroom, I tried to connect with Danielle woman to woman. "Thank you for taking time to meet us today. How's your pregnancy been? Not too hard I hope."

"Oh, I've been sick a couple of times. That's really hard when you're pregnant." I could tell she appreciated the opportunity to have my undivided attention.

"That is hard. I'm sorry to hear that. I hope you're feeling better and that you stay healthy."

"Well, I've already started having contractions," she said before heading into an open stall. "They happen in the middle of the night. It hurts and wakes me up."

"That's difficult. Did it scare you the first time it happened?" It was awkward carrying on a conversation through the bathroom stall walls. I would rather have done my business in peace, but I didn't want to be rude.

"Why would it scare me?" she asked over the sound of the toilet flushing. "They said it might happen in our birthing class and if it did to call the doctor. So, I just get up and call the doctor."

I laughed at myself. I suppose it really could be as simple as that. We stood at the sink and while washing our hands Danielle turned to me and said, "I want you to come to my doctor appointments. I go every week."

"Oh! Thank you for inviting me Danielle," I said as I turned off the water and grabbed a couple paper towels. "But we live several hours away and I work full time. I'm sorry, but I can't be here for your appointments." Seeing the disappointment on her face I continued, "But you're welcome to call me after the appointments to tell me about them."

"Well you need to be here when the baby is born." I could tell she wasn't happy with the alternative I had offered.

"Of course. We'll give you our phone numbers so as soon as you go in to labor you can call us and we'll drive over." We stood by the sinks in the restroom. Danielle was between me and the door and showed no intention of moving. I took the signal for what it was and figured we'd have the conversation right where we were, even though other patrons were now coming and going.

"What if you don't make it over in time?" I was touched by the question.

"Well, often a woman's first labor is long. With Theo it was over 12 hours. So hopefully we'll have time." I was careful not to give any guarantees. "Will Mark be with you in the delivery room? Will you have family with you too?"

"We want it to be just us," she said. Her eyes narrowed and her tone changed. I got the feeling I had inadvertently stepped where I shouldn't have.

"It was just Nate and me when Theo was born, too." I said, trying to break the tension that hung in the air as

I took a step closer to the door. We'd been gone almost ten minutes. "Should we catch up with the guys?"

"I guess. Have you called Joyce yet?"

"Not yet, maybe Nate did," I replied, holding the door open for her.

Both guys were standing in the entry way as I suspected they would be. Mark was holding the basket we'd brought for Danielle. I walked over to Nate and put my arm around his waist, giving him a quick squeeze.

"Did you call Joyce already?" I asked, looking up at him.

"You can just drive us," Danielle said as Mark handed the basket over to her. I wondered why they brought that up again.

"Yes, she said she'll be here in about five minutes," Nate said.

"Why don't we give you our phone numbers while we wait," I suggested, then turned to Nate. "Danielle and I talked about her calling after her doctor appointments over the next couple of weeks to let us know how they went."

I found a small piece of paper in my purse and wrote down our phone numbers. As I handed the paper over to Danielle, Mark asked for his own copy. I hunted through my purse for another piece of paper, wrote out our numbers again, and handed it to him wondering why they each needed a copy.

"It was very nice meeting you both," I said as I saw Joyce pull into the parking lot. "If you have more questions you can call and ask us."

"Yes, good to meet you," Nate said. "Hope you guys have a good weekend."

"We don't know what we're going to do. We wanted you to take us where we wanted to go next." Mark said as we walked toward Joyce's parked car.

Wow, we aren't going to live that down are we, I thought. Why was he giving us attitude? It was Joyce who had said she would pick them up and take them home.

Joyce got out of the car and opened the door to the backseat for Mark and Danielle.

"How'd it go?" she asked cheerfully.

"We had a nice time getting to know each other," I replied. Mark and Danielle were already buckled in.

"Everything go okay?" she asked looking first at me and then at Nate.

"It went fine. They are characters," I said. "They were quite concerned that we keep the baby safely away from our dog. And they seem upset that we aren't taking them somewhere now." I shrugged.

"I'll call you later this weekend and we can talk more!"

"Sounds good," I grabbed Nate's hand, smiling and waving goodbye. I wondered about the reason for Joyce's tone. It sounded like there was something she wanted to tell us out of Danielle and Mark's earshot. If I was right, history showed it probably wasn't anything good.

I pushed any negative thoughts out of my head and returned to the more important matter at hand – we were going to have a baby! I couldn't believe that after all this time, it was actually happening – and now, it was all happening faster than I ever imagined.

We waited until Joyce pulled out of the parking lot before walking slowly back to our car. I glanced at my watch while Nate leaned over to unlock the door. It was 12:30. The past two and a half hours had passed quickly and I felt as if we'd just completed a marathon marked by a delirious mix of excitement, exhaustion, and wonder.

As Nate pulled out of the parking lot I wondered how we had done. It was all so surreal. They were definitely a quirky couple and quite different from us. It was clear Mark and Danielle cared deeply about the baby and were taking their responsibilities as expectant parents seriously. It was strange how they had talked about their daughter as if planning their lives together, the three of them, while at the same time interviewing us to make sure we knew what we were doing when it came to parenting. They had named their baby, gone to classes to learn how to care for a newborn, and hadn't they mentioned going to a charity to get clothing and diapers for her? I had a hard time wrapping my mind around it.

"What do you think Joyce wants to talk to us about?" I asked.

"She probably just wants to know how it all went," he said looking over his shoulder before changing lanes.

"You think that's it?"

I wasn't convinced. Nothing in this process had been straightforward or simple. I doubted Joyce's pending phone call would be either. What did she want to know? Had we made it another step forward only to take two steps back? I couldn't ignore my growing sense of uneasiness as we drove back to my parents' house. Something didn't feel right. Joyce was holding something back, something she planned to spring on us at the final hour. And I couldn't imagine it was something I wanted to hear.

Chapter 23

One Month

We returned home late Sunday evening from our trip to meet Mark and Danielle. Earlier in the day, while celebrating my grandmother's birthday at her nursing home, I received a call from Joyce. She asked how things went at brunch, what we thought of Mark and Danielle, and gave me the contact information for Danielle's mom encouraging me to call her. I had the feeling she was trying to make sure we wouldn't back out as the previous adoptive couple had. I knew there was something Joyce wasn't sharing with us, but couldn't figure out how to ask about it. But asking the question directly wouldn't matter if I couldn't get a straight answer.

I told Joyce that Mark and Danielle seemed to care deeply for the baby and were doing everything they could to be good parents during Danielle's pregnancy. I also shared my concerns that they seemed to be planning to care for the baby after she was born. Joyce assured me it was all very normal and not to worry and encouraged us to talk to them over the coming weeks, get to know them, and even come back again for another visit.

"Thanks for your time Joyce," I said feeling my frustration grow. "It's unlikely we'll be able to come back again before the baby is born. We have a lot to get ready and I need to get things in order to take my maternity leave." I took a deep breath. "I need to get back to my grandmother's birthday celebration. I'm sure we'll talk soon."

I knew the adoption agency didn't like that I was the bread winner in our family and was unwilling to take a year off work after we adopted. The fact that Nate was only working part-time and could take the time off to be the lead parent didn't count for much in their eyes. If they had their druthers, the mother would stay home fulltime. That wasn't how our family worked.

There was a lot to do, but I felt confident we had plenty of time to get it all done. One of the nice things about becoming a parent for the second time was I didn't feel the same pressure to have everything perfectly in place before the baby arrived. And the list of must-haves was significantly shorter. All we really needed to be ready were some sleepers, diapers and wipes, a few receiving blankets, and a car seat. Although in the excitement of having a baby girl, the list of what I *wanted* to have was much longer. I wanted a drawer full of brightly colored outfits, little socks with lace trim, and bright pink diaper covers. And I wanted to accessorize the bright yellow walls of the nursery with flowers and butterflies to give her a dreamy and peaceful place to sleep.

After dinner on Sunday, with Theo dressed in his pajamas, my parents drove us back to the airport. It had been a whirlwind trip.

"Your dad and I would like to help you get ready for the baby," my mom said looking at me over her shoulder from the front passenger seat.

"Wow, thanks mom," I said feeling a lump grow in my throat. "But we don't need much. We'll figure it out."

"No, we want to do something for the new baby." She had the determined look in her eye that told me to just let her have what she wanted.

"Kimberly, listen to your mother," my dad warned from the driver's seat. I could see the smile in his eyes as I saw them reflected in the rear-view mirror.

I smiled. "What did you have in mind?"

"Why don't we get you a travel bassinet. That way she'll have a place to sleep when you stay with us after she's born."

"That sounds like a great idea, Mom," I tried to blink back the tears I felt building up behind my eyes. "We really appreciate it."

"Well it's not every day that we get a new granddaughter."

"Nope, it's not every day ..." My words hung in the air as I watched the trees and low hills rise and fall as we whizzed past on the way to the airport. If I said another word, I knew I'd start to cry.

* * *

The calls from Mark and Danielle started on Monday. They called me at least a couple of times a day; if I didn't answer, or wasn't available, they would call Nate. Sometimes they would call to tell me about the results of a doctor's appointment, sometimes it was to tell me something I needed to do to get ready for the baby, and sometimes it was just to chat.

Every time they called I felt I needed to drop whatever I was doing to take their call, even though most of the time it meant I was interrupted at work and had to go searching for a private place to talk. I felt both indebted to them for the incredible gift they were giving us and worried that if I made one misstep they would dump us. It was an entirely new and unexpected kind of stress and one I hadn't been prepared for.

In the weeks following our meeting with Mark and Danielle, our free time was filled with preparing for the new baby. Theo helped me paint the nursery a bright, creamy yellow. After I cut in along the baseboard, he followed along behind me with a roller painting the wall as high as he could reach, which was about three and a half feet. To our surprise he was a remarkably good painter and I was the one who got paint on the floor.

Nate designed a font for the baby's name and we painted it on the wall above where her crib would go. No matter what the agency had told us, we decided that we would choose the baby's first name. It was an important and emotionally charged decision we weren't comfortable leaving to others. And we would be the ones saying it dozens of times a day—Rhys. Rhys is a Welsh name meaning enthusiasm and was one of my favorite characters in a book series with a strong female heroine I had read after graduating from college.

Seeing her name in glossy white paint, in the rounded, yet strong script that Nate had designed, brought tears to my eyes and made my heart swell with joy. I was so grateful for the baby we were waiting to meet and could hardly stand to wait another day to hold her.

A coworker gave us her daughter's crib with all the accessories and a box of newborn baby clothes. It was a gracious gift and provided more than enough to get us started. As the days until Danielle's due date ticked by I continued to search for ways to get Theo used to the idea he was about to be a big brother.

On a bright, cool Saturday morning a couple weeks before Danielle's due date, I took Theo with me to buy clothes for the baby and pick out a birthday gift for her. I hoped he would feel involved in the process and it would make his sister's impending arrival more real for him.

"Hey buddy, let's go to the store and buy some things for your baby sister," I said, trying to make our errand sound more fun than the *Bob the Builder* episode he was watching. "I need your help picking out some clothes and a birthday present for the baby!"

"We can get her some trucks!" He said with his eyes wide with excitement and a smile that spread across his face. "And some race cars too!" He stood up and walked over to me giving me a big hug, his forehead hitting my belt buckle.

"Oh my goodness, buddy, you're getting so tall. Be careful when you hug mommy," I bent down to examine his forehead to make sure he was okay. "Do you think your sister will like trucks and race cars?"

"Or do girls only like dolls and stuff? Emily at daycare always plays dolls and dress up."

"I don't think girls *only* like dolls," I said as we laced up his tennis shoes and I helped him pull a sweatshirt over his head. "Why don't we go to the store and see what we can find."

At the end of our shopping trip we had a package of soft, brightly colored plush blocks, a pink jogging suit, and a new race car. Admittedly the race car was for Theo, but he had promised to let his sister play with it "when she was old enough."

One afternoon while chatting with a couple of coworkers, my phone rang. It was Danielle. "Sorry guys, I need to take this." I sighed deeply, stood up, and walked over to the window. The sky was filled with dark grey clouds and large raindrops bounced off the windows as the wind picked up.

"Hi Danielle," I said. trying to sound cheerful. "What's up?"

"It's *Mark* and Danielle," Mark replied. I could tell by his tone he was not happy.

"Oh, hi Mark. I saw it was Danielle's home phone..." his tone instantly set me on edge, suddenly feeling shame for some unidentifiable reason. I was annoyed at my reaction.

"The guardian ad litems haven't called us yet to sign the papers!" he said, cutting me off mid-sentence.

"The guardian ad litems?" I didn't have any idea what he was talking about and why his anger was directed at me. The only time I had heard of a guardian ad litem was to represent juveniles in divorce or custody proceedings. It wasn't clear to me why they would be contacting Mark and Danielle.

"Yes," he said as if I was stupid. "They need to call us to have us sign the papers and they haven't called."

"I see. What papers do you need to sign?" I was trying to be patient and find a way to be helpful. But his tone was pushing my buttons. I had to fight back my growing frustration and the urge to tell him to speak to me respectfully.

"The adoption papers."

"Okay. Well I'm not involved with the paperwork you and Danielle need to sign. Have you talked to Joyce about this? Is there a deadline they gave you?"

"We called them. They said just wait. But they're the ones that said we needed to sign the papers." His voice got louder and the words came more quickly.

"Well, you should probably wait for the guardian ad litems to call you then, just be patient."

"They said they would call us," Danielle broke in. "And we've been waiting and they haven't called. We need to sign the papers."

I decided to try a different tack, to see if I could calm them down and get them off the phone. "I understand you're waiting and you want to sign the papers, but the baby won't be here for a couple of weeks. I think you have time. If it was urgent, I'm sure Joyce would make sure they called you."

"They. Said. They. Would. Call!" Danielle spoke so loudly I had to pull the phone away from my ear.

Oh. My. God! I nearly lost my patience. It was like talking to a five-year-old who wasn't getting the toy she wanted. I took a deep breath.

"Okay, I understand. Would you like me to call the agency and see what I can find out?" My adrenaline was really pumping. I resented being spoken to the way they were talking to me but I felt like I had to take it. This was an uncertain time for them, I'm sure they were just trying to be responsible. And they were preparing to give away their child for Heaven's sake. *Compassion, Kim. Compassion and patience*, I reminded myself.

"Yes!" They hollered in unison.

"Alright, I'll call Joyce and then I'll let you know what she says. I'll call you later."

"Call us right back," Mark ordered.

"I'll talk to you *later*." *What in the hell did he just say to me?* My heart began to race. This hadn't been the first time he had tried to tell me what to do, and I didn't appreciate it. I was at work. I wasn't at their beck and call. I wasn't their servant!

But clearly they thought I was.

I called Joyce and told her about the call. "Kim, they need to *wait*." Joyce said, emphasizing the last part of the sentence. *Was she giving me attitude too?* "The guardian ad litems have been appointed and will call." Her tone reminded me of a middle-school teacher impatiently explaining an assignment to a student for the third time. And it was remarkably close to the one I had just heard from Danielle and Mark. *Why was she talking to me like I'm an idiot? This isn't my job!*

I hate it when people start a reply by using my first name. It's always aggravated me and put me on the defensive, because it always signals a lecture of some sort. And Joyce's words stung in a particularly potent way. I felt once again that I had to defend both myself and my ability to parent to this woman.

At the agency's suggestion, I was bending over backwards to quickly establish a relationship with total strangers in what was possibly the most stressful time of their lives. I could understand the attitude I got from Danielle and Mark. However, Joyce's failure to offer any useful help left me feeling both frustrated and increasingly defensive. *What part of the situation did she fail to understand? What more did I need to communicate to her so that she would provide the support and guidance that were currently missing?*

"Joyce, I don't even know what paperwork they're talking about," I replied. I tried to stay calm and explain my concern, trying to keep anger out of my voice. "But I received a call from them in the middle of the workday, they are very upset, and clearly there's a misunderstanding."

"You can tell them there's no hurry and they'll be contacted soon."

Why is she expecting me to tell them to wait? She was the birth parent advocate, not me. That was her job, not mine. The familiar cocktail of stress, frustration, and fear rose to the surface.

"Joyce, it's not my place. I don't know what process they need to follow. *You* should call them and straighten out the misunderstanding."

"I've already told them they would get a call before the baby is born and they will."

The call ended shortly after that. Again, I wanted to throw the phone I was so frustrated. *Why did talking to that woman make me want to do that?* My heart raced at the thought of having to call them back. This whole exchange had already taken too long, and I shouldn't have even been involved in the first place. I had work to do.

I decided to wait to call Mark and Danielle back until I drove home. They would just have to wait. It felt good to put my foot down but at the same time I felt guilty for not calling immediately. I knew they were stressed too.

A few days later, after having resolved that crisis, I was walking from the parking lot to my building before work, enjoying the feeling of the springtime sun on my face when my phone began to ring.

I figured it was Nate calling to say good morning, so I stopped and fished around in my purse hoping to answer before it went to voicemail. Seeing it was Danielle, my heart sank. I didn't want to think about Mark and Danielle that morning. Every time I spoke to them it was another demand, another scolding, or another complaint. That close bonding I'd once imagined having with the birth parents of my child just wasn't happening—and the warm and fuzzy relationship the agency had painted felt more like a Brillo pad. They never told us to expect power struggles and resentment, that our role would be to serve the birth parents' needs and desires, or that we had to be on call to calm them at all hours. I was neither prepared, nor trained, for what I was experiencing, and the agency seemed to be doing nothing to help either us, or Danielle and Mark.

The sunshine and warm spring air was soothing my bruised soul. I wanted my day to go smoothly, to focus on work, and get prepared for my maternity leave. I knew if they sucked me in first thing in the morning, I would be distracted by the interaction for hours and I really needed to focus. But the guilt of not answering would gnaw at me for hours, too.

"Good morning," I said cheerfully.

"We have a doctor appointment today," Danielle said.

"Oh, you do? I didn't know. I hope everything goes well. You can call me tonight and let me know how it goes."

"You should come over and go to the appointments, too," I heard Mark's muffled voice. Danielle didn't have him on speakerphone, but he was clearly standing next to her.

"I appreciate you inviting me, Danielle, but I can't be there. I'm working until the baby comes and then I'm taking time off." I did appreciate that she wanted me there and I felt guilty that I had to say no. But I had a job, a home, and a family to take care of.

"But you need to visit the hospital and we need to show you where to go," Mark said closer now to the receiver but still not talking directly into the phone.

Mark wasn't usually with Danielle in the morning. I had learned over the course of our daily calls that he didn't stay at Danielle's apartment because his parents expected him home every night. Mark's usual routine was to get up and take the bus to school. After his classes he met up with Danielle and they hung out until nine or ten when he left to take the last bus home.

"We know you're concerned about that, but we still have the map you gave us. If we have any questions when we get there, the hospital has people who can show us where to go." Again, I tried to be understanding. I knew how important this was to them. But even if we had never been to the hospital before, I was confident we'd find our way.

"But they told us at our classes that you need to visit the hospital, tour the maternity ward, and know where to go when the baby comes," Danielle explained.

Joyce had told me that one of the ways the seizures had impacted their brains was that they were concrete thinkers. I was only now beginning to understand what that meant. The world was black and white to them. They wanted to be good parents to their baby. Good parents were prepared. Part of being prepared was to visit the hospital and know how to get to the maternity ward. That was how it was, there was no other way to be prepared and in turn be a good parent.

"I know they did, Danielle, and I'm very glad that you and Mark have taken the time to get familiar with the hospital. It *is* important for you to know." I started walking the last half block toward my building. "I'm almost to my office, so I need to go. I hope you both have a good day and you can call us tonight to let us know how your appointment went."

Before I could say goodbye, the call was disconnected. Shaking my head, I looked up one more time and felt the warm spring sun on my face and muttered, "I can never win with them."

I took the silence of the sky as tacit agreement.

I didn't receive any calls the rest of the day. I stayed late trying to get things wrapped up and ready for the people covering my work while I was out. Danielle was 39 weeks pregnant so the baby could come at any time and I didn't want to leave my coworkers in a lurch. I had only been working at my new job for six months and was still proving myself.

When I was about ten minutes from home, and Mark and Danielle still hadn't called, I decided to call and check-in. I wanted to extend an olive branch, even though I didn't feel like I had done anything wrong. I was also curious about why they hadn't called as was their habit, and I wanted to know if the doctor had given any indication whether the baby was likely to arrive on time.

"Hi, Danielle, it's Kim. You hadn't called so I thought I'd call to see how your appointment went."

"We didn't call because we are busy," she said in a clipped tone.

"Oh, okay," I replied, taken aback by the severity of her tone. "Well, I'll let you go."

"We'll call you when we have time."

"Okay, have a nice night." I hung up the phone knowing I was being punished.

With only a week to go until Danielle's due date I tried to focus my full attention on Nate and Theo. Life was soon going to change significantly for all three of us and I wanted to enjoy the luxury of giving my undivided attention to Theo. He would never have the opportunity to be the only child again.

We raced his oversized Tonka trucks around the yard and I pushed him on the swing set as the sky turned pink on the cool spring evenings. When it was too dark or rainy to be outside we raced Matchbox cars around the living room floor or snuggled on the couch, munched popcorn, and watched *Cars* for the thousandth time.

I spent extra time on his bedtime routine, lingering in his room a little longer, snuggled beside him in the bottom bunk of his bed, reading him one more story than usual. I wanted to cherish this time with my son before my attention would be unevenly divided as I cared for our newborn daughter.

Since receiving the first email from Joyce about Danielle and Mark I had grown steadily attached to the baby Danielle was carrying. I no longer thought about a baby, or the baby. I thought about our baby, our daughter. Not unlike how I had thought about Theo before laying eyes on him the first time, I thought about Rhys. *How big will she be? Will she have hair? How tiny will her fingers be as I hold them in my hand for the first time?* It felt like I had always known our unborn child, the only question left to be answered was when I would cradle her in my arms.

I was excited to meet our baby, while at the same time I wondered if I was up to the challenge. *Could I handle being a working mom with two kids? Could I successfully juggle an increasingly challenging career and motherhood? Did I have enough energy to do it all?*

Theo was an amazing kid and was getting to be a lot more fun and independent. I wondered if I was ready for the sleepless nights, poopy diapers, and spit up.

Even as the doubts ran through my mind, I knew the answer was yes. I had longed for another baby and it seemed to take an eternity to have one. It felt surreal to finally be so close.

In the final weeks of my pregnancy with Theo I had twice a week visits to my OB. I knew whether or not I was dilated and effaced. I could pepper her with questions about whether or not my baby would come early. And then thanks to pregnancy-induced hypertension that required an induction, I knew for sure the day our baby would arrive.

This time another woman was experiencing the more frequent visits to her doctor. She was learning whether or not her body was preparing to give birth. And maybe she was even asking her doctor the odds of delivering early. There was no way for me to know because I wasn't there. And since I wasn't willing to make the multi-hour drive to attend, Danielle chose not to share information with me. I respected her decision and I didn't ask.

The lack of information left me feeling excluded from my child's birth. The feeling slowly gnawed at me and filled me with uncertainty and helplessness. I wanted to know the baby was doing fine. Instead, I was being treated as if it was none of my business.

* * *

On the Friday before Danielle's due date I made sure everything at work was handed off and my desk was clean and organized.

"Okay, I think everyone has what they need. But I'm sure I'll be here Monday," I said feeling nervous as I placed my laptop into my briefcase.

"We hope not to see you," Stacie said giving me a reassuring smile. Stacie was a great support to me as

I prepared for our daughter's arrival. She had given us the crib and baby clothes. She was also taking over the biggest project I owned.

"Thanks, I appreciate that." I said returning her smile. "I'll let you know if we hear anything."

With a few more well wishes from my coworkers I headed to my car. We had a busy weekend ahead. Nate was hosting an Xbox night with his three best friends from high school as a last hurrah before baby number two arrived. And on Saturday, Nate had planned one last date night while Theo spent some time with Nate's parents.

Friday night after dinner, while Nate hung out with his friends, Theo and I decided to put the crib together. We had waited to put it up to give plenty of time for the paint fumes to dissipate because I was concerned the fumes might linger in the mattress or crib sheets. Theo, almost four and a half, and I were quite the pair as we struggled to build the crib. It looked simple enough. There weren't many pieces, but without the instructions, I hoped I was doing everything in the right order. But, of course, two of the screws didn't seem to line up.

"How's it going in here?" Nate asked as he poked his head into the room. "Oh, Kim," he said when he saw what we were up to. "I said I'd take care of that."

"I know. I just really want to get it done." I wasn't sure why, but I felt the need to have the nursery all set up and ready to go. The thought of the crib sitting just outside the nursery door in pieces made me nervous. "We got this," I said as a bead of sweat ran down my forehead.

"Here, let me give you a hand."

"I got it. You go hang out with your friends."

"Let me just help you with this part and then you'll be good to go." He gently took the Allen wrench from my hand and took over.

I was glad Nate took the time to help. I didn't know how I was going to make it work with Theo's help. But I was bound and determined to figure it out. Ten minutes later, with the crib put together, it only took a minute to put the sheet on the mattress and lift Theo in to try it out.

"How's it feel, buddy?" I asked smiling at him as I tussled his hair.

"I'm not a *baby*," he said.

"I know you're not, buddy. Do you think your baby sister will like it?"

"Yes, but where are the blankets?"

"Good question, buddy. It isn't safe for babies to have blankets. Your sister'll sleep in a sleep-sack," I explained.

"Did I sleep in a sleep-sack?"

"You did."

"That's silly," he said giggling as I lifted him out of the crib and set him on the floor.

"It is a silly name isn't it?" I knelt down and enveloped him in a big hug, kissing his cheeks over and over again. "Too many kisses, too many kisses on your cheeks, on your cheeks," I sang to him.

We spent the rest of the night racing cars around his bedroom floor. At bedtime, I laid next to him and read him book after book until he finally fell asleep snuggling his stuffed dog, Watch.

* * *

The next morning as I was putting laundry away our home phone rang. I looked at the caller ID; it was an unfamiliar number but the area code was from the same city as the adoption agency.

"Hello?" I said wondering who was calling.

"Hi, Kim, this is Kathy, Danielle's mom," her voice was light and cheerful.

Danielle had said little about her mom, other than she lived in the same town and was a nurse. At Joyce's urging I had called Kathy and left her a message after we'd returned home from meeting Mark and Danielle. We had been unable to connect for the last few weeks and I figured we'd meet when the baby was born.

"Oh hi, it's so nice to get to talk with you," I said as I walked into the nursery and leaned against the wall. "I'm sorry we've had such a hard time connecting."

"No problem, it's a busy time for everyone."

Kathy and I chatted for about forty-five minutes. She told me she hadn't seen Danielle recently and hadn't seen our portfolio. I took the time to tell her about Nate, Theo, and me. I told her where we lived, what we liked to do, and talked to her about my career. I told her about what a great big brother Theo would be, about our extended family and not to be left out, I told her about Chinook, our lovable furry four-legged child. I mentioned the concerns about the dog Mark and Danielle had shared at our first meeting.

"Oh my goodness, really?" she asked as she laughed quietly. "I heard they had taken the classes offered at the hospital. Danielle interprets what she learns quite literally."

"We've come to understand that they both do." I wasn't sure how well Kathy knew Mark, but I figured from the little Danielle had talked about her mom, she hadn't shared much with her about her boyfriend. I decided to steer clear of the subject.

Kathy shared the story of Danielle's seizures, when they began, and the multiple doctors they visited in search of a diagnosis and cure. She told me about her career, Danielle's siblings, and the little she knew about Danielle's pregnancy. It was clear Kathy was a caring mother.

Our conversation was a remarkably easy one for two people who had never met in person and Kathy was talking to the woman soon to be the mother of her first grandchild. As the call wound down, Kathy asked if we had big plans for the weekend.

"Oh, we're going on one last date night before the baby comes," I said. "We'll probably go to dinner and a movie."

"Oh that'll be nice. You might not have that opportunity again for a while," she said. "We'll be doing the same thing tonight, too."

"I hope you have a wonderful time," I said, as Theo ran into the room. "And we look forward to meeting you."

"Look forward to meeting you too, Kim."

I hung up the phone, relieved to have had the opportunity to talk with Kathy. The relationship we began to build during our call was like the one I had imagined building with our child's birthmother so many months ago.

"Hey, buddy, let's go find Daddy," I said to Theo as I steered him out of the nursery. I felt comforted by the call that created a spark of kinship. It felt like we were in this together and shared a common bond. What that bond was exactly I couldn't yet define, but I knew it was more than the fact we were united by our relationship to Danielle.

The day passed quickly as we went about our ordinary Saturday routine. I felt like I should begin packing our bags in case we got the call that the baby was on the way, but I just couldn't bring myself to do it.

It was a beautifully sunny spring day. I wanted to be outside playing with Theo, cleaning up the garden and getting ordinary stuff like laundry done. I was excited to relax and spend time with Nate, just the two of us. As Danielle's due date had neared I found myself missing Nate and our time together as I focused more and more on Theo.

"Have a great time with Grandma, buddy," I said, bending down to kiss him goodbye. "You be a good boy, okay?"

"He's always a good boy," Linda, Nate's mom, said. "What should we do tonight?" she asked him. She took his hand and began leading him into the living room.

"We'll be back around ten. Is that okay Mom?" Nate asked.

"That's fine, sweetheart. You two just have a good time," she said over her shoulder. "Should we build a castle with the blocks?"

"Thanks. See you later buddy," I said as we stepped out the door.

We decided to head back to the same restaurant we'd gone to the night we'd talked about whether or not to move forward with meeting Mark and Danielle. The food was great and with where we were now in the process it felt like we were bringing things full circle.

The restaurant was busier on a Saturday night than it had been a few weeks earlier. We sat in the bar while we waited for a table, watching an NBA game on the TV above the bar. When our table was ready the hostess sat us by the window where we could enjoy the setting sun which cast everything in a pinkish hue. There was a large family of at least twelve sitting across the aisle from us celebrating. The noise from the two large parties on either side of our table made it difficult for us to have a conversation so we sat in companionable silence.

"Wow, big difference since the last time we were here, huh?" I said after the food arrived to surrounding tables quieting their conversations. "A lot has happened in the last few weeks."

"Kinda crazy isn't it?" Nate said as he reached across the table to hold my hand. "Did you hear from Mark and Danielle today?"

"I did. They were just hanging out," I said before changing the subject. I wanted to forget about Danielle and Mark for the evening and enjoy time with Nate. "What movie do you want to see after dinner?"

We debated whether to see a comedy or an action movie, got caught up on what was happening at work, and talked about Theo's latest antics. After our food came we ate in silence, both trying to enjoy a leisurely dinner and not eavesdrop on the family sitting across from us.

As Nate handed his credit card to the server to pay the bill, I reflexively checked my phone. Whenever we were out in the evening without Theo I always tried to keep my phone close in case something happened. There were missed calls from both Danielle and Mark's numbers.

"Wow, I missed a few calls from Mark and Danielle," I said casually, figuring they were bored and wanting to chat. Nate reached into his coat pocket and pulled out his phone.

"Um, I've missed several too," he said, looking up at me with his eyes wide.

Over the last month they had called Nate only when they couldn't reach me. Mark had called Nate first only once about a video game. Clearly, something was up – maybe Danielle was in labor.

"I think you should call him back," I said as my heart beat quickened. "I'll call Joyce and see if she's heard from them, too."

When Nate reached Mark, he said that Danielle had begun to have contractions and she was getting checked in. Joyce confirmed this information during my short call with her and advised us to head over as soon as possible.

"Sounds like we better head out," Nate said.

I called my parents on our way to pick up Theo from Linda's house, but they weren't in, so I left a message letting them know we were on our way.

As we headed to Linda's I started making a mental list of everything we needed to pack and began to calculate how long it would take to get on the road.

"I'll pack for myself, the baby, and Theo if you can grab what you need and snacks for the car. Sound good?" I said as we pulled in to his parents' neighborhood.

"Sounds good, babe," he said with a smile. He knew when I got into 'get it done' mode I am fast, efficient, and focused. And it was best to just stay out of my way.

Theo and Linda walked into the kitchen as we opened the sliding glass door. While Nate updated her on our plans I knelt down, kissed Theo on the cheek and said "Guess what buddy? The baby's coming! We gotta get home, pack, and drive to grandma and grandpa's house!"

He quickly turned away from me, walked over to Linda, gave her a big hug and said, "Sorry Grandma, I gotta go. We're goin' to get my baby sister!"

My heart melted and a lump formed in my throat. I loved our son so much and I was over the moon that he was excited to meet his sister. My family, after years of working on it, was finally going to be complete.

We were home and packed in a little more than an hour. As we drove home from Linda's house, we heard there was a winter storm warning for the mountain pass we had to cross. I hoped we'd be lucky enough to beat the storm, the last thing we needed was a delay which would surely mean more stress. As we hit the road, I called Mark to let him know we were on our way.

"Hi Mark, it's Kim. How's Danielle doing?"

"She's fine. She's in the bed and has an IV. When are you going to be here?" He sounded equal parts bored and annoyed. Clearly the excitement of an hour earlier had already worn off.

"We should be there just after midnight."

"That's too long, we need you here now."

"We'll get there as soon as possible Mark. Nate will drop me off at the hospital. Let Danielle know we're thinking about her, okay?"

"We want you here."

I didn't appreciate his tone, but I reminded myself that he didn't understand it was physically impossible for us to get there any sooner. Part of his concrete reasoning meant that all he understood was what he wanted and what was preventing him from getting it. The time it took to drive across hundreds of miles didn't even enter into the equation.

"I know Mark, we're on our way. Call us if there's anything we can do or you want an update on where we are." I tried to reassure him and acknowledge his frustration. But there was nothing I could do to change the situation. Even if I got on the next flight, it would still take a couple hours to get there.

As we drove along the dark and empty highway Theo drifted off to sleep in the backseat. While Nate drove, I called our friends and family to let them know we were headed to meet our baby. I finally reached my mom and confirmed our plan to drop me at the hospital and have Theo and Nate sleep at their house. I didn't want Theo to wake up alone at my parents' house the next morning. As we headed into the mountains it began to rain and further up the pass the rain turned to snow and traffic slowed.

I tried to keep my nervous energy to myself and reminded myself of what we could control and what we couldn't. But I knew that any delay in my arrival would cause more stress for Mark and Danielle and that I would be the target of their frustration. I wondered what would happen at the hospital, who would be there, and what I would do while I waited for our baby to be born.

For the first time, I found peace in the fact that there was no way for me to be prepared for whatever came next. We had no other choice but to take it as it came. Joyce had promised to be at the hospital and I looked forward to her active participation in helping us all through this next phase of the adoption process.

We had another three hours of driving if everything went well and I wanted to enjoy the time with Nate. We could finish our date night driving across the state. Whatever would come, would come. And we would soon meet our baby girl.

Chapter 24

Eighteen Hours

Once over the mountain pass the road was clear, the drive smooth. Theo continued to sleep peacefully in his car seat, while Nate and I spoke intermittently to stave off the boredom of the straight, dark highway. Except for the occasional big rig, we were alone on the road.

"So, what do you think about a middle name? Any ideas yet?" While we had decided on Rhys for her first name we hadn't decided on a middle name.

For Theo, we had steered clear of family names, concerned about hurting someone's feelings. This time around, we wanted to hold to the same principle. We tried to think of options as the miles ticked by but neither of us liked any of the names we came up.

"How about Rhys Mile post two hundred seventy seven...." Nate suggested, trailing off in a fit of laughter.

"That's perfect!" I said, joining in his laughter. "But I don't think she'll like it when she gets older." I looked over at him with my lower lip jutting out in an exaggerated pout.

"Yeah, you're probably right," he said, returning the pout.

I was feeling pressure to make a decision. I wanted to include our daughter's full name when we announced her arrival to family and friends sometime the next day. *Should we take the agency's advice and pick one of the names Mark and Danielle had chosen for the baby?* I wondered. My thoughts travelled back to the morning we first met them and how proudly Danielle had shared the name they had chosen for their baby, Saraclairehannah. A sigh escaped my lips. I hadn't changed my opinion of any of the names since we had first heard them nearly a month before.

Bringing myself back to the present I decided to ask Nate his opinion. "Do you think we should consider Sara?" My heart skipped a beat as I said it. "That way we're doing what the agency advises. And we can tell them that at least one of the names they picked is part of her name?" I knew telling Danielle and Mark we'd chosen to name the baby Rhys would cause some consternation.

"No, I don't," Nate said flatly, not taking his eyes off the highway. "She's our daughter and *we* will name her." I detected a hint of "screw them" in his tone and found it comforting.

"Yeah, just asking you the question made me nervous." I continued looking into the darkness and wondered how and what we would ultimately decide on, and what the ramifications of our decision would be. Our headlights lit the road directly in front of us, narrow reflective posts illuminated the road's edge. Just like life, we couldn't see what was behind or to either side. But we knew where we were headed and just wanted to get there safely.

* * *

As we approached the outskirts of town my cell phone rang. I scrambled to answer it before it woke Theo. "Hello?" I said in a loud whisper as Theo stirred.

"How much longer until you get here?" It was Mark.

"We're probably about thirty minutes away," I guessed. "How's Danielle doing?"

"She's fine, her brother just left and we don't want her mom at the hospital."

"Oh, Danielle's mom is coming to the hospital? That will be nice." I was reminded of Theo's birth and how much I missed my mom during the long hours before and after his delivery.

"We don't want her here," he said simply.

Oh boy, I thought, *what's going to happen?*

"Well, I suppose that's all up to Danielle." I wanted to change the subject as quickly as possible. "Nate will drop me off at the hospital and I'll check-in with the night nurse to see how you guys are doing."

"Just come straight to the room. It's room 728."

"Well, I should be there in about half an hour," I said, trying to end the call. "Please tell Danielle I hope she can get some rest."

As I hung up the phone I began to wonder what I was getting myself into and how I would manage without Nate by my side. It was one thing responding to their needs over the phone, what would it be like in person?

I figured after letting them know I had arrived I would have a long night in the waiting room. We knew Mark and Danielle expected us to be at the hospital, but we'd never talked about anything more than that. I was glad I had my laptop and a good book with me. I hoped it was enough to keep me busy until Nate joined me in the morning.

As the lights of the city grew brighter and the tall buildings of downtown rose toward the sky, so did my anxiety. Up until that moment, the evening's events all occurred in such rapid succession that the reality of what I was about to experience hadn't had time to sink in. Now the inevitable was bearing down upon me. Thoughts about what it would be like when we arrived were about to be replaced with reality.

I began silently running through our game plan. I was nervous to leave Nate and Theo. I worried they would both be uncomfortable at my parents' house without me. I worried that Theo would wake up after his long four plus hour car ride and not want to go back to sleep. I worried that Nate would be worried about me and would lay awake wondering what was happening at the hospital. *Maybe I should just run in, say hello and tell them that we would see them in the morning,* I thought.

I knew my worries were illogical. Nate had known my parents for fifteen years and he, Theo, and I had been to their house many times, including several over the last year. I was scared and my anxiety was quickly becoming laced with fear.

I had no idea how the next several hours were going to play out. *Did Danielle and Mark really want me there? Would they decide they didn't want us as the baby's parents after all? Would they try to keep the baby? And what about the baby, would she be born healthy?* With the fear growing with each passing mile I was lucky it was nearly pitch-black outside, because I might have jumped in fright at the sight of my own shadow.

We exited the freeway and I guided Nate through the deserted streets to the hospital emergency room entrance. The familiar numbing sensation down my arms, quickened pulse, and tightness in my chest grew the closer we got to the hospital. I took deep breaths in an attempt to slow the familiar spread of anxiety through my body. It was no time for a panic attack.

You've been waiting years for this Kim. You can handle this. Just think, you'll be holding your baby soon. This is such an exciting time. Try to enjoy the moment, it's your last time becoming a mom.

I tried all the positive self-talk I could think of to spring my mind and body back to a peaceful state. But I was out of time. Nate had pulled into the circular drive in front of the emergency room doors. I needed to get out of the car.

"So you know how to get to my parents' from here?" I asked as I leaned over to give him a kiss.

"Yes, I'll be fine," he said with a smile.

"And you'll make sure Theo is comfortable before you leave in the morning?" I asked looking into the backseat as my eyes filled with tears seeing our son sleeping so peacefully, his *Cars* blanket pulled up under his chin.

"We'll be *fine*." Nate had lived through my panic attacks before and he knew what I was battling. "You just go and see what's up. Text me an update."

"Okay," I said taking a long deep breath. "Wish me luck." I opened the passenger door, grabbed my backpack and headed toward the sliding doors. The emergency room sign lit the side of our car and was reflected in the wet asphalt. I stood there shivering in the thirty-degree weather, blew Nate a kiss, and watched until the car was out of sight.

I slowly turned around and walked through the automatic sliding glass doors. Just inside the second set of doors a security guard sat behind a tall, brown laminate counter. "Can I help you miss?"

"Yes, our birth … um, well…" I stammered. *What was I supposed to say? How much did he need to know? Why wouldn't my brain work?* I cleared my throat and tried again, "Can you direct me to labor and delivery please?"

"Sure, just go through those doors to my left and follow the signs to the southwest elevators." He smiled reassuringly at me. "Go to the seventh floor, take a left as you exit the elevator, go across the sky-bridge, take two rights, and check in with the night nurse on the floor."

"Okay, thank you," I said returning his smile. All I remembered him telling me was to go through the doors and up the elevator. I headed off and figured if I got lost, I'd eventually find someone to point me in the right direction.

The hospital felt cold, sad, and spooky as I wound my way through the empty, dimly lit hallways to the elevator. My memories of working at the hospital were in stark contrast to what I was feeling. When I had volunteered there two decades before it had felt light, vibrant, and full of activity. Of course, my volunteer hours were on weekday mornings and my limited life experience had brought with it the bright lens of youthful naiveté. It wasn't just the hospital that had changed; I had changed, as well.

After about five minutes of winding my way through the sleepy medical center, I saw the check-in desk for the Labor & Delivery Department. Taking a series of deep breaths, I steeled my nerves for what I expected to be another awkward encounter. I would surely have to explain to the night nurse who I was and who I was there to see.

"Good evening, my name is Kim Severn," I said, squaring my shoulders and standing as tall as possible trying to buoy my confidence. "I'm here to see Danielle Lansing, I'm the adoptive mother."

"Oh yes, they said you were on your way. Let me check with her nurse to see if you can go back."

"Thank you. I know they're anxious to have me and my husband here. Oh, and can you point me to the nearest restroom please?" I suddenly realized I hadn't gone to the bathroom since before we left the restaurant and couldn't wait another minute.

"Sure, it's just to the left inside the waiting room," the nurse pointed across the hallway. "I'll be right back."

I went to the restroom and while washing my hands, examined my face in the mirror. It was just after midnight and the adrenaline of the last several hours was beginning to wear off and dark circles were forming under my eyes. I returned to the waiting room where I sat down in an overstuffed, vinyl covered armchair.

I surveyed my surroundings. There was a low table with four small chairs in the far corner. Bins of toys and a small bookcase had been placed under the windows nearby. Through the windows stood the dark skeleton of the deserted multi-story parking garage. The remainder of the room was filled with a mix of loveseats, lounge chairs, and side tables covered with magazines. I was surprised to be the only occupant.

"Ms. Severn," the nurse said to get my attention. "They would like to see you."

"Oh, okay. Thank you."

"Down the hall, fourth door on the right."

"Thanks," I said giving her a quick nod and a closed-mouth smile as I threw my backpack over my shoulder and headed down the hallway.

As I walked toward Danielle's delivery room I heard the quiet crunching sound from the tread of my shoes on the freshly polished linoleum. The sound breaking through the silence made me feel like an even bigger intruder into Danielle and Mark's experience of their baby's birth. I knocked lightly, and upon hearing a faint, "Come in," I slowly opened the wide, heavy door.

The first thing I saw was the pink and beige striped fabric curtain that separated the entrance of the room from the hallway. Pushing the curtain aside, I poked my head into the dimly lit room.

As my eyes adjusted to the dark, I saw a nurse at the head of the bed entering information into a computer. Danielle was in the bed laying in a semi-seated position, a white sheet pulled up under her arms and her pink hospital gown falling from one shoulder. Mark stopped talking and stood up when he saw me.

At the sight of him, a wave of nausea washed over me. My legs felt suddenly weak and I thought my knees were going to buckle. I wanted to turn and run from the hospital as fast as I could, but my feet were cemented to the ground. I was suddenly filled with terror. *I can't raise their baby! I don't want a child like them!*

In what felt like hours, but was less than ten seconds, I experienced terror, then shame, and finally embarrassment. The challenges of the last several months came flooding back all at once and joined with the fear that the baby would have the same challenges as her birth parents. *You can still back out*, came a voice from the back of my mind. *Just say sorry, turn around, and bolt. You don't even have to wait for Nate to come get you, you can just call a cab.*

"Hi, I'm Kim," I said in the direction of Danielle's nurse. "The nurse at the desk said it was okay for me to pop in to say hello."

The words came out of my mouth as if I was a ventriloquist's dummy and someone else was speaking for me. As I spoke, I walked toward the bed to greet Danielle. "Hi Danielle. Hi Mark. How're you guys doing?" "I *finally* got my epidural," Danielle said. "Now we're going to get some sleep."

"Oh, good. I bet you feel much better now," I said feeling a tenderness toward her and remembered the relief that an epidural could bring. "Well, I'll be in the waiting room. I hope you can get some rest."

"No, we want you in the room with us," Mark said.

"Oh, it's okay," I said, looking at Mark and then Danielle. "I'll be fine in the waiting room. And you both need to get your rest before it's time for Danielle to start pushing."

"Yes, remember Danielle," the nurse said looking directly at her. "Now that you're comfortable, you need to get some rest so you have the energy to push."

"I think that's my cue to go. Hope you both get some sleep. I'll be in the waiting room."

I wished the nurse well and told her to let me know if there was anything they needed me for. The nurse followed me to the door.

"When it's time for her to start pushing we'll come get you," she said as I reached for the door.

"Oh, you don't have to come and get me, but I'd appreciate knowing that things are progressing," I said, giving her what I hoped was an appreciative smile.

"They said you're her birthing coach."

What?! We had never talked about that. I didn't know the first thing about helping someone through labor. I wanted to meet our daughter as soon as possible, but I felt no right to be in the room when she was born. It felt much too intimate, and much too sad. My legs began to feel weak again and I began to tremble.

"Oh, wow. I didn't know ..." I trailed off dumbly.

"Well, I'll be in the waiting room in the meantime."

As I walked back to the waiting room, unsteady on my feet, I tried to calm my quickly fraying nerves. They never ceased to amaze me at every turn. I was dumbfounded by the complete turnaround in their attitude. They had gone from freezing me out to wanting me in the room throughout her labor. I wanted to be there from the moment our daughter was born, while at the same time I felt like an intruder on a very important moment between mother and child. Danielle and Mark had conceived their baby and I felt strongly that they should experience her birth together, without distraction. And I was convinced I would be a distraction.

I wanted to tell them I didn't want to be in the room, but I didn't feel I was in a position to advocate for what I wanted. Or for what I needed. They were making the sacrifice, and I was receiving the greatest gift. I didn't see how I could say no.

I figured I had several hours to relax, maybe even drift off to sleep. *Did I hope that when it came time to start pushing the nurse would forget to come get me? Would Joyce have arrived by then to help?*

When I arrived in the waiting room there was another couple sitting in a loveseat by the window. I smiled politely as I sat down in a chair and dug in my backpack for my cell phone. I wanted to let Nate know what had just happened.

I texted: *OMG, got so nervous when I first saw them. Everything is fine. Danielle wants me to be her birthing coach. WHAT?*

Nate texted right back: *Normal to be nervous. I love you. Wow, what a surprise.*

I sat in stunned silence for a minute just staring at my phone screen. When I finally looked up I saw that the other couple was looking in my direction.

"Good evening .... Or should I say good morning," I said with a smile. It was nearly one in the morning.

"Are you Kim by chance?" the woman asked. "I'm Kathy, this is my husband, Dan."

Oh my God, this was Danielle's mom and stepfather. I was not expecting to meet them in the middle of the night, in a darkened waiting room. They sat close together, Dan's hand resting lovingly on Kathy's leg. He was dressed in a button-down shirt, dark jeans, and loafers. She was wearing a brightly colored blouse, slacks, and dress shoes. I suddenly remembered they had been out on a date, as well.

"So nice to meet you," I said standing up to shake their hands. "When did you arrive?"

Kathy explained they had enjoyed a nice dinner, followed by an evening of live music at a club. They were just getting ready to head home when their youngest son had called to report that Danielle was at the hospital. They must have arrived just after I left the waiting room.

I let Kathy and Dan know I had seen Danielle and Mark, that she had had her epidural, and was going to try to get some sleep. The nurse said to expect it to take several more hours before Danielle would be ready to push.

We spoke for about twenty minutes, providing me a glimpse into their lives. They told me about Danielle's two younger siblings, the recent late spring snowstorms, and their plans for their upcoming vacation. Our conversation was winding down and they were just getting ready to leave when the night nurse came into the waiting room.

"Kim, Mark and Danielle would like you in the room. It's time for her to start pushing."

"What?" I asked tilting my head to the side and narrowing my eyes. I was confused and wondered if I'd heard her correctly. "I just saw them less than half an hour ago and she was going to get some sleep."

"She's progressed very rapidly and it's time for her to start pushing. She wants you in the room."

I looked over at Dan and Kathy, and I could see the hurt in Kathy's eyes. I couldn't imagine what she must have felt. Her daughter was about to start delivering her first grandchild and she wanted a strange woman in the room with her instead of her mom. Once again, I felt like a terrible intruder.

"I'm so sorry," I stammered.

"Oh, it's fine. We'll be waiting out here. Just let us know how it's going," she said, giving me a soft smile. Her kindness and understanding showed not only in her smile, but in her big blue eyes. I was suddenly struck by how much Kathy had been through with Danielle over the years as they dealt with her seizures. I could see her strength and tenacity come through and admired her for it.

"Do you mind if I leave my backpack here with you?" I asked. There was plenty in Danielle's room already between all the medical equipment and Mark and Danielle's belongings.

"No problem at all," Kathy said.

This woman is incredible, I thought as I quickly grabbed my cell phone. Walking back down the hallway, I heard my shoes crunching lightly on the linoleum again. Before I opened the door, I quickly texted Nate *Danielle's ready to push, I'm going in. Oh, and I met Kathy. Text ya later.* Pushing my phone deep into the back pocket of my jeans, I walked into the room.

"Wow Danielle, that was fast!" I said as I pushed the curtain aside and saw Danielle laying on the bed, Mark holding one leg and the nurse holding the other. "What do you need me to do?" I asked the nurse.

"Come over here!" Mark said sternly. I noticed he was white as a ghost.

"Why don't you help Danielle push," the nurse replied and gestured for me to take over for him. "And Mark, sit down on the bench and put your head between your knees. We don't want you fainting on us."

He sat down obediently and I listened intently as the nurse gave me the rundown on what I could do to help Danielle through this stage in her labor. As soon as she stopped talking I heard soft snoring from behind me.

I turned around and he was lying on the window seat fast asleep. *Oh for heaven's sake.*

Danielle pushed for over an hour, making little progress. Then she started vomiting. This took a tremendous toll on her emotionally. As the nurse tried to reassure her it was normal, and actually helpful in the delivery process, I did my best not to add to the mess.

I have a very weak stomach and I'm a sympathetic vomiter. With my nerves now in tatters it was all I could do not to begin retching too. Now more than three hours into the pushing, I needed a break. I'd been up for over 20 hours, I was emotionally exhausted, and didn't know how much longer I could keep myself together.

I found an opening when another nurse came in to check on Danielle's progress and to see if she could help.

I politely excused myself and went out in the hallway to catch my breath. I didn't want to text Nate again, hoping he was getting some sleep, so I decided to call my dad.

"Hi Dad," I whispered into the phone as I walked past the waiting room and into a deserted hallway. I didn't want Kathy and Dan to know I wasn't in the room with Danielle.

"Hi kiddo, what's up?" he asked groggily. I could hear the rustle of sheets as I pictured him sitting up in bed. It was about three thirty in the morning. Hearing his voice, I started to cry.

"It's just so stressful, and I'm so scared," I said, wiping at the tears that streamed down my face with the back of my free hand. "Danielle's pushing, but it's not working. Now she's throwing up ... and you know how I am with that ... I don't want to be in the room ... Kathy's here, but Danielle wants me ..." I was taking shallow breaths as I tried to get everything out. "I just need somebody here who's on my side."

"It's okay sweetheart," he said soothingly. "Just let me get dressed and I'll be down."

"Thanks so much Dad," I said. I felt my shoulders relax and I was able to take a deep breath. It felt good knowing someone was on their way, someone who I could share my concerns with and not have to worry about saying the wrong thing to or offending.

"I'll see you soon, sweetheart. You're in labor and delivery?"

"Yes, I might be with Danielle, so just go to the waiting room and text me when you arrive."

My dad and I had been through some rough times, not always seeing eye to eye. But he came through when I needed him, and I was grateful. I also knew he appreciated that I called on him when I needed support. That night, arriving thirty short minutes after I'd called, his presence delivered the reinforcement my weakening spirits needed.

Danielle pushed with all her might, but in the end she needed to have a C-section. Mark woke up and was ready to join her in the operating room. I felt a sting of jealousy. I had been by Danielle's side for hours, supporting her, cheering her on. And I now wanted to share the moment with her when we met our baby for the first time as two mothers, welcoming a new life into the world. She was having a baby girl we both couldn't wait to meet.

The nurse had explained that the operating rooms were small and there was only space for one person to join Danielle. I respected it was Danielle's choice and I understood how much Mark wanted to be there for the big moment. I sent a text to Nate to let him know what was happening as Danielle was readied for surgery.

My phone chimed: *Theo is up playing with your mom, I'm on my way. C U soon!*

Nate found us in a waiting room by the entrance to the operating rooms. As he entered the waiting room in his sweats, blue microfleece pullover, and a baseball cap he had never looked more handsome.

I stood up and walked over to him. He wrapped me in his arms and I began to cry into his shoulder. I didn't need to stay strong any longer. All of the emotions and fear were released through my tears. I relaxed my body and let him hold my weight, sharing the burden I had held for the last several hours.

After introducing Nate to Danielle's mom and stepdad, I sat between Nate and my dad, as we all waited for news that the baby had arrived and Danielle was doing well. The sun was up, the hospital was now brightly lit and the day shift was in full swing. The hallway buzzed with activity, nurses and doctors whizzed by. Orderlies pushed carts filled with food to patients waiting for their breakfast.

We took turns catching Nate up on the overnight events. After about half an hour, the large doors to the surgery wing swung open and Danielle's doctor walked to the waiting room entrance.

"Everything went great. Baby Sara is here and healthy. They're finishing up with Danielle and she'll be in her room in about an hour." He looked at each of us in turn, smiling confidently before he turned and walked back through the doors.

"Congratulations," we all said to one another in a cacophony of joy and relief.

I leaned over and gave Nate a tight hug and a kiss. "Our girl is here," I whispered in his ear. "She's finally here!"

After hugging my dad and thanking him again for joining me in the wee hours of the morning, I stood and walked over to Kathy.

"Congratulations," I said to her through tear filled eyes.

Mark came out soon after, told us Danielle would be moved soon, and that Sara was in the nursery and we could meet her there.

Sara. I looked over at Nate making my eyes as big as possible hoping to communicate what I was thinking.

What are we supposed to do now? I knew that now that the baby was here we had to navigate through the maze of our new reality. We had to find a way for two couples, who both felt a responsibility for the new baby's life, to move forward peacefully.

I called Joyce to let her know that the baby was born and Danielle was in the recovery room after her C-section. Then I asked when she would arrive at the hospital to help us through the first hours of this new phase of the adoption process.

"I have a lot to take care of today. I'll be there later," she told me. My heart sank. I was emotionally overwhelmed and exhausted. *Hadn't she promised to be at the hospital? Wasn't this what we'd paid her to do?* We had hired the agency for their assistance and support adopting a baby. We were also paying the agency tens of thousands of dollars to provide the support and counseling the birth parents needed to help them through this experience. Part of the reason we had chosen this agency was because of their promise to provide this support.

"We really need you, Joyce," I told her, as tactfully as possible. "You told Mark and Danielle you'd be at the hospital when the baby arrived, and we could sure use your help right now. I've never done this before, and they're –"

"Yes, Kim," she said, cutting me off, "and I will be there, when I can get to it. The baby isn't going anywhere; just get some rest and I'll see you later today. Goodbye."

I shook my head as I hung up the phone. I knew we were about to be disappointed again.

Chapter 25

Meeting Our Baby

Waiting to meet our daughter for the first time I tried to make sense of two distinct realities. For a few sweet moments at a time, I lived in a peace-filled bubble created by the love I felt for our newborn baby girl. The bubble muffled the noise and blocked the emotions of everyone else. It was the same endorphin rush I had felt when I first held Theo and just as then, time seemed to stand still as I took in the glory of new life. It was all about the family Nate and I were creating, our family that had just grown from three to four.

And then there was the reality of how we'd achieved our dream. This reality included the experiences Danielle, Mark, Kathy and Dan were living. Their experience bumped up against me, poking a tiny hole in my bubble letting escape a bit of the peaceful air surrounding me. They were all excited to greet the baby they'd created and welcome her to the world. But we were there, interrupting their celebrations.

How was I supposed to honor their experience? How was I supposed to stay out of the way and let them have their special time? How could I get the time to begin to show our daughter how much she was loved? How could I honor both realities?

After hearing that everything was okay in the operating room we made our way to the postpartum ward where the nursery was located. There we all were, Nate, my dad, Kathy and Dan standing in the hallway, looking just like any other extended family waiting to meet the newest member of the family. We all silently jockeyed for position in front of the two large nursery windows.

Each of us stood in anticipation of the moment we would see our baby for the first time. Anxiety hung in the air like a heavy fog, everyone aware of it but no one impacted enough to acknowledge it.

There I was, after over a year of waiting, holding Nate's hand, squeezing it from time to time in silent attempts to release the nervous energy and excitement that grew with each passing minute. I couldn't wait to cradle my baby in my arms, see her face, feel her tiny hand wrap around my finger. Most of all I couldn't wait to touch my lips to her soft cheek and whisper in her ear, "Welcome to the world my little one. I'm your mommy and I love you."

I wondered at the depth of love and attachment I felt for the baby girl who had grown in another woman's womb. It was by pushing through the emotional turmoil, dashed hopes, and a strong commitment to my dream that I had gestated our daughter into being. The tears, physical pain created by the fear, anxiety, and frustration were the labor I had experienced to bring our daughter into our family. It had been so stressful, so confusing, and so infuriating at times, but none of it mattered anymore. I would do it all again, a thousand times, if it brought me to the moment I was about to experience.

As the nurses and doctors came and went from the patient rooms that lined the hallway, my dad stepped away from our little group to talk quietly on his cell phone with my mom. He let her know everyone was fine, Rhys was here, and promised to be home soon to watch Theo so she could come meet her newest grandchild.

I finally caught his eye and said, "Please make sure Theo is okay for me, okay?" I wanted our son with us, but I knew it was best to wait until later in the day to introduce him to his sister. None of us was entirely sure what would happen over the next few hours.

Kathy and Dan were only a few feet away, silently awaiting the first look at their first grandchild. I wondered what was going through her mind. I wondered what the correct protocol was, whether or not we should let them meet the baby before we did. I wondered if she resented me being there, resented that I was going to be her granddaughter's mom. I didn't know what the right thing was to do and had no clue what she was thinking. All I knew for sure was that I could hardly stand to wait another minute to meet my daughter.

We heard footsteps and the sound of wheels along the linoleum of a hallway we couldn't see. Everyone tensed and peered into the nursery. A moment later a door at the back of the nursery opened and a baby lying peacefully in a clear acrylic bassinet was wheeled in front of the window. The anonymous newborn was tightly swaddled in a white hospital-issue receiving blanket with a plain white cap on its head. We all instinctively oohed and I looked at Kathy, "Do you think that's our girl?"

It was hard to tell, there was no nametag visible, no outward sign of whether the baby was a boy or a girl. As the nurse checked on the newest resident of the nursery, Mark joined us in the hallway.

"That's Sara," he said to the group of us before turning to face Nate and me directly. "You can go in to see her. But you have to wash your hands before you touch her."

"Thank you, Mark," I said as I reached up to give him a quick hug before grabbing Nate's hand and pulling him toward the nursery door.

The nurse greeted us with a smile. "I understand you want to meet this beautiful baby girl," she said, indicating the baby we'd all just seen through the windows. I wondered if she knew who we were and why we were so anxious to meet her. I wanted everyone to know that our beautiful baby girl was here and I'd tell anyone willing to listen that I was a mom for the second time.

"We do," I said as tears sprung to my eyes. "We're her parents and can't wait to hold her. Is there a sink where we can wash our hands please?"

"Absolutely, it's over there in the corner. You can sit in here for as long as you'd like, and if you want privacy, feel free to pull the curtain." She gestured to the curtain pressed back along the far wall and nearly out of sight. "I'll wheel the baby over while you get settled."

"Thanks," I whispered, afraid to speak and release the torrent of tears waiting to fall.

I quickly washed my hands and sat down in the high-backed wooden rocking chair sitting next to the sink. Nate washed his hands, reached in to the bassinet, and placed our daughter in my arms.

I stared down at our baby, as tears of joy and relief streamed down my cheeks and fell onto her blanket.

She was beautiful and absolutely perfect. Her eyelids and tiny eyelashes glistened from the medicine the nurses had applied after she was born. She was so small, a little over five and a half pounds. I held my breath as my breasts began to ache, just like they had when Theo was born. Our daughter was finally here.

I held her tightly in my arms, slowly rocking back and forth. After a few minutes, she opened her eyes and looked at me. I looked down into big, round, dark blue eyes that looked so familiar, although I had never seen them before. "Can you get a picture of us?" I asked Nate when I was finally willing to take my eyes off her. The tears had subsided and were replaced with a smile so wide my cheeks ached. I knew I needed to share her, but I didn't want to let her go, not even to let Nate hold her. I had waited so long to meet her. I had dreamt of her all my life and she was finally here.

There it was again, a little pin prick to my bubble as the reality of adoption broke through the magic of the moment. We wouldn't have custody until Danielle and Mark went before the judge and signed away their parental rights. That was days away. I knew they could change their minds. They could decide to try to keep custody of their daughter or could even decide they didn't want us as her family. I was devastated by the thought of either of those possibilities. I was already deeply in love with the baby girl in my arms.

I looked back down into her big blue eyes and knew that there was no way I could let that happen. *But what if I had no choice? What if Joyce dropped another bombshell on us and they took this baby from us?* We were just tottering on the edge between a prayer and a court ruling, and I was scared to death.

Chapter 26

Navigating New Waters

After half an hour with our daughter we saw Danielle arrive in her postpartum room directly across the hall from the nursery. It was time to put our baby down and congratulate Danielle. Mark saw us standing to leave and came into the nursery.

"I'm going to rock Sara now," he said to us.

"Okay," I said watching Nate stand up to give the rocking chair to him. I tried to push down my annoyance at hearing our daughter called Sara. In fairness, Nate and I hadn't told Mark and Danielle that we wouldn't be naming her Sara. I knew I couldn't expect them to call her anything different, but it still bothered me. I feared it was a sign that they may not let her go.

I already felt bonded to our baby. I knew legally we still had no right or obligation to her, but emotionally she felt as much our daughter as Theo was our son. To hear Mark calling her Sara and telling us what to do, where she was concerned, annoyed and worried me. *Was this how people acted who had agreed to give their child up for adoption? Was allowing him to be alone with her, to bond with her, the right thing to do? Were my feelings normal or was I being selfish and unreasonable?*

"We'll go check on Danielle and see how she's doing. She is beautiful, isn't she?" I said in an effort to build a bridge across the rift I felt continuing to grow between us. *Was I now talking to a potential adversary?*

Once he was settled in the rocking chair holding Rhys, I grabbed Nate's hand and we headed out the door. My dad had gone home to watch Theo so my mom could come meet our girl. Kathy and Dan were in with Danielle. The hallway that had been filled with people was now deserted. Less than an hour had passed, but it felt like a lifetime. I felt a calm and fulfillment that I hadn't felt in a very long time.

We knocked lightly on the door that was closed but not latched. "Knock, knock. It's Kim and Nate, mind if we come in?"

"Come on in," Kathy replied.

We pushed back the curtain and saw Kathy sitting next to Danielle on the bed as Dan stood by the window. Kathy was smiling, but her face was full of concern for the wellbeing of her daughter. I was grateful that Kathy was there to help Danielle through whatever the next few days might bring. Danielle not only had to recover from her C-section but would also have all the other pain and discomfort that came from having a baby. My heart ached for her as I thought about all of the changes her body would go through in the days to come.

Suddenly my chest tightened as I thought about her milk coming in. I remembered how much my breasts had ached as they became engorged with milk for the first time. What would she do without a baby there to ease the pain?

I pushed my thoughts aside and tried to convince myself it was not my job to care for Danielle, or to fix her pain. I tried to find comfort in the fact that Kathy was there and Joyce would hopefully arrive soon to begin helping both of them through the coming transition.

"How are you feeling Danielle? You've had quite a long night!" I said as I walked over to the bed. "Is it okay if I give you a hug?" I was trying to protect myself against getting too close with her emotionally, but I cared about her and her well-being. And I was incredibly thankful for her; she had made me a mom for the second time.

"Yes," she said as she sat up a little taller.

"That is one beautiful, perfect baby girl you just delivered," I said as I hugged her gently and then took a step back toward the end of the bed. "Mark's in the nursery with her now."

Nate leaned over and gave Danielle a quick hug and congratulated her on the birth. He stepped back and looked at me, his eyes communicated that he expected me to make the next move.

"We'll give you guys some time to talk," I said to Danielle, Kathy, and Dan. "We'll be outside in the hallway waiting for my mom to arrive. I'd like her to meet the baby before I go back to her house to get some rest. I don't know about you Danielle, but I'm exhausted."

Dan followed us as we walked toward the door. When we were all three in the hallway and the door to Danielle's room was closed, he spoke. "So, we plan to stick around for a few more hours until Joyce arrives. Then we'll head home for some sleep and plan on coming back tonight."

"Sounds good," I said, then looked at Nate for his agreement. "As I mentioned in the room, we really want my mom to meet the baby and then we'll leave for a while. Do you want us back before you leave?"

"That would be great," Dan said.

"Okay, so why don't we plan to come back around one thirty or two and we'll bring Theo with us. We'll plan to stay until about dinner time and then we'll be back around breakfast tomorrow. Does that work?"

"Perfect, we can tag team this," he said with a smile.

A few minutes later my mom arrived. As soon as I saw her I rushed over to give her a hug. It was such a relief to have her there and I instantly felt like I was standing on more solid ground. As I stepped away to lead her over to the nursery window I noticed her eyes were rimmed in red. She was crying.

"That's Rhys, right there," I said gesturing to our daughter lying once again in the acrylic bassinet near the window. "I'll knock on the door and see if they'll let me hold her up to the window for you."

Once inside the nursery I quickly washed my hands again, walked over to our daughter, picked her up, and cradled her in my arms. I stood as close to the glass as possible, my mom on the other side with her head tilted to the side, looking lovingly at her newest granddaughter. I was filled with pride and love. There we were, three generations, finally united.

As I stood holding Rhys by the window, swaying gently from side to side, I saw a couple in their late fifties, maybe early sixties, stop in front of the nursery. Mark appeared and walked up to the couple, the woman gave him a quick hug. I watched for a moment trying to decide who these new people were.

The man was well over six feet tall and heavy set. He had dark brown hair streaked with grey and stood with great authority. The woman was also tall, yet slender, with short mostly gray hair. Her shoulders were curved slightly forward as if she was cowering.

The three of them gestured in my direction and stood staring at me as I continued to hold Rhys. *That must be Mark's parents,* I thought.

"I think those are some people interested in meeting you," I said to Rhys before turning to the nurse. "I'm going to set her back in her bassinet. I think I need to go meet some folks." I gave Rhys a quick peck on the forehead before laying her gently in the bassinet.

I left the nursery and joined them in the hallway. I noticed Nate and my mom standing a few feet away. It was clear Nate was going to let me handle this encounter.

"Hi, I'm Kim," I said extending my hand to the man.

"I'm Frank, Mark's father. This is my wife, Rebecca," he said gesturing to the woman standing meekly beside him.

"Nice to meet you." I could tell instantly this man was sizing me up. Mark was tall like his father and slender like his mother. Mark and his mom had the same slim nose and I noticed her glasses slide down her nose like Mark's often did.

"Are you a Christian?" Frank asked.

"I'm Catholic," I replied taken aback. *I am the woman who is going to be his grandchild's mom and that's the second thing that comes out of his mouth?* I had heard little about Mark's parents and wondered how much they knew about Danielle's pregnancy, let alone Nate and me, the couple who would become their granddaughter's parents.

"We're Christian and expect the child to be Christian," he said. I noticed his eyes narrow slightly.

His tone of voice left no doubt where Mark's assuming and often pushy tone of voice came from. I had heard it many times over the previous month.

"Well, I *am* Catholic, and our daughter will be raised Catholic as well," I wasn't about to be bullied by this guy. After my reply he turned to Mark and began talking. Clearly I was dismissed and no longer needed. *What an ass*, I thought as I walked over to Nate and my mom, shrugging my shoulders as I walked. "What in the hell?" I whisper to them both.

A few minutes later, after saying goodbye to everyone, Nate and I headed back to my parents' house. It was time to get some sleep. My emotions were all over the place, I wasn't sure whether or not we were doing what we were supposed to be doing, and I was growing increasingly fearful that Mark and Danielle were beginning to change their minds about the adoption.

Theo was waiting for me at the top of the stairs when we arrived at my parents' house. I ran up the stairs to greet him with a huge hug. "Congratulations buddy! You're a big brother now!"

"I know!" he said excitedly squeezing me back. "Grandma told me. We watched a movie this morning and then Grandpa let me play with his Star Wars Legos."

"That's very exciting buddy! After Mommy takes a nap we can go meet your sister, okay?"

I greeted my sisters, nieces and nephews, thanked my dad again for coming to the hospital, and went to take a nap. I laid down on the bed, still dressed in my clothes from the day before, too tired to change, yet unable to stop my mind from racing. I finally fell asleep but stirred every time I heard the word baby from my family all gathered in the living room. After a couple of hours, I simply gave up.

My sisters, nieces and nephews joined us as we headed back to the hospital. Rhys would finally get to meet her brother and cousins. We stood outside the nursery window and pointed her out to the crowd waiting to see her. There she was a celebrity, her fans all waving and cheering.

The nurse finished up caring for the other babies in her custody and when she saw us all at the window she invited me in to hold our baby. I was once again on the inside of the glass, holding Rhys and gently rocking from side to side as my family continued to ooh and ah.

And so began the delicate dance of getting to know our daughter and figuring out how to adjust our relationship with Danielle, Mark, and their families. We had hoped Joyce would join us at the hospital, provide us choreographed moves so we would step on each other's toes as little as possible, but throughout Rhys's three-and-a-half-day hospital stay, we saw Joyce and Barbara only once, and only after the bombshell had been dropped.

* * *

The morning after Rhys was born we headed to the hospital in time to take Mark to breakfast. As we wound our way through the brightly lit hallways to the cafeteria he turned to me and declared, "Danielle and I talked last night. We're Sara's parents and we want to keep her."

My eyes must have swelled to quadruple their normal size as I stared back at him, my mouth wide open. *Did he just say what I think he said?* I wondered if Nate had been paying attention enough to hear the comment. I wasn't surprised to hear him say they wanted to keep the baby, it was his timing and casual tone that had taken me off guard.

I finally found my voice, "We know you love her deeply," I said and kept walking. There was nothing more I could say. *This is why Joyce should be here*, I thought.

Barbara came by later that day to talk to Mark and Danielle after we contacted her to say that they had begun talking about keeping the baby. It was understandable that they were having second thoughts. They were in love with their baby and felt confident in their ability to care for her, especially under the watchful eyes of the nurses and Danielle's family. We figured this was likely to happen at some point. But it was scary.

Joyce finally arrived two days after Rhys was born. We were told to go and wait in the waiting room while she talked with Mark and Danielle, and then she would come find us afterwards.

Nate and I sat nervously in the now full waiting room, wondering how the conversation was going. We knew that Mark and Danielle would not be allowed to keep a baby they couldn't care for; the State would intervene and prevent that. But if that happened, it could take weeks, if not months, before we got custody of our daughter, and in the meantime, she might be put in foster care or left with Kathy to care for her. Far worse, Mark and Danielle could punish us by deciding they no longer wanted us to adopt her—and would Joyce go along with it and just pull another portfolio from her stack and take our baby away from us? I squeezed Nate's hand and leaned against him as all the possible disasters ran through my brain, and I did my best to bat each one away with logic.

After about half an hour Joyce arrived and sat down next to me.

"So, how's it going?" she asked in a chipper voice.

"Stressful," I said figuring honesty was the best policy. "We thought you were going to be here to help us navigate through these first few days. And now they want to keep the baby."

"Oh, you guys are doing just fine," she said. Her dodge of my concerns didn't go unnoticed by either Nate or me as we exchanged looks. "I talked with them. They know that they can't keep Sara."

"That's another thing," I said diving right in. "Her name isn't going to be Sara. It's Rhys. We need your advice on how to tell them that." For the last two days we'd been careful not to refer to the baby by either name, unsure how to broach the subject. We didn't want to start a fight or do anything that might tip them over to trying to keep the baby.

"I see." Her tone said it all, I heard the reproach in her voice. "You should consider including them in naming the baby. If you aren't *willing* to name her Sara, then make it her middle name."

"Respectfully Joyce, we've talked it over, considered your advice," Nate said, not bothering to soften his tone, "And we're going to name our daughter. Her name is Rhys and we're considering a middle name." I noticed he had sat up a little straighter and had waited to speak until he made direct eye contact with her, "And Sara is not on the list."

I was taken completely by surprise and I was so grateful that Nate had stood up for us that I wanted to cry. My heart pounded as we waited for Joyce to reply.

"Well, then if that's the case, I suggest you wait to tell them. Until they go to court, Sara is legally their child." She then abruptly changed the subject. "Here is the open adoption agreement. Let's go over it and have you both sign it so everything will be ready to go when Danielle is released tomorrow. They've already signed it."

I exhaled deeply, relieved they'd signed the agreement. "And when she's released, the baby comes home with us, correct?" I wanted to be sure I understood what to expect since I doubted Joyce would be around to help.

"Yes, that's right," and Joyce began to go through the open adoption agreement. It was printed on the agency letterhead and I saw it contained all the standard language we had reviewed over a year before.

And then my eyes stopped, about two-thirds of the way down the page, the printing was crossed out and changed with a black pen.

"What's that?" I said pointing to the change. In the section that laid out the in-person visits the standard two visits were crossed out and replaced with three.

"To help reassure them that they would continue to be part of Sara's life we agreed to change the visits to three times a year."

You agreed! Who the hell do you think you are holding negotiations about our life and our daughter's life without including us in the decision! And Sara, we already told you that won't be her name! Should we just walk away now? What … in … the … $@!*

I was raging inside and felt the heat rise up my face so fast I was dizzy. And then I suddenly felt nauseous and light-headed. What was going on?

"Excuse me?" I said, shocked and unable to form a coherent sentence. *Breathe, just breathe!*

"It will be fine," she said casually. "You're over here anyway to visit family, what's another hour visit with them?"

"Have you …" I stopped myself. This woman was unreal. She clearly had no sense for what she was asking us to take on. It was totally clear to me that she had no idea how much energy it took to spend time with Danielle and Mark and constantly ignore their jabs and their demands. How much time had she really spent getting to know them?

In the stress of the last three days we'd come to an even deeper understanding of the impacts of their 'concrete thinking' and it had ramifications way beyond what Joyce had previously explained. In reality it meant that they were totally inflexible and had no ability to understand that sometimes things happened and life didn't go to plan. If we were two minutes late, no matter the reason, we heard about it. If we didn't do something exactly the way they wanted it, we were scolded. How in the world could they grasp the nuances of open adoption?

"We need you to sign this and then everything will be ready to go for tomorrow. Whenever the hospital is ready to release Danielle, she'll go home, and as long as you have a functioning car seat, the baby will go home with you."

I was already deeply in love with Rhys, I couldn't imagine my life without her. I had little choice but to sign. I took the pen from Joyce's hand and signed the paper. Just like a mother would run into a busy street to save her child from oncoming traffic, I would sign this agreement so Rhys could come home with us the next day. She was our daughter, I felt it in my heart. We'd come too far to turn our backs on her now. Nate signed the paper as well, before we stood and bid Joyce a good day.

I needed to clear my head, but I knew that Mark and Danielle were expecting us back in her room. We had the day shift and that meant entertaining them while they parented Rhys.

As we walked slowly back to Danielle's room I wondered how many couples Joyce had done that very same thing to. The bait and switch to appease the birth parents rather than helping everyone to address the challenges that had presented themselves. Emotional blackmail, that's what I felt like I just gave in to. At the same time, it was a small sacrifice to make for the perfect baby girl with the waft of reddish blond hair and the biggest blue eyes I had ever seen.

For the last two days we had arrived in time to have breakfast with Mark. At lunch, as Danielle ate her hospital meal, we took him to the cafeteria and bought him lunch. We hadn't expected to be feeding Mark while Danielle was in the hospital, but Barbara assured us it was standard practice. Just another item to add to the growing list of things the agency never bothered to tell us until we had no other choice but to comply.

In between buying Mark meals we would sit in Danielle's hospital room with the Nickelodeon channel playing on the television for background noise. Danielle sat in her bed and held the baby. She and Mark would begin to bicker, and he would take the baby for a while. We listened to them talk about how they would raise her and how they were going to care for her.

Part of me was glad to see them so proud of the life they had created. I also felt sad that they wanted to have a family and an ordinary life, but I knew they never could.

At the same time, I was also annoyed and scared. To them we were second-class citizens and they very much knew they held the keys to our dream. I was already a mother, had experienced caring for a newborn, and wanted to share my experience for the benefit of my daughter. The power struggle between Danielle and me had begun.

To keep things from unraveling, I continued to endeavor to keep my patience, and tried to focus on finding common ground from which to form a healthy relationship with them.

The nurses on the wing must have seen the stress on my face, because as I asked them for more wipes for Rhys, one of the nurses working at the desk asked me if I'd like some time alone with the baby.

"Really?" I asked in disbelief. "If you could swing that I would be so grateful."

"Sure, you can use one of the empty rooms on the wing," she said smiling at me. "I can't leave you unattended, but I have some paperwork to do so you can take all the time you'd like."

She escorted my parents, Nate, Theo, and me to an empty room at the end of the hall and brought Rhys in. We sat on the cushioned bench by the window, I cradled Rhys in my arms and we all leaned over her talking gently. Theo peeked over my shoulder and reached out to touch her hand that she'd managed to get out through the top of her swaddling blanket.

"Hi little sister," Theo said. "I'm your big brother." He was holding her hand as I leaned over and kissed him on the top of his head. "I love you little one." He sounded like he was forty, not four.

We spent a peaceful thirty minutes with our baby. Nobody telling us what to do, nobody fighting for my attention. I sat with both of my children close as Nate took pictures. This was the feeling I had fought so hard to experience.

At four o'clock Dan and Kathy arrived for the evening shift. I quickly caught Kathy up on the conversation with Joyce and we talked about the logistics for leaving the hospital the next day. The nurses had informed me that they expected Danielle to be released about ten thirty after rounds. The plan was for Kathy to be there to take Mark and Danielle home. She would help Danielle get settled in her apartment and make sure she had everything she needed to continue her recovery. And Nate and I would take Rhys home to my parents' house.

As we walked to the car I was a jumble of emotions. I was nervous about what the next day would bring. I was frustrated at the lack of assistance the agency was providing us, and I was so grateful for the love and support that Kathy was extending. This had to be an incredibly stressful time for her, yet she was welcoming us into her family, and willing to work with us to accomplish what was best for her granddaughter.

I clung to the short half an hour we had alone with Rhys that afternoon and hoped the restorative effect would power me through the days to come. I had hope, but I doubted it.

Chapter 27

Our Baby Comes Home

I rolled over and draped my arm around Nate's shoulder. I had slept fitfully all night, my sadness over losing my last opportunity for an uninterrupted night's sleep eased by the excitement of bringing our daughter home from the hospital. I laid listening to the deep rhythmic breathing of Nate and Theo, feeling a bit envious of their ability to sleep so peacefully.

The first rays of morning light appeared through the window. There was an unexpected brightness to the morning. There was little point in trying to fall back to sleep, my mind was fully engaged in making a mental to-do list in preparation for the day ahead. I rose quietly and tiptoed out of the room, wandered into the living room and saw the newspaper laying on the coffee table. It was April 1st.

Today was the day our daughter was coming home. The baby I had yearned for every day for more than 18 months. I had been patient, persistent, and driven to realize this goal. I silently prayed, or more correctly pleaded, that the events of the day would bring no surprises. The irony of bringing our baby girl home on April Fool's Day, after all our struggle, was not lost on me.

"Good morning, how'd you sleep?" My dad asked as he came around the corner from the dining room with a mug in his hand. "Want some coffee?"

"Yes, thanks Dad," I said following him into the kitchen. "It was kinda hard to sleep last night. I'm excited to bring Rhys home today."

"What do you think about the snow?"

"Snow?" I looked out the window above the sink. That explained the glow I'd noticed through the bedroom window. It was April Fool's Day and there were a couple inches of wet snow blanketing the landscape. *Hopefully that's the only joke the heavens will play on us today*, I thought.

"Do you guys mind keeping Theo this morning while Nate and I go get Rhys?" I said as I leaned against the counter and took a sip of coffee. I hoped the caffeine would give me the energy and not just power my growing nervousness.

"We were planning on it. We're going to meet the other grandkids at the children's museum. We'll meet you here whenever you get back." I set down my coffee cup and walked over to give him a hug.

"Thanks for having my back, Dad. We really appreciate how much you and Mom are doing for us." I gave him a quick squeeze before grabbing my coffee and heading back to the living room to try to relax for a few more minutes.

The night before my mom and I had gone shopping to buy an infant car seat and some preemie outfits. We hadn't anticipated Rhys would be so small and knew she would be swimming in the newborn outfit we originally planned to bring her home in. At only a bit over five and a half pounds, we needed a few preemie outfits to get her through her first couple weeks.

It was important to me that we had a special outfit to bring her home in. My mom was with me almost five years before when we bought Theo's coming home outfit. And I was glad to have her there when we bought Rhys's too.

My mom joined us in the living room a few minutes later, freshly showered and ready for the day. I greeted her and headed for the shower. I wanted to be ready to go before Theo woke up. I needed to get him ready for the outing to the museum with my parents, make sure the diaper bag was packed, and install the infant seat in the car before we headed to the hospital. There was a lot to get done in the next hour and a half and I knew it was going to get more challenging as I also battled the storm of emotions that had begun to take shape inside me.

The plan was to arrive at the hospital by eight thirty, treat Mark to breakfast and then wait for Danielle to be released. Kathy would be there, too, so while we had breakfast with Mark, she would have time alone with Danielle to prepare her for the day ahead.

Kathy was our partner and I couldn't imagine how the last three days would have gone without her involvement and support. She attended to Danielle's needs, supported us in caring for our daughter, and helped us address the gaps Joyce and Barbara had left open for us to fill. It was up to the three of us, Kathy, Nate and me, to make it through the impending separation.

Once again I was struck by the havoc we were about to create. I had a mixture of dueling emotions that couldn't be avoided if we went through with making that beautiful baby girl our own. I felt the jubilation of bringing our daughter home, completing our family, fulfilling a dream. And I felt the devastation of breaking a family apart, of preventing the realization of another woman's dream, separating a baby from the people who created her. The conflicting emotions swirled within me, as the thrill of our new baby collided with the guilt of taking her from her birthmother.

Nausea grew, and my stomach grumbled threatening to betray me as the power of the devastation grew. I had to focus on Rhys, on our family. It was my job to care for my family and me. It was Kathy's job to care for her daughter. We knew that Danielle and Mark, no matter how badly they wanted to, were unable to raise a child.

I tried to pull myself together before I had to be bright and cheery in front of Mark, Danielle, and Kathy. I wanted the day to be all about us. Not that I wanted to be the center of attention, but I wanted to focus on welcoming home the newest member of our family. I wanted to bathe in the joy of our first hours of finally becoming the Severn Four.

But I felt like I didn't have a right to experience joy when there was impending heartache just around the corner for them. Their needs trumped ours. We were gaining, they were losing. Our family was coming to completion, theirs would have a hole where a daughter had been.

We both slowed our pace as we turned the final corner that led to Danielle's room. I squeezed Nate's hand harder and leaned into him hoping to gather courage.

"You ready for this?" I turned and saw a smile spread across his entire face. From his lips to the outer edge of each eye where smile lines formed a little deeper than usual. *He's excited,* I thought, feeling delighted.

"Let's do this." He squeezed my hand, pulling me toward him and into a tight hug.

Our shoes squeaked in unison on the waxed vinyl flooring as we walked the last few feet to Danielle's room, each breathing deeply to calm our rapidly firing nerves. The door to her room was open a couple of inches and we heard voices as we approached.

"Good morning," we said in unison as we knocked on the door.

The talking stopped. We looked at each other apprehensively as we waited for permission to enter. The few seconds that passed felt like an eternity. Were the heavens about to play a trick on us? Was this the moment it all came crashing down, the culmination of a three-day long April Fool's Day joke? My knees felt weak, are we about to be the fools?

Just before my mind dove off a cliff of despair, we heard Danielle reply, "Come in."

"Hi," I said as I moved the privacy curtain aside and surveyed the room. There were a couple of bags at the foot of Danielle's bed, and the flowers she had received a few days earlier were in a small box under the television. Kathy stood by the head of the bed, Mark sat by the window with his eyes narrowed at us, and Danielle was rocking Rhys. "How are you doing this morning?"

"I'm hungry," he said as he glanced at the clock on the wall. "You're late."

"We are?" I looked at my watch, eight thirty-two.

"You were supposed to be here at eight thirty," he said as he stood. "I'm ready for breakfast."

I wanted to argue with him, I wanted to defend us, to explain all that we'd had to do that morning. But I knew there was no point. I knew enough by now to know that Mark judged the world by whether or not the people in it were fulfilling his needs. Nothing I said would change his current mood. I swallowed my feelings, reminded myself that this was a difficult day for him, and took a deep breath.

"Well, let's go to the cafeteria and get you something to eat then," I smiled as I met Kathy's eyes. She nodded at me and I knew she understood the challenge we were facing. "We'll give you three ladies some time together," I said, referring to Kathy, Danielle, and Rhys.

I turned and headed for the door, hoping he and Nate would follow, and they did. Mark brushed past me and speed-walked in the direction of the cafeteria. As I tried to keep up, tears stung the back of my eyes. *Not now!* I commanded the tears to retreat.

"You know we could keep Sara," he said as his plate, full of scrambled eggs, hash browns, sausage, and bacon clunked loudly on the table. He sounded like a five-year-old taunting an older sibling.

The first shot across the bow, I thought.

I knew he would continue to throw verbal barbs at me until I responded. In an effort to move this part of the conversation along I replied, "You think so?" I hoped to sound more probing than threatening. I didn't know what else to say. And I was not going to remind him that the State would intervene if they decided to try to keep the baby.

"We made her. She's our daughter," he said challengingly. He looked me directly in my eye, ignoring Nate. *And the battle has begun. How do I get out of this one,* I wondered?

"Yes, Mark. You and Danielle made her. She will always know that." I hoped providing some reassurance might work. Over the last three days they had made it very clear that they saw themselves as Rhys's parents.

We had consistently assured them, whenever the subject had come up over the month we had known them, that Rhys would always know she was adopted and we would tell her about them. That was part of what it meant to have an open adoption.

"We want you to take us home from the hospital," he said taking a bite of eggs.

"No, Kathy is going to take you both to Danielle's apartment and make sure Danielle gets settled in." That was the plan Kathy suggested and we fully supported. Danielle's release from the hospital was an important transition in the process. That was when the roles changed and Nate and I took the lead as Rhys's parents. The doors of the hospital would signal the closure of one chapter and the beginning of another.

"No, we want *you* to drive us to Danielle's."

I tried to stay patient. I reminded myself again what a stressful day it was. I switched to my mom voice, slowing my speech just enough to make sure my words didn't run together. "I understand that is what you want, Mark, but that is not the decision that was made."

"How's your breakfast this morning?" Nate asked before Mark could respond. I looked at him, grateful he stepped in to try and change the subject.

It worked, and he was on to talking about a show he and Danielle watched the night before. As he finished his last sausage, he told Nate about a new video game he couldn't wait to play.

An hour later, we all sat in Danielle's room, waiting for the discharge papers to be completed. I stood next to Nate, leaning against the wall, Danielle sat rocking Rhys. Kathy finished packing the last of Danielle's belongings.

It was painful watching Danielle as she held her baby, rocking her softly in the wooden glider. She so clearly loved her baby and felt confident that she could provide what the baby needed. And she wanted to be her mom. I was sad because I knew no matter how much she wanted to be a mother, it could never happen.

I had never before witnessed a scene where I knew for certain, no matter how much a person tried, their dream could never be achieved. My heart was heavy, the lump in my throat made it hard to swallow, the air so thick with sadness it was hard to breathe.

"I'm going to take some of these things to the car," Kathy said, looking from Danielle to me.

"Do you need a hand?" Nate offered.

"Nope, I have it thanks," she said. I wondered what she sensed. I wondered if Danielle had asked her to leave the five of us alone at some point before she was discharged.

Nate held the door for Kathy and for a split second I thought he might just follow her out.

"Do you want to try to feed the baby before we go?" I asked Danielle.

"No, she isn't hungry," she said.

"Okay, but we probably want to try to feed her before we go," I said again. I was trying to give her another opportunity to care for the baby like she enjoyed.

"Mark and I were talking last night," she said, looking at Nate and me. "We want Sara to call us Mom and Dad."

I felt light headed and the room darkened as if someone had suddenly turned off the lights. My lungs were suddenly starved for oxygen. *BREATHE!* I commanded myself. *It's going to be okay, just breathe!*

"I'm sure we can find a special name for the baby to call you when she is old enough," I said, forcing my voice to sound calm.

"No, we are Sara's mom and dad," she said.

This is a time when Joyce should be here, I thought. *Why couldn't she have taken the time to be here for the difficult moment when they had to relinquish their baby to us?*

"Danielle, she will always know that you and Mark are her birth parents." Just as I had done with Mark during breakfast I tried to reassure her. Maybe I was just being naive, but I hoped that was what this sudden command was about. "And remember, the baby won't start talking for many months."

"We are her parents." He stood up and walked next to Danielle. They were a united front.

I looked at Nate not knowing what to do next. Mercifully, we heard a knock on the door and a nurse walked in the room.

"We're almost finished with your paperwork, Danielle. Why don't you try to feed the baby and change her diaper before you get her ready to go?" She smiled at each of us before she opened a drawer in the bassinet stand and took out a bottle of formula. "Oh, you can take all of this with you as well," she said looking at Nate and me.

"Thanks," I said, hoping my response wouldn't ignite a fire.

The nurse opened the small bottle of pre-mixed formula and handed it to Danielle. "Do you have any questions before you go?"

"No," Danielle said as she brought the bottle to Rhys's lips. "Kim and Nate are going to take us to lunch and then bring me to my apartment."

What? Not her too! I thought. *Are we being too harsh? Should we be taking them to lunch?* I began to feel guilty for how much I wanted to grab Rhys and run as fast as possible from the hospital. I remembered the initial punch of fear that hit me when I entered the delivery room three days before when then too I had wanted to turn and run away, even without our baby.

As we stood in awkward silence, it felt like the moments before the bell rang to start a prize fight. Nate and me in one corner, Mark and Danielle in the other. I wondered how many rounds we had already completed. And how many rounds there were to go.

I was grateful when Kathy returned from her trip to the car. She was gone less than fifteen minutes, but it had felt like hours.

"Kim and Nate are taking us to lunch before we go home," Danielle said to her mom as she looked up from feeding Rhys.

"No Danielle," Kathy said, her voice full of warmth. "They need to get the baby home. You've had a full morning. I'm going to take you home and help you get settled in. Your brothers are just finishing setting up your new bed for you."

I looked at Kathy and smiled. I hoped she knew how thankful I was that she was there and helping us through the morning.

The nurses finally came in and reviewed Danielle's discharge information with her. Nate had returned with the car seat we had kept in the car for as long as possible, trying to be sensitive to Danielle and Mark.

"An orderly will be here soon with a wheelchair, Danielle, he'll escort you to your car," the nurse said and patted her shoulder. "Do you want to get the baby ready to go?"

"Do you mind if we put her in her car seat?" I asked Danielle. "It might take us a little while to get her comfortable."

"Nate can do it," she said. I was clearly the enemy and I didn't blame her.

"Thank you," I said and nodded to Nate.

Rhys was dressed in a one-piece white outfit with delicate purple flowers. Lilac fabric added to the feet made it look like the baby was wearing Mary Janes. When Nate picked her up she wriggled, passed gas, and filled her diaper.

"Oh, guess she needs a change," Nate said, laughing. "Ooh, and a new outfit."

"No worries," I said unzipping the diaper bag we had brought with us. I had learned with Theo never to leave the house without a spare outfit. I pulled out another one-piece outfit. This one was light green with big white and pink flowers. The same faux Mary Janes, white this time, on each foot.

Ten minutes later we were traveling through the hospital corridors to the main entrance. Nate and Kathy had gone ahead to get the cars. Mark led the way, followed by an orderly pushing Danielle in a wheelchair as she held Rhys in the car seat on her lap. I walked beside Danielle.

"You know you can take Mark and I to lunch," she said looking up at me.

"Your mom is looking forward to taking you home and helping you get settled," I said loud enough for Mark to also hear. "What kind of car does your mom drive?" I realized as we saw the hospital entrance in the distance that I had no idea what model car I was looking for. It was still just above freezing outside so we waited for Kathy and Nate to pull up in front of the entrance before going outside.

"It's silver and looks like a shoe," she said.

I laughed. "Looks like a shoe?" I couldn't think of any car that looked like a shoe.

"Yes," Mark said, once again narrowing his eyes at me.

The patient pick-up and drop-off area reminded me of an airport on Thanksgiving weekend, with long lines of cars slowly making the way through the one-way loop through the main Medical Center entrance. We waited ten minutes before I saw our car appear in the drive. Kathy stepped out of a non-descript silver car two in front of our burgundy Subaru. I hadn't seen her drive by. *That car looks nothing like a shoe*, I laughed to myself.

"There they are," I said to the orderly who began to roll Danielle out the two sets of automatic sliding doors. "So we'll see you at the Agency tomorrow after lunch for a visit, okay?"

I wanted her to know the next time she would see the baby. We had agreed with Kathy to meet at the agency for visits over the next two days before we hopefully received permission to return home. We had to wait for Danielle and Mark to go before the judge to relinquish their parental rights. Until then, they were still legally responsible for the baby.

Kathy appeared at Danielle's side and handed Rhys, tightly buckled in her car seat, to Nate.

"We'll see you guys tomorrow afternoon," she said to us. "Drive safely."

I leaned over and gave Danielle a quick hug. "We'll see you tomorrow. Thank you!"

Kathy gently helped Danielle out of her wheelchair and into the front seat of her car. I followed Nate to ours, watched as he latched our new baby into the backseat and softly shut the door. I got in the passenger's seat and buckled myself in.

It had finally arrived, the moment I thought might never come. I looked over at Nate and smiled, rubbing my hands together as the heater worked to warm the rush of cold air that filled the car. "Let's go to my parents' house and get some lunch."

We were now responsible for the beautiful baby girl in the backseat. We finally had the freedom to fully care for her. And we were entering the next phase of our relationship with Danielle and Mark, where their hold on us would finally begin to loosen.

Or so we thought.

The tension between us was far from coming to an end. And in the days to come we'd realize it was only the beginning.

Chapter 28

So You Want to See My Daughter

Less than 24 hours after leaving the hospital, it was time for our first post-hospital visit with Danielle and Mark. The all too familiar feeling of dread washed over me as I tried to eat a bowl of cold cereal while Nate showered, and my dad fed Rhys her bottle. I was exhausted from a mostly sleepless night but looked forward to our first day as a family of four.

Even though Rhys had fallen asleep around ten I was awake until after midnight. No matter how hard I tried, my brain would not shut off. I worried about helping Theo transition to his new role as big brother, I worried that Rhys wasn't healthy, and I worried about helping them understand that *we* were Rhys's parents and that they were not.

It seemed as though I had just drifted off to sleep when I woke to Rhys's first stirrings. I didn't want her tiny whimpers to turn to wails and wake up Theo so I rolled out of bed. I peered over the edge of the portable bassinet and two big blue eyes were staring back at me. Even if she had yet to form a smile, her eyes communicated her pleasure at having roused a companion.

"Why hello baby girl," I whispered as I picked her up. I rested her head on my shoulder and her diapered bottom on my arm. The firmness of her diaper was my first clue to what had woken her. "Feels like you need a dry diaper," I said as she nuzzled into my neck.

I wandered into the living room and turned on the lamp that sat on an end table next to the couch. I wanted to keep the room as dark as possible hoping that a clean diaper and a full belly would restore her to her previously sleeping repose.

I changed her diaper, pulled down her nightgown, and swaddled her tightly in a receiving blanket. I cuddled her close, trying to hold her ear close to my heart as I fed her a bottle. Even though I rocked her softly she seemed to get more alert with each passing minute. After an hour I knew we were up for the long haul.

"So, you're going to be a night owl are you?" I whispered in her ear as I patted her back. She gave me a large burp in reply. "Ooh, good one sister, you have another burp in there?" A few minutes later she responded by filling her diaper. *Oh the blessings of motherhood,* I thought as I changed her diaper again, this time trying not to gag.

We bonded until about four in the morning when Nate woke up and took the next shift. Even with less than two hours of sleep earlier that morning, it took me almost an hour to finally drift off. I woke up just after seven to Theo talking softly "Morning Mommy, where's my sister?"

Getting up and following Theo into the living room, I longed to stay in my sweatpants, my hair pulled back in a ponytail, and spend the day cuddling on the couch with Nate and our kids. I wanted to have the comfort of my parents close by to lend a hand and my mom's loving ear to soothe the new worries that had sprouted during the wee hours of the morning.

Rhys and I had spent a couple of hours staring at each other during the night. I had studied her features from the height of her forehead, to the shape of her eyes, to the point of her chin. I wondered at the wrinkles of her fingers and the shape of her tiny fingernails. But most of all I prayed that she was truly as healthy as the hospital pediatrician told us she was—followed by prayers that she would stay that way. I tried not to let my mind wander to the possibility that our healthy baby girl might one day, in the not too distant future, become stricken with the seizures that her birthmother had suffered. I did my best not to imagine what an infant seizure looked like and what I would do if and when I witnessed one. And I tried not to wonder if finally having our baby girl was too good to be true.

Nothing had stayed peaceful for long in our adoption process, so I didn't dare to let myself settle into comfort even as I held our newborn in my arms. Something could happen to pull the adoption out from under us at any moment, and if Mark and Danielle's comments were any indication, that something might be just around the corner.

* * *

With a new set of worries on my mind I headed to the shower hoping that the hot water would rinse away the worst of the anxiety. Before leaving the hospital the day before, we agreed to meet them at the adoption agency just after lunch for our first post-hospital visit.

The agency had assured us that the visits during the few days we remained in town would help Danielle and Mark with the transition. I was doubtful; wouldn't the visits only make it harder for them to let go? Wouldn't they increase the chances that they would start to bond with the baby they'd just brought into the world? On the bright side, at least we were meeting at the agency so we didn't have to have the visit in public with who knew how many unknowns to manage.

At Danielle's request, and against my better judgment, we brought Theo along with us. Until she and Mark went to court to relinquish their parental rights, there was still a chance the adoption would fall through or at least be significantly delayed. So, in order to try to keep things moving forward, I was trying to agree to as many of their requests as possible, without ceding total control. It was a delicate balance that I wasn't sure was working. At the same time, I didn't see a better option. I was willing to trust that it was important to give them time with their baby girl to help them through the transition, although that was just the problem, I couldn't see that they were transitioning into a new role. Their confidence in their ability to care for the baby seemed to increase the more time they spent with her.

The sun shone brightly into the car as we wound our way through town to the agency. I turned again in my seat to make sure the sun wasn't bothering either of my children who both sat quietly in the back seat. Theo was busy trying to entertain his sister with the soft rattle attached to the handle of her car seat. The scene warmed my heart and brought me an unexpected surge of strength and patience.

Even though the early April day was sunny, the temperature was only in the high 30s. As I helped unbuckle Theo from his car seat, Nate bent into the car to readjust the fluffy pink blanket so it rested around

Rhys's shoulders to protect her from the cold. As he lifted her out of the car, he quickly adjusted the canopy to provide a barrier against the cold and the blinding sunshine.

I took Theo's small hand in mine and led him to the front of the car where Nate joined us. We all instinctively paused. I looked up at Nate with my heart racing and in a near whisper I asked, "You ready for this?"

"Yes. Try not to worry, Kathy will be here to help us," he said gently rubbing my shoulder before resting his hand on my lower back and giving me the gentlest of pushes toward the front door.

"I think I'm going to throw up," I whispered. My nerves were all firing and adrenaline raced through my veins as if my body was host to the Indy 500. I suddenly felt weak.

I don't want to do this, I thought. I was too tired, too weak, too filled with fear. These were the people who could take my baby from me. These were the people who thought they were Rhys's parents, who thought her name should be Sara, who thought we were mere babysitters, raising their daughter as they directed. And experience told us that they could be unpredictable, unreasonable, and unaccepting of limits.

Instead of clarifying healthy boundaries, it seemed that Joyce and Barbara's actions had only reinforced their point of view. The more I thought about it, the more I viewed Mark and Danielle, and the agency, not only as the ones who had given us Rhys, but also as the ones who could take her away at any time.

I tried to swallow hard and continued taking deep breaths as we walked the twenty feet to the front porch of the building. I saw Kathy's car in the parking lot and knew they were waiting for us inside.

As I walked up the stairs I tried to put my game face on. I would be patient, understanding, and loving to the couple who were bound to be hurting. I would be grateful to them for the sacrifice they made. I would be thankful to them for giving us the baby they had so lovingly cared for throughout Danielle's pregnancy. I would be gentle; we were all in new territory and it would take time for everyone to find their place in this complicated arrangement that open adoption had created.

I opened the door and allowed Nate, who held Rhys in her infant seat, to enter the building first. The interior looked darker than it had before. As my eyes adjusted from the bright outside to the dim light of the waiting room, Danielle and Mark quickly advanced on us.

"We want our daughter," Mark said as he stopped directly in front of Nate, blocking his way. Theo and I were trying to squeeze inside so we could shut the door and stop the flow of cold air that rushed in. My heart stopped, I couldn't breathe. *Had we just stepped into a trap? Had we just put our daughter into our car for the last time? Was Joyce about to appear with more of her platitudes about how this sometimes happened and we just had to be patient?*

"Give them a little room you two," Kathy said as she joined us in the tiny waiting area. "Let's go up the stairs to the room Joyce showed us."

I found my breath and willed my nerves to calm down so I could follow Nate up the stairs. *Stop overreacting. Enough of the doom and gloom, Kim.* I tried hard to give myself a pep talk, but my logical brain couldn't communicate with my emotional one.

"Follow Daddy," I said to Theo in as cheerful a voice as I could manage. I could feel his body tense beside me. He held my hand as he walked up the narrow staircase. The treads felt unusually shallow and the gray walls closer than they should.

There was a room at the top of the stairs. It was large and took up nearly the entire width of the front of the house. The ceiling followed the contours of the roofline, high in the center and low at either end. There was a large quilt covering a window in the center of the wall opposite the door. I wondered why natural light was blocked from this room.

"We want to hold our daughter," Danielle said as she sat down on one of the three overstuffed couches that were arranged in a u-shape in the center of the room.

"Just a sec and we'll get her out of the car seat," Nate said as he set the infant seat down on a table that sat under the gables at one end of the room.

"We can do it," Mark said as he advanced on him.

"Why don't you have a seat next to Danielle," Kathy said meeting Nate's eyes.

I tried to concentrate on Theo. Participating in handing my daughter over to them felt like a betrayal. It felt like handing over my child to the enemy. Shame flooded over me. These people were not my enemies, I reminded myself; they are the grantors of a dream. My logical brain fought with my emotions and it seemed the battle was raging in my stomach and squeezing the air out of my lungs.

"Look Theo, there are toys over here," I said spying a toy box behind one of the couches. "Let's see if we can find some cars."

I watched out of the corner of my eye as Nate picked up our beautiful baby and walked over to Danielle; cradling Rhys protectively, he set her down gently into Danielle's awaiting arms.

"I want to hold Sara," Mark said the instant Nate bent in Danielle's direction. *Her name is not Sara!* I wanted to scream.

"Ladies first," Nate said cheerfully.

I was envious of his ability to be so warm with them. I looked up and smiled at Kathy who sat on the edge of a couch, clearly ready to jump in if she needed to help Danielle hold Rhys. The gratitude I felt for her made me feel even worse about my growing resentment toward them.

Once I was confident Theo was settled and happily racing cars around the floor I forced myself to join the group. I didn't want Kathy to think that I was the enemy too. I wanted her to know that I was a good person and I would be a wonderful mother to her grandchild.

"Turns out we have a night owl on our hands," I said smiling at Kathy before meeting Mark and Danielle's eyes. "She was up from about three until six this morning."

"Why didn't you change her diaper and feed her? That's what babies need when they wake up at night," Mark said.

That tone!

A new rush of frustration quickly morphed into anger as it struck my heart. *Does he think we're idiots?* I wanted to scream at the top of my lungs. *WE'VE DONE THIS BEFORE! WE KNOW WHAT WE'RE DOING!*

"Well, sometimes even when you do that babies just don't want to go back to sleep." I tried to push away the anger and keep the conversation open and friendly.

"How was your night last night Danielle? How are you feeling?" I figured she was still managing the pain from her C-section and her milk had likely come in by now causing additional discomfort. "How is the new bed your brothers got for you?"

"It's fine," she said. She clearly did not want to take her attention from the baby in her arms. I could relate to that feeling. My heart broke and my guilt grew.

Danielle gave up Rhys to Mark to hold. When Rhys began to fuss, I stood up to comfort her. Danielle moved quickly to take the baby. I swallowed hard.

We had been there for close to an hour when Theo began to get antsy. Nate and I had both tried to keep his interest by bringing out additional toys from the toy box. But he was four and in a strange place. He wanted to be back at his grandparents' house where he was free to run around.

"I want to go home," he whined. "I wanna go."

"We'll go home soon buddy. They just want a little more time with baby Rhys."

Oh shit! I had said it. I said her name in front of Mark and Danielle. Nate and I knew we needed to tell them that we had decided not to name her Sara, but we hadn't agreed on when or how we would deliver the news. I looked around the room and it was clear that Kathy had noticed, but Mark and Danielle did not. *We dodged a bullet, but we'll have to tell them tomorrow.*

"We want more time with Sara," Danielle responded as she narrowed her eyes at Theo.

"He's just four Danielle," I said standing up and moving in Theo's direction. That was the final straw, she had fully activated the mama bear in me. "He's been very patient and played quietly for a long time."

"He's trying to take Sara away."

"Danielle, he's *four*. It has nothing to do with you. He's bored and wants to leave," I kept my voice as level and calm as I could.

Kathy stepped in. "Danielle, we've been out and about for quite a while. Why don't you say good-bye and we'll see everyone again tomorrow?" Kathy came to the rescue again.

"Let's get the toys picked up buddy. We need to put everything back where we found it." I helped Theo get the toys in the toy box and generally straightened up the room as Danielle and Mark covered Rhys with kisses.

It was time to move things along. "Kathy, would you mind helping get the baby back in her seat?" I just couldn't take it any longer. I wanted to cry, scream, and vomit. If I didn't get some air fast, I was afraid I might do all three. Strangely, at the same time I was both ashamed of my reaction and fully accepting of it.

I hoped Kathy understood my offer for her to participate as the only amount of control I could concede. I was trying as hard as I could, but I struggled mightily.

I didn't know how to make things work with Danielle and Mark. I didn't know how to move our relationship from a power struggle to one of mutual respect. I didn't know how to help heal Danielle's pain. The agency hadn't talked about any of the emotions I was experiencing. They hadn't ever said that the birth parents wouldn't want to let go, that the birth parents would want to be called mom and dad, that they would be ill-prepared to face the realities of giving up their child. And they hadn't said a word about how hard any of that would be on us, the adoptive parents, who would live in a state of constant fear that at any moment, their baby could be taken.

Instead, everything had been framed as a win-win situation with a few bumps along the road, to a wonderful and unique bonding of two sets of parents who understood and respected their unique roles. But that was a far cry from what was unfolding for us as Mark and Danielle's stern faces spoke volumes—they resented us as much as I resented them. They weren't going to let go. And neither was I.

What if this is the way it's always going to be, how will I survive? I had no idea what to do next to fix the problems we were facing. I had built a career around identifying a problem and building a plan to address it. I was known for my ability to find people's strengths and designing ways to help them use those strengths to solve a problem. I had a reputation for showing people respect and enjoyed their respect in return.

What we were experiencing didn't seem at all similar to what we heard about during our workshop. Had we misunderstood? Were we doing something wrong? How could it be that these two people, who helped me realize my dream, had become my kryptonite?

The dark of the windowless room took residence in my heart, so stealthily that I wouldn't recognize it for months to come.

Chapter 29

Back on Home Turf

A week after Mark's call that Danielle was in labor we had permission to return home. It was a bright, sunny, mild spring day as we packed up the car, gave tight hugs to my parents, and with the kids safely strapped in the backseat, headed for home.

The first few hours of the drive were uneventful. We stopped for lunch at McDonald's, giving everyone a chance to eat, go to the bathroom, and walk around a bit. Forty-five minutes later, we were back on the road. Only an hour and a half left to go. With a full tummy and a dry diaper, Rhys quickly fell asleep in her infant seat and Theo soon dozed off as well. Nate and I sat in companionable silence, my body relaxing with every mile that passed.

And then, just ninety miles from home, traffic ground to a halt. All three lanes of traffic which had been flowing at a smooth 70 miles per hour were at a standstill. After half an hour, we'd moved less than twenty feet. People turned off their engines and got out of their cars to stretch their legs. A group of teenagers tumbled out of a Suburban and began playing catch on the wide shoulder.

"Are you kidding me? What's going on?" I asked aloud as anxiety began to set in. How was it possible that our journey had hit another snag?

"Probably an accident ahead or something," Nate replied. I could hear the exhaustion in his voice, but my own emotional exhaustion was getting the better of me.

"Seriously, how far back do you think we are from it?" It was a rhetorical question because of course there was no way for him to know. If Nate was right, and there was an accident, how long were we going to be stuck? How long before the kids woke up and got cranky? A screaming newborn I couldn't nurse, and a tired, hungry preschooler were the last things either of us wanted to deal with while stuck in bumper to bumper traffic with nowhere to go.

"I'll call the traffic report line while you try to find something online, okay?" I said as I dialed the number for the automated State transportation line. Maybe some information would help calm my nerves.

It wasn't an accident, but avalanche control that had damaged the highway that cut through the mountain pass. During the past week the mountains had received a couple feet of fresh snow and then temperatures rose rapidly increasing the avalanche risk. The automated voice on the information line relayed that the avalanche crew was expected to reopen the road in an hour, but we would be stuck for a while since we were still about 45 miles from the summit of the pass.

Our six-hour drive ended up taking ten hours. So instead of arriving home in the middle of the afternoon, we pulled into our neighborhood at nearly eight o'clock. We were all tired and anxious for the drive to be over, but I felt a refreshing wave of pride as we turned onto our street. We would soon be carrying our daughter across the threshold of her new home.

As I opened the car door I was momentarily transported back to the moment, four and a half years before, when Nate and I had arrived home with Theo for the first time. I was stunned by the stark contrast between my physical condition then and now. With Theo I had struggled to stand and walk through the door on my own. This time, having been spared the physical strain of childbirth, I was strong enough to carry Theo in one arm and Rhys, in her infant seat, in my other arm. If I'd given birth to Rhys, walking through the door would have been a test to my physical endurance. Instead, the test had been a mental and emotional one. But a test nonetheless.

And I had done it. I had overcome numerous obstacles, both physical and emotional, to get to that dream moment. And I thoroughly enjoyed the sweet rush of victory.

"We're home everybody!" I said feeling happier than I had in years. "We did it Daddy," I said leaning over to give Nate a kiss as he caught up to us in the kitchen, arms full of bags.

I set Rhys down on the dining room table, unbuckled her from her infant seat, and picked her up. Reflexively I felt her bottom to gauge the urgency of another diaper change.

"Welcome home, Baby Girl," I said as I snuggled her close. Theo had quickly disappeared around the corner and into the living room. "Where did your brother go?" I asked as I turned toward the living room and glimpsed a banner hanging on our fireplace mantel. There it was, our award for graduating from the Severn Three to the Severn Four; "Welcome Home Rhys!" in large curly letters surrounded by flowers.

I had the homecoming I had dreamt about since becoming pregnant with Theo. *Maybe everything will be okay*, I thought. Maybe now the hole in my heart will be filled. Maybe now that I had realized my dream of a family with two kids I could begin to heal.

I prayed that the anxiety that had gnawed away at me would finally come to an end. But what if I was wrong? What if Mark and Danielle continued to challenge us, determined to parent the child that his sperm and her ovaries had formed? Their determined, upset faces lingered in the back of my mind, but I did my best to push them aside, to focus on our new daughter, and our family of four.

No matter how hard I tried, I couldn't let go of my concern about their suffering and the difficulty they were having with the adoption. The worry was a constant buzz in the background of our day. I knew Mark and Danielle loved Rhys. I knew they wanted to keep her. And I knew they were unable to fully understand why they couldn't parent her.

Was open adoption an appropriate choice for them? How had the agency thought they would be able to understand that access to information didn't give them rights to parent the baby? It was hard enough for me and Nate, with all our education, to understand how to establish healthy boundaries and expectations of an open adoption. Could we form a healthy relationship with a couple who couldn't grasp the concept of boundaries?

I held Rhys closer to my chest, feeling her tiny heart beating against mine. And I prayed that they would heal and find peace. And that they wouldn't find a way to take our daughter away.

* * *

We soon figured out the new rhythm of everyday life with a preschooler and a newborn. I once again found a way to survive on only five hours of interrupted sleep each night. As I sat on the couch feeding Rhys, Theo snuggled in next to us. He draped my arm over his shoulders and leaned in to hold the bottle for his baby sister. Or sometimes he stood directly in front of me, leaning his elbows on my legs to cover her soft cheeks with kisses. After her bottle was done and her head lay on my shoulder as I burped her, Theo would climb into my newly vacated lap and hug her. "Rhys sandwich," he declared through his giggles.

I focused on building a strong foundation of love and safety for our family. I wanted to maintain a peaceful, sunny bubble around us. I wanted time for the four of us to get to know each other and settle in to our new life. I wanted a reprieve from all the unexpected emotional work of the adoption.

We didn't get out much at first, afraid to expose Rhys to too many germs. Nate was back at work, but I was on maternity leave for three months. When we ventured out, I was so proud of my two kids. I looked forward to having them with me when I ran errands, enjoying the opportunity to have some adult interaction, and reveling in the smiles we received as we walked through the aisles of the grocery store. I wanted to brag to the world about my kids and share how beautiful and amazing they were with anyone who would listen. I was as thrilled to be a new mom as if Rhys had been my firstborn.

For weeks, when I shared news about our daughter and how wonderful she was, I felt that I had to put an asterisk next to every positive thing I said. I wasn't the one who had created her, yet I was the one witnessing her milestones. I felt like I was leading people to false conclusions about my contribution. When people complimented me on her "beautiful blue eyes" or her "gorgeous long lashes" I said thank you, followed silently by "they came from her birth parents." And every time I thought those words, I felt a small piece of my mom-ness drift away.

The truth was, for as hard as I tried to convince myself that having a second child via adoption was no different than giving birth, it was different. I didn't feel like a mom the same way I had when Theo was born. I knew that Theo and Rhys were my children, but I was haunted by the thought that someday Rhys could wake up and decide that I wasn't her mom. If Theo wanted to disown us someday, at least he could never erase my genes. I was devastated by the thought that someday Rhys could just disown us as her parents.

I was incredibly sad that I hadn't had the privilege of creating her amazing life. As the days passed and I cared for Rhys's every need, I increasingly felt like I had known her forever. There was no difference in the depth of love and commitment I felt for my children. I felt a primal urge to protect and care for them both. Would she grow up to feel the strength of our bond?

Whether or not I carried Rhys in my womb, I felt she was always meant to be my daughter. But if that was the case, why did I still feel so sad about not being pregnant with her? Would the sadness ever go away?

If I had her now, why wasn't that enough? Why did it matter how she came to join our family; wasn't the fact that she was part of it now all that mattered?

I was surrounded by love and in awe of the two lives Nate and I were now responsible for. However, even though there was a feeling of contentment, there was an unmistakable emptiness too. *Why do I feel so alone? Am I just missing my work? Why does my heart feel so full of love on the one hand and so devastatingly empty on the other?* Sitting on the couch with my kids each night before bedtime I routinely felt waves of love, followed by sadness, loneliness, and frustration.

As my happiness grew, so, too, did my worry that the bubble of fulfillment I had created would soon burst. I began to notice the first hints of gloom when Rhys was a couple weeks old. Every time I laid her down to sleep I said a prayer. "Please God keep Rhys healthy and strong. Please help her brain develop normally." I still dreaded the possibility that seizures would begin wracking our daughter's body. I feared that at any moment our healthy baby could encounter a health crisis that would turn our world upside down.

In the evenings, I stood beside the crib with my hand over her heart, gently rocking her swaddled body back and forth, my eyes closed tight. I stood in the quiet of her room, feeling her breathing change as she drifted off to sleep. The minutes filled with silent pleas that our daughter would develop normally, and happiness would continue its residence in our home, while the hours passed with a convoluted mixture of exhaustion, bliss and worry.

It wasn't only Rhys's health that I was worried about. Theo began to show more signs that he was having trouble adjusting. He rarely wanted to leave my side, fought to sit on my lap every time I sat down, and only wanted me during his bedtime routine which Nate and I both used to share with him. After the first two weeks, we decided to have him go back to daycare three days a week. We hoped a return to his daily routine would help to settle him down and I yearned for at least the possibility of fitting in a nap while Rhys napped.

"Hey buddy, you ready to go to Miss Allie's?" I asked as cheerfully as my sleep-deprived brain could muster. Miss Allie had been his daycare provider for the past two years. "She's excited to see you and your friends have missed you." I could tell immediately he didn't want to leave the house.

"I don't wanna go," he whined. "My tummy hurts."

"Your tummy hurts?" I wasn't sure whether to believe him. He had been acting completely normally and eaten a good breakfast without any issues. "Buddy, your friends miss you and are looking forward to seeing you."

I grabbed his shoes and finished getting him ready to go. He followed me out to the car without further complaint. But after I strapped Rhys into the car, Theo just stood next to the rear car door, holding his blanket, looking like a lost puppy.

"What's the matter buddy?"

"I don't wanna go!" He began to wail.

What was going on with my boy? Theo had never acted this way before. I knelt beside him in the middle of our garage and hugged him tightly.

"Take deep breaths buddy; you're alright." I kissed his cheeks, wiped away the tears streaking his cheeks, and rubbed his back to try to help him calm down. As I gently pushed him back so I could look him in the eye he began gagging. "Buddy, what's going on? Take deep breaths, you're fine."

We never made it to daycare. This same scene happened every day for over a week. We tried everything and not knowing what else to do we took him to his pediatrician. The diagnosis was panic attacks.

I could hardly believe it, a four-year-old with panic attacks? I had no idea that children so young could have them. *How would we help our son? How had I not anticipated this?* Was this something I had given him? Had he inherited my biological vulnerability to anxiety? The worry left me at the edge of a panic attack of my own.

There was Rhys's health to worry about and now Theo's, too. Both of my kids needed my full attention to help them have happy, healthy childhoods.

And there was the continuing challenge of managing Mark and Danielle. Just as I'd feared, no sooner had we settled in at home, then they started calling, texting, and sending emails. The calls started out sporadically, but within no time they began calling multiple times a day and always with a complaint or a new demand. As the days turned into weeks and there was no change in their behavior, my frustration and anxiety over our new relationship grew. *How were we ever going to have an amicable relationship with these two? Nothing is working to help calm these stormy waters! Why am I solely responsible for finding a way to make this work?*

That was the question that ate at me the most. I was holding up my end of the deal, taking their calls and answering their questions about how Rhys was doing. I thought this extra effort would provide evidence of my commitment to our end of the adoption agreement and would help improve the situation. And maybe the additional proof that my extra efforts weren't working would convince the agency that they needed to step in and help me out.

I was not only willing, but felt compelled, to do whatever I could to help Rhys's birth parents make the transition to the current phase of the adoption. I felt responsible for their hurt, constantly unable to please them, and powerless against the onslaught of demands they sent my way. I had called the agency to share my concerns with both Barbara and Joyce about the escalation of their behavior. I was told to be patient and shower them with information and photographs. When I asked them to speak with Danielle and Mark to assess the situation for themselves I was told there was no need.

When the agency wouldn't engage, I wondered whether I should build a stronger relationship with Kathy. *Was that appropriate? Was it fair? Could she help manage Danielle and Mark?*

Their most common concern was that they didn't know how Rhys was doing, and they wanted reassurance that she was fine. Hoping to reassure them that she was okay, I sent them a letter full of as many details as I could think of for a month-old baby. I also included a dozen pictures. I addressed the envelope to both Danielle and Mark and sent it to Danielle's apartment. I hoped that providing detailed information about how Rhys was doing along with pictures would help them feel better. I also knew they were incredibly proud of Rhys, or as they called her, Sara, and I hoped that the pictures would give them something to brag about to their friends, which they had made clear to us was important to them.

I had just put Rhys down for a nap, Nate was at work, and Theo was quietly playing Legos on the floor of the playroom. Just as I sat down to relax and thumb through a magazine our phone rang. The caller ID showed Danielle's home number.

"Hello?" I said tentatively.

"Hi, thanks for the letter and pictures of Sara," Mark and Danielle said in unison.

Anxiety instantly filled my body. Something in the tone of the greeting sent a chill through me. *Take a deep breath. Be patient, be kind, don't forget they're hurting,* I reminded myself.

"You're welcome," I said, hoping to fend off any attacks. "We took them on Easter. Hope you like them."

"We need more," they said, once again in unison.

"You need *more?*" I stammered. "I sent *twelve* pictures. That's a lot." I struggled to keep my tone even and volume low as I stood up from the couch and started to pace. I had downloaded, printed, and trimmed the pictures. I had written a detailed letter, found an envelope that would protect the pictures from damage, addressed and stamped it, and gotten it out to the mailbox. All with a preschooler and a newborn demanding my full attention. I was utterly exhausted, sending a dozen photos was more of an accomplishment than I thought possible at that point.

"We *need* copies. We can't share," he said. There was that tone, the one I'd come to know so well, the one that implied I was a thoughtless idiot. The tone was all it took for me to let go of the last calm, empathetic thoughts within my sleep deprived, worry-filled brain.

That's it! Are you f'ing kidding me? You need copies?! You can't share?!

I couldn't believe what I was hearing. My anger was rapidly morphing into rage. The weeks of resentment and frustration that had built up with each and every one of their demands, each and every one of their putdowns, and each and every one of their attempts at manipulation, threatened to burst through my calm exterior. I yearned to yell and point out all our efforts to hold up our end of the adoption agreement, but instead I swallowed my feelings and took another deep breath before responding.

"Well, I sent so many so you could split them between you," I calmly replied, hoping an explanation would resolve the issue. But as I fought to control my roiling emotions, the phone to my ear, I paced back and forth across the room like a caged animal. I was trying to stay calm so Theo wouldn't sense my frustration.

"We ... *can't* ... share!" he spat, angrily, demandingly, as if their limitations were my failings. I had failed to accommodate their never before communicated requirements.

That tone again! I'm going to lose it!

"We just fight because we both want them all," Danielle said.

What the hell have I gotten myself into? I thought, as I reflected on all the agency had promised. They'd assured me Danielle and Mark wanted adoption, understood the concept of open adoption, would accept that their role as Rhys's parents had ended. Instead, I was getting demands to comfort and placate a couple who couldn't be comforted or placated. A couple who couldn't cognitively grasp that they were not Rhys's parents. A couple who couldn't even grasp the concept of sharing. *This can't be real. Holy shit!*

"Well, you're just going to have to work that out," I said in my most authoritative mom voice. I no longer cared how guilty or responsible I felt for their hurt. I'd gone above and beyond. "If you need copies, then I'll only be able to send a couple of pictures in the future."

I didn't want to be stingy or heartless. But the truth was, I was exhausted. And I knew I had to set limits, or the next eighteen years would be nothing but increasing demands—demands that had nothing to do with Rhys, and everything to do with their personal issues. I hoped this warning would work, while at the same time knew it would likely have no effect. But I had to find some way to stand up for myself.

The demands continued unabated for months. I could do nothing right. I appealed to the agency for help, but instead, they just encouraged me to send more pictures, so I did. I didn't answer every time the phone rang, but with multiple calls per day, I eventually answered just so the phone would stop ringing. I continued to hope that my efforts would provide whatever it was they were looking for in order to begin healing.

Every time, within days of sending pictures, I'd get a complaint call.

"You used the wrong paper. We need photo paper." *Sister, you're lucky I even found time to print pictures. Do you have any idea what it takes to care for a baby and a four-year-old? There's no way I have time to switch out the paper in the printer.*

"You printed the wrong size pictures. These don't stay in the album." *Not my problem!*

"We don't like the way Sara looks." *Don't scream, don't scream. Her ... name ... is ... RHYS! And she looks adorable!!! Can't you see that? She isn't a decorative ornament!*

"We can't see Sara's face enough."

That was it; that was the straw that broke the camel's back. I lost it. When I heard that, I hung up the phone, throwing it on the couch so hard it bounced back and landed on the floor with a thud. With Rhys napping in her crib and Theo playing on the living room floor, I walked into my bedroom, closed the door and screamed "SUCK IT!" as loud as I could to an empty room. I knew, it was totally childish, but I was done. I'd had enough of Mark and Danielle; open adoption be damned.

For months, I ignored what my gut told me to do. I devalued my own wisdom and perspective, instead bending to the "experts" at the agency. I had repeatedly shared my concerns with Barbara and Joyce. They both said the same things: "Oh, they're still just working their way through the transition." Or, "Just shower them with pictures of Sara, that will keep them happy." Or "Well, just don't answer the phone when it rings." *Sara?*

I justified my acquiescence because Danielle and Mark had given me the greatest gift a human could give, and I showed my gratitude through peaceful acceptance of their abuse. I felt forever indebted and required to bow to the altar upon which they had firmly taken residence. But enough was enough.

And on top of it all, I was sinking into a deep, thick darkness, that no amount of maternal love and family happiness could alter.

I had serious concerns about the health of my children, my energy was draining faster than I could replenish it, and the color of life was dimming with each passing day. I had felt this darkness before, but I denied its meaning. I hadn't been pregnant with Rhys, but there was no mistaking it. I was depressed. Deeply, profoundly, and unbiologically, post-adoptively depressed.

Chapter 30

Is She Really Healthy

A few days after returning home, we had brought Rhys to the doctor for her first well baby checkup and we were assured she was fine. With Danielle's condition potentially hereditary, we felt it was important to partner closely with our doctor to monitor her health and development. There were too many unknowns that came along with the mystery of Danielle's seizures. Was there anything we could do to lower the chances that Rhys would be affected? What did we need to know in case she had a seizure? Was there truly no way to know, without waiting two years, whether she would stay seizure-free?

The only other thing to do, besides wait it out, was to try to get an appointment with a geneticist. Fortunately, we had a world class children's hospital in our area. Unfortunately, it took six weeks to get an appointment.

Rhys slept soundly in her car seat during the hour drive to the medical center. It was an unusually warm, sunny day in early June. Brightly colored hanging baskets hung from the light posts lining both sides of the narrow drive that wound through the campus. The beauty of the baskets helped to calm my nerves.

We found a parking spot on the ground level of the garage and as I pulled on the parking brake I turned to Nate's mom, Linda, "Thanks again for coming with me. I really appreciate it." I stopped talking abruptly as tears unexpectedly sprung to my eyes. I was scared. The possibility that Rhys would begin having seizures transformed in that moment from the constant worry of an overprotective mother to a real possibility that needed to be guarded against in any way possible.

I swallowed hard as I reached for the door handle. "If you wouldn't mind carrying the diaper bag, I'll get our girl."

"It's going to be okay. And I don't mind at all," she said giving me a reassuring smile.

As we entered the building and checked in at the front desk, I took long deep breaths to try to calm my nerves. *We're here to get more information. The doctor can help us keep Rhys healthy.*

Since she had been born ten weeks before I had used a mixture of positive self-talk, prayer, and distraction to combat the always present worry that our otherwise ordinary life with two young children might come crashing down. I frequently admonished myself for spending so much time worrying about something that I had no control over and was wasting energy trying to change. But now I was worrying as if at any moment I would receive the news that would change my life forever.

Linda and I checked in with the receptionist and took our seats in the lobby. While we waited, I looked down at my baby daughter. "How're you doing baby girl?" I asked swinging her gently and rearranging the lightweight blanket that covered her legs. "What're you thinking about, huh?" I said gently tickling her belly as she smiled up at me.

I loved it when Rhys smiled. A few weeks before, as she and Theo laid on the floor playing she had smiled for the first time. I had thought my heart would burst. My two children, laying side by side on the floor, Theo making funny faces at his baby sister.

When Rhys smiled her entire face lit up. Her tiny lips curved upwards, dimples appeared in her chubby cheeks, and her huge blue eyes, now framed by lashes so long they touched her eyelids, grew to twice their normal size. *This is the joy both my head and my heart were searching for*, I thought each time I caught a glimpse of her smile.

Just then, a nurse appeared in the doorway. "Mrs. Severn," she said brightly looking in our direction. "Hi, I'm Marcy, it's so nice to meet you." She reached out her hand to shake mine.

"Nice to meet you," I said before turning to Linda. "And this is my mother-in-law, Linda. And this," I said turning slightly so Rhys was facing the nurse, "is Rhys." I felt the gentle warmth of pride fill my chest as I introduced my daughter.

"Very nice to meet you all. Please follow me this way and we'll get you ready to meet Dr. Reynolds."

The brightly lit corridor was lined with doorways on both sides. On our left the doors were plain white and utilitarian. On the right were wooden sliding doors, stained a rich chocolate brown. Each door had a narrow window inset next to the door handle with a wave pattern to match the ocean themed building.

"You'll be here, in room number eight," she said as she slid open the door to reveal a small room, approximately six feet wide and ten feet long. "If you'll please take Rhys out of her seat and completely undress her, we'll take her measurements."

All three of us stepped in the room. An upholstered bench was built in along the length of one wall, a whiteboard covered the wall opposite the door, and two chairs were placed next to a counter that served as a changing table and held the infant scale. Linda walked over and sat down at the end of the bench, waiting quietly while I got Rhys undressed.

"Out you come, baby girl," I said as I gently lifted Rhys out of the infant seat. "Oh my goodness, you need a diaper change." I quickly got her undressed and cleaned up. "We better make this fast before she goes again," I smiled at the nurse. "She's kind of unpredictable."

"No problem," the nurse said smiling back. "Let me get her weight and then you can put a diaper on her. But keep her undressed. The doctor will want to examine her when he comes in."

The nurse quickly took her height and weight and then stepped out of the way so I could put a clean diaper on her.

"The doctor should be here shortly," she smiled one more time before leaving the room and sliding the door shut behind her.

Linda and I sat quietly in the room. I wondered if I was being impolite not making small talk. I was too nervous. "Do you mind taking notes for me while the doctor's here?" This was the fifth or sixth time I had asked her that question since Nate asked her to join me at the appointment.

"I'm glad to," she said as she pulled a notebook and pen out of her purse.

"Thanks again," I said before looking down at Rhys who sat on my lap loosely wrapped in her blanket. *Is she as worried about Rhys as I am?* I wondered. *Does she worry about Rhys as much as her other four, biological grandchildren?*

I tried to refocus my thoughts on the task at hand. Those were useless questions; questions I wasn't going to ask. But still, they were questions I wrestled with as I tried to understand the realities of adoption for all the people involved.

"She's smiling a lot lately," I said as I picked Rhys up and kissed her several times on the cheek. "I just love her so much." My voice cracked and I pushed my lips tightly together. It was no place to have a breakdown. That would only make the situation even more uncomfortable.

We sat in silence for another couple of minutes. I cleared my throat before trying to talk again. "I let Kathy know we had an appointment to see the geneticist. She couldn't come over for the appointment but offered to talk to the doctor in advance. I gave them her contact information when I scheduled the appointment."

"That was generous of her. Do you know if they've spoken?"

"I don't, but I hope so." Danielle's mother, Kathy, was the only one who could provide the medical history pertinent to our current situation. We hadn't asked Mark or his parents because when the adoption agency inquired before Rhys was born, Mark's parents refused to answer.

After what seemed like hours, but was only ten minutes, we heard three quick knocks on the door before it slid open. "Hi, I'm Dr. Reynolds." A man in his mid-to-late fifties, with salt and pepper hair and reading glasses on top of his head, stepped into the room and extended his hand toward me. He was wearing a cotton button down shirt, khaki pants, and brown loafers. He was dressed more like a golfer than a doctor, and his informal dress helped me to relax. "And this is my assistant, Melanie."

Melanie looked to be just a couple years older than me. She was tall, slender, and wore a short-sleeved wrap dress. "Nice to meet you," she said extending her hand to me as I stood up.

I once again introduced Linda and proudly introduced Rhys to them before sitting back down, this time perching on the edge of the bench and lightly bouncing Rhys on my knee.

"Well, Rhys looks to be a beautifully healthy baby," Dr. Reynolds said with a smile. "Congratulations."

"She is beautiful, and we sure hope she stays healthy," I said surprised by how openly I spoke the unguarded truth about how I was feeling.

"We reviewed the information Rhys's doctor sent over and I had the opportunity to have a conversation with Kathy, who sent us Danielle's medical records." He showed us several pages of information in Rhys's file.

"Oh wow," I said as a tear escaped down my cheek before I had a chance to stop it. I was overcome with gratitude that Kathy had taken the time to both talk with the doctor and send over the detailed medical information. "What do you think?"

"Well, let's take a look at Rhys and have a conversation." He reached out to take Rhys from my knee. He gently laid her on his lap and unwrapped her blanket. Dr. Reynolds and his assistant took additional measurements, checked her from head to toe, talking softly between them. "She indeed appears perfectly healthy," he said as he wrapped Rhys back up in her blanket and cradled her in the crook of his arm. He nodded to his assistant.

"We reviewed all the information and unfortunately, we don't have enough information to give you any indication of whether or not Rhys is likely to have a similar type of seizure disorder," Melanie said as she looked directly at me. "What we know is likely the same as what you've already learned. If she remains seizure free for two years, she'll be no more likely than any other person to experience seizures."

I felt my heartbeat quicken and felt slightly short of breath. *How will I survive two years of constant worry?* I wanted to cry in frustration and fear, but I was also relieved to know they had found no obvious health issues.

"Let's talk about what a seizure looks like in an infant, things to watch out for, and what to do in case you suspect Rhys is having a seizure," Dr. Reynolds said. He described what a seizure might look like, told us seizures usually stopped on their own, and if we suspected one to call our doctor as soon as possible. We would only need to call 9-1-1 or get her to an emergency room if the seizure didn't stop.

I could hardly believe I was sitting there with my two-and-a-half-month-old baby learning to identify infant seizures. This experience had never crossed my mind. Not even after we made the decision to move forward with the adoption had I ever thought about sitting in a doctor's office learning about the subtle signs of infant seizures. And among the things we learned was that they can be so brief that Rhys could suffer one without us even realizing it.

We were told that the thing to worry about was if the seizure didn't stop. That would mean we'd need to get medical intervention as quickly as possible to prevent brain damage. Physical, emotional, and cognitive delays and impairments could occur depending on the area of the brain a seizure occurred in and how long it lasted.

I asked a few questions to make sure I understood the information that both Dr. Reynolds and Melanie shared with us. I probed a little further hoping to glean any additional information I could about our chances that Rhys would continue to develop normally. If I couldn't be comforted by knowing that chance was in our favor, I wanted to be sufficiently armed with instructions on exactly how to respond should our world begin to fall apart.

"We know this is difficult information to hear. I wish there was something I could tell you that would help you feel better. Something that would help you not worry. I can only imagine how stressful this situation is for you. We're here to help where we can. Feel free to call me if you get any additional information or think of more questions." Dr. Reynold's acknowledgement of how stressful the situation was provided unexpected comfort.

Linda and I thanked them for their time and we worked together to get Rhys dressed and safely strapped in to her car seat. My mind was reeling, and I wasn't sure what to think or how I felt. There was so much to try to sort out. We hadn't received any bad news and that was good. But nearly two more years of wait and see felt nearly impossible to survive.

The drive home was uneventful and I thanked Linda one final time as I dropped her off before heading to pick up Theo from daycare. The next few hours I would be distracted by our new evening routine; dinner, a walk through the neighborhood, bedtime stories for Theo and a bottle for Rhys. Nate and I typically watched an hour of TV together before collapsing into bed. And if I was lucky, I would enjoy a couple hours of sleep before Rhys needed me again.

I knew I needed to fill Nate in on what we'd learned at the doctor that afternoon. But I wasn't sure what there was to say. In truth, the only thing that was different than when we'd said goodbye that morning was what an infant seizure looks like. We still had twenty-two more months to go. Twenty-two months of waiting, over 650 days of not knowing, 15,600 hours until we would hopefully know the risk had passed and our daughter was indeed healthy.

As I pulled into the driveway of Theo's daycare, I wondered if I had the energy to survive until bedtime.

Chapter 31

This Won't Work

According to our open adoption agreement, we had to visit Rhys's birth parents three times a year and send pictures twice a year. It was early June, Rhys was almost three months old, and with only six months left in the year we were trying to figure out how we would squeeze in the three visits.

We were accustomed to family road trips. For several years we went to see my family in July for my nephew's birthday and in October to celebrate Theo's birthday. We figured we'd make our third visit to coincide with Rhys's birthday. So April, July, and October, that was the cadence we thought would work.

What I didn't know was whether the visits at the agency after Rhys was born counted as one of our three visits. I didn't figure asking the agency would get us any different answer than they'd given us about anything else. Since our first introduction to Mark and Danielle it was some answer to the effect of "more is better" or "shower them with attention, it can't hurt."

I wanted to live by the letter of the open adoption agreement, but it seemed the agency consistently asked us to do more. At some point if we did enough 'more,' we were assured that everything would be fixed. The frequency of calls had slowed down, from several a day to several a week. But we had no other evidence that more was better, at least when it came to pictures. The more we sent, the more they complained.

They were just as demanding and unhappy as ever before. And as for "what will it hurt?" I knew for sure it was hurting. It was hurting *me*.

I was in a constant state of high alert. If I wasn't on the lookout for signs of infant seizure, or bringing Theo down from a panic attack, I was preparing myself for the next demand for photos or information.

I was lucky to get five interrupted hours of sleep each night. Rhys was a night owl, sleeping from eleven until two, then up until five thirty or six, when she would fall back to sleep until eight. But with Theo up at six thirty, that meant half an hour to doze on the couch before I needed to be up again.

Coffee and candy became my two best friends. The energy boosts they provided propelled me through the day. With stress, anxiety, and exhaustion my constant companions, depression had once again settled in.

I didn't want to leave the house unless I absolutely had to. It became increasingly difficult to motivate myself to get ready every day; I only wanted to wear sweats and pull my hair into a ponytail. I did my best to deny the feelings of sadness and disinterest, telling myself *I'm just exhausted like every other mom with an infant. I want to stay close to home while I can, I'll be back at work soon and wishing I could just hang out at home. This can't be postpartum depression; I didn't have the baby!*

I knew I felt depressed, but I couldn't understand why. I had finally achieved a dream I'd had for as long as I could remember. And I couldn't believe it could be postpartum depression; I hadn't given birth to the baby, I thought it was physiologically impossible.

I felt like I was failing. I knew I wasn't failing as a mother. I was a loving, attentive mom taking excellent care of her children. I was failing as a woman. I was incapable of being healthy and caring for two young kids. *Plenty of women manage with kids much closer in age, I told myself, while I only have one in diapers, for goodness sake.* I was home with my kids, on paid leave no less. *I should be able to do this,* I thought time and time again.

Then came the final straw. I had woken to a text message from Danielle's phone saying: *We wish we never picked you for Sara's mother* followed by their initials in all caps, including SCH. SCH, Sara Claire Hannah. While I thought that their complaints about the pictures had been the last straw, I was wrong. This was the text that capped it. As I read the message over and over again, in my sleep-deprived state, my heart raced and bile rose up my throat. The abuse had to stop. This relationship would no longer be on their terms only.

* * *

In the middle of June, after finding out my nephew was scheduled to play in a rec-basketball tournament, I asked Nate about making the drive over to see my family and squeeze in a birth parent visit. It would mean two trips in less than a month, but it also meant we would manage to fit in the three birth parent visits in the first year and have one less thing to worry about. He agreed readily, wanting to get the visits over with as soon as possible. The agency had agreed to let us have the visits there, so all I needed to do was call and let them know when we'd be in town.

After Rhys and I returned from dropping Theo at daycare the next morning I called Joyce.

"Joyce, it's Kim Severn. I'm calling to let you know we'll be over in a couple weeks and would like to use a room there for a visit with Mark and Danielle."

"Sure Kim, what day will you be here?"

"Why don't we make it Friday, the 24th at 11. That should be a good time for Rhys."

"Okay, well if you and Nate want to come 30 minutes early we can do your post-placement visit and begin the adoption finalization."

"That would be awesome!" I wasn't expecting that. Normally the post-placement visits were in person at the adoptive family's home. Nate and I had wondered when we would host Joyce again. Hope surged through me, maybe this visit was going to be a turning point.

I hung up the phone and looked down at Rhys who was rocking gently in her swing. "Well how about that, baby girl. Let's write Mark and Danielle a letter and let them know we're coming for a visit."

I had two goals in mind when I sat down and wrote them the letter. I wanted to let them know we would be in town for a visit and put them on notice that the way they'd been communicating with us needed to change.

Dear Danielle and Mark,

We hope you're doing well. We want to let you know that we will not be responding to text messages, emails, or phone calls from you.

The messages you recently sent are mean and not appropriate. We will send you a letter to let you know when we will have our visits. Along with the trip in a couple of weeks, we plan to see you in July and October.

We will see you on the 24th at the agency from eleven to noon. If you would like to visit, we will see you then.

Regards,
Kim and Nate

I hurried to make a copy of the note, address an envelope to Danielle and one to Mark and get them in the mailbox before the mailman arrived.

Four days after mailing the letter my phone chimed as I was putting away the dishes. It was a text from Danielle: *Are you mad at us?* Followed by their initials and SCH.

I knew we were headed for an eventful visit.

We decided to make the drive across the state after dinner on Thursday night. With little traffic, Theo playing quietly in the backseat and Rhys sleeping most of the way, the drive to my parents' house had gone flawlessly and I was determined to take it as a good omen. *This weekend will go great!*

I was up early the next morning with Rhys, although she had slept later than usual, waking up at four rather than two. When it was clear she wasn't going back to sleep at 6:30, I got the stroller out of the back of the car and took her for a long walk through my parents' neighborhood.

I didn't really mind that she was up, I couldn't sleep anyway. I was increasingly anxious about the visit with Danielle and Mark. I wondered what it would be like and whether they would see us as Rhys's parents now that a few months had passed.

The day was already beginning to heat up and it felt good to work off a little nervous energy. As we walked through the residential streets I pointed to the houses where my high school friends had lived. By the time we returned to my parents' house Nate and Theo were both up.

"Good morning," my dad said in his booming voice from the couch where he sat reading the paper and drinking a cup of coffee.

"Morning," I said walking up the stairs with Rhys on my hip. "Hi guys," I said to Nate and Theo. "How did you guys sleep?" I leaned down and gave them both a quick kiss.

"Nate, can you get Theo some breakfast? And Dad, do you mind hanging out with Rhys while I take a shower?"

"Not a problem," he said, smiling. My dad was great with babies and babies loved my dad.

Just after ten, with everyone fed, dressed and ready for the day, we left Theo building a Lego set with my dad and Nate and I headed to the agency.

We met with Joyce in her sunny office in what used to be the kitchen of the old house. She sat in her office chair holding Rhys and intermittently cooing at her and asking us questions.

"How's Rhys doing?"

"Great," I answered, smiling.

"How's she developing?"

"Perfectly."

"Are you taking her to her well child checks?"

"Absolutely."

"Any concerns?"

"Well, since you asked," I hesitated and looked over at Nate as if to ask *should we go for it?* "We have no concerns about Rhys. But is there anything you can do to help Danielle and Mark with the transition? They really don't seem to understand that we're Rhys's parents now."

"Well, I encourage you to send them lots of pictures, give them lots of information about how she's doing. Help them understand how she's developing, tell them when she hits important milestones."

"Um," I paused and swallowed hard, *here we go again*. "That's not working ... and if I may, that's not the deal, Joyce."

"What do you mean that's not the deal?"

Is she kidding me?

"Respectfully Joyce, you said you'd help them through this transition. And I don't think that's happening. Our agreement says pictures twice a year and visits three times a year. We've sent pictures several times already, and with each set of pictures their demands only grow. I'm very nervous about how this visit is going to go today." My palms had begun to sweat and I wiped them down the tops of my thighs as I willed myself not to start crying.

"Well, what's sending pictures cost you? Flood them with pictures. Whenever you get them developed, get doubles and send them the duplicates," she said as if the solution was obvious.

"I'm not trying to be argumentative. But I don't think you understand how demanding they are. And frankly, we don't get pictures developed. We take the pictures with our digital camera and print them on our home printer. Toner's not cheap. Again, we're not trying to be difficult. This is really stressful, and we're not comfortable with how things are going."

"Kim, you need to understand. This is how this population parents."

Screech! Like a driver in rush hour traffic having to brake unexpectedly to avoid an accident, her comment forced me to stop and let my brain process what she had just said. I felt like I was swaying back and forth and a high-pitched scream filled my ears. Did she just say what I thought she did? Did she just refer to the way they were behaving as "parenting"? Was she encouraging them, telling them that they still had a parenting role to play? *Oh God ...*

I was speechless and wasn't sure what to say next. We needed this interview to go well so we could move forward with the adoption finalization. After Danielle and Mark released their parental rights a week after Rhys was born, we had legal guardianship and the adoption agency had legal custody. So although we'd received permission to take Rhys home, we still had to appear in court to finalize the adoption. Rhys was our daughter and I wanted her legal status to match our reality – and now it was up to the agency how soon that could happen.

We heard the receptionist greet Danielle and Mark as they arrived and direct them to the waiting room. As soon as I heard their voices my heart began to race.

We finished our interview and after checking Rhys's diaper, Nate carried her into the waiting room. They both jumped to their feet the minute they saw us turn the corner. Nate stopped a foot in front of Danielle who reached out and grabbed Rhys from his arms.

"Whoa, Danielle, be careful," I said stepping forward and placing my arms underneath Rhys's bottom. "She's still a baby. You can't grab her out of Nate's arms." My voice was stern, my fear and anxiety barely held in check. *What was she thinking? I understand she is excited, but she can't just grab her!*

I wanted to take my daughter back, declare this relationship permanently broken, and revoke their privileges. I had said the visit would last an hour, but maybe it would be less than 30 seconds. I knew I would survive, but I wasn't sure how.

"I want to hold Sara," she said looking me directly in the eye.

"I get that, but you can't grab her. That isn't safe," Nate said patiently. "Why don't we go into the waiting room and have a seat. Be really careful, please."

I swallowed hard as I watched Danielle carry Rhys into the small waiting room and sit in a chair next to the windows. I sat down directly across from her and set Rhys's car seat and diaper bag next to my feet. Mark sat next to Danielle.

"I want to hold Sara," he said to no one in particular.

Her ... name ... is ... Rhys! I placed my stare directly between them and watched the traffic wiz through the busy intersection.

"We've been showing all Sara's pictures to our friends. But there are a lot of them that you can't see her face clearly," he said trying to make eye contact with me. His words sounded like an accusation, as if I'd broken the law.

"Well, I'd hoped you would appreciate that we were able to send you so many pictures," I shot back. I wasn't going to let this guy bully me. *And her name's RHYS!* "Listen guys, we need to tell you something. We know that you called her Sara while you were pregnant. But we've decided her name is Rhys." They both just looked back at me as if I hadn't spoken. I knew I'd just dropped a potential bomb, but I didn't know any other way to break the news. We couldn't think of any gentle way to break the news, so I had taken the opportunity to just rip off the Band-Aid.

"And the album we got from our friends is almost full. We're going to need another one." Mark said as if I hadn't just spoken.

"Oh, your birthday's coming up, right? You can put that on your gift list," I said, this time I met his eyes and tried to make my voice sound light. *Be nice!* I reminded myself.

"Or you could send us one. You're the one sending pictures."

"Excuse me for a moment," I said as I stood up and patted Nate's knee as I walked by. "Please keep an eye on Rhys while I go to the bathroom," I said to him.

I was so furious I could hardly see straight. I didn't actually have to go to the bathroom, what I needed was to calm down. Why was I letting this guy push my buttons? As I sat on the closed toilet lid, with my head in my hands, I listened to the angel and the devil battling as they perched, one on each shoulder.

You need to understand they think differently than you do. You need to remember they experience the world differently. They've made a tremendous sacrifice and they're still healing, be patient, the angel advised.

They need to appreciate that they've received more than was agreed to. They need to show some respect. They need to move on! The devil argued back.

My face burned with shame at the devil's final statement. "You have to pull yourself together sister," I whispered to the empty room. "You are kind, caring, and can be patient. This relationship is hard on everyone and will take time." I wanted to believe what I was telling myself, but I didn't.

I wanted to be a good, caring, understanding, and appreciative person. But I wasn't. I was angry, resentful, and increasingly jealous. I didn't want another couple taking credit for our amazing daughter. I was the one constantly on guard, up in the middle of the night, cleaning poopy diapers and spit up. I didn't want to be relegated to ghostwriter while they claimed to be the authors.

And Joyce's comment continued to gnaw at me – *this is the way this population parents.* I could sense the impending doom.

When I walked back into the room they were bent with their faces almost touching Rhys's nose cooing at her. It was a heartbreaking scene. Their tremendous love for her was undeniable. But while I was touched and saddened by what I saw, my fear also grew. I couldn't put my finger on exactly what it was that they were doing, but somehow the strength of their conviction as her parents seemed to be growing, not diminishing. The more we gave into their demands, the more their view of their role and their rights expanded.

"You alright?" Nate whispered as I sat down next to him.

"No," I said quietly and shook my head. I sat in stunned silence until Rhys began to fuss. It was getting close to lunchtime and I knew she would be needing a bottle soon.

"Why don't you give her to me for a few minutes, let me calm her down, and then I'll let you hold her for a bit longer before we have to leave," I said, making sure to hold eye contact with Danielle.

"No," Danielle said as she put Rhys up to her shoulder and bounced her up and down.

"Danielle, please. That's not how we do it," I was almost pleading and felt my distress increase. "Let me just calm her down and then you can have her for a few more minutes."

"I'm going to hold my daughter," she said, looking me directly in the eye as if challenging me to a duel. "It's okay, Sara. Shhh, it's okay."

I looked over at Nate in desperation. What was I supposed to do? Rhys continued to fuss and my breasts began to ache. I couldn't breastfeed our daughter, but I often got the familiar ache when she cried. *She needs her mom … and that's me!*

"It'll be okay," Nate whispered, reaching over to put his hand on my knee that bounced up and down uncontrollably. I had never felt a sadness quite like what I felt that day. It was a mixture of desperate yearning to soothe my child, sympathy for their experience, and anger.

"You know that Sara can find out we're her real parents when she's twelve. I checked, it's the law." She continued to bounce Rhys on her shoulder as Rhys continued to cry.

"Danielle, *Rhys*, will always know who you are. It is an open adoption, it's not a secret." Is this what this whole thing is about? I wondered. They don't want to be anonymous?

"And when she wants to come live with us, Mark and I will be ready."

"Oh," I said in shock. I didn't even know what to say. "Danielle, you need to give me Rhys so I can calm her down. We need to leave in ten minutes or so and I don't want to have her upset when we put her in the car seat." I fished in the diaper bag for a pacifier. I calmly stood, walked over to Danielle, and put my hands on Rhys's sides. "Please hand her to me so I can calm her down. As soon as she's quiet I'll give her back."

Danielle reluctantly let go. I gently took Rhys into the crook of my arm and gave her the pacifier. I swayed gently back and forth, while I bounced two times on the left, two times in the middle, and two times on the right. It had taken us weeks to perfect this dance and I knew it would work. "Shh, pretty girl. You're okay. Are you getting tired?" I asked making eye contact with Rhys the whole time. After a minute she was sucking on her pacifier and her body had relaxed. I kissed her on her cheeks and looked at Danielle.

"Alright, if you'll hold her like I'm holding her, she should stay relaxed." I bent down and gently placed Rhys back in Danielle's arms.

"But I wanted to hold Sara," Mark complained.

"I told Danielle when I took the baby to calm her that I would give her back to her."

The visit lasted fifteen more minutes. When Nate said it was time to go they took several photos on their cell phones and covered Rhys with kisses.

With Nate holding Rhys, who was strapped in her car seat, we walked to the front door.

"We'll be back in three weeks for another visit," I said. "I'll send you a letter letting you know what time and the exact date we'll be here. I hope you guys have a good weekend."

"Have a good weekend guys," Nate said as he reached for the doorknob. "See you in a few weeks."

"Bye, Sara," they said one after the other.

It took several hours for the adrenaline to wear off after the visit. I was shaken by Mark and Danielle's reaction to seeing Rhys, the depth of their parental feelings for her, and my strong reaction. I also wasn't sure how to think about their complete lack of response to the news that we'd changed her name.

They clearly still felt strongly that they were our daughter's parents. The fact that they called her Sara throughout the visit was evidence they had no intention of moving on, whatever that actually meant. And there was no doubt in my mind that I was their enemy number one.

The other thing I knew for sure was the only support the agency was going to give us was a place to have our visits. Other than that, we were on our own.

On my own. Alone. No one to turn to who understood what I was thinking, no one to help guide me through the minefield.

It was time to duck and cover. When other people were looking, I'd find a way to act as if everything was fine. And in the safety of my own home, after everyone was tucked in for the night, I could fall apart. I hoped five interrupted hours of sleep a night would be enough to put me back together again each day. But so many times, it wasn't.

Chapter 32

So Many Awkward Moments

After three months it was time to go back to work. Even though I was constantly exhausted I hoped the change of pace and atmosphere would be enough to kick me out of what I'd decided was my stay-at-home blues. *Just fake it 'til you make it*, I thought. If I forced myself to act like everything was great, then maybe it would be.

After all, what did I have to complain about? I had a great job that provided me paid time off with my children, a house in the burbs, and two healthy and thriving kids. Wasn't that what I'd been working so hard for? I figured with more mental stimulation and adult interaction I would soon be back to my pre-adoption self.

With both of us back at work beginning the next day, I figured it was a good time to begin establishing a new bedtime routine. The frequency of Theo's anxiety attacks had finally declined so I was weary of putting him through too much change. I didn't want my return to work to impact the progress he had made.

Talking over my concerns with Nate, we decided I would continue to put Theo to bed and he would get Rhys down. That would also give me 30 minutes to an hour each night to pack lunches, refill the diaper bag, and catch up on things around the house.

Amazingly, as if she knew I had a big day ahead, Rhys was only up for an hour in the middle of the night. Just as Theo had done the night before I went back to work when he was an infant, she gave me the much-appreciated gift of a little extra sleep the night before I returned to work.

I woke up with a jolt when the alarm clock switched on and the morning news filled the quiet air. I quickly showered, put on make-up for the first time in a month, and got dressed in clothes that didn't include any jersey knit. Nate was already heading out the door when I went in to wake Rhys.

I tiptoed past Theo's bedroom, hoping to give him another half hour of sleep, and quietly opened the door to Rhys's room. My breath caught in my chest. There was my beautiful baby girl, her cheeks slightly flushed, her short wispy curls framing her round face. *There is nothing more beautiful than a sleeping baby.* As if hearing my thoughts, she opened her eyes and blinked up at me.

"Good morning, baby girl," I said with a wide smile as I leaned down over the rail of the crib and put my hand on her belly. "Thanks for the extra sleep last night."

Rhys smiled, and my heart melted. When Rhys smiled the corners of her mouth went up and her lips parted showing her pink, toothless gums. And her beautiful sea blue eyes glistened.

"Today's a big day sweet girl," I said lifting her out of the crib and setting her on the changing table. "You get to go with brother to daycare while Mommy goes to work."

The spit bubbles she blew in response, made me laugh. *Maybe this is all going to work out just fine.*

A half hour later, with Rhys changed and fed, we went up to wake Theo. I stood beside his bed for a moment taking in his sweet sleeping figure. I knelt beside the bed with Rhys in the crook of my right arm and began to sing the *Good Morning Song* my mom had sung to me when I was a kid.

"It's time to get up, it's time to get up, it's time to get up in the morning. It's time to get up, it's time to get up, it's time to get up today." I leaned over and gave him kisses on his soft cheeks as he slowly opened his eyes.

"Good morning, Mommy," he said putting a hand over my shoulder for a quick hug. "Hi Rhysie," he continued patting his sister on the head. Rhysie was the nickname Theo had given his sister soon after her arrival.

"It's time to get up buddy," I said. "We have to leave for Miss Allie's in half an hour."

"I don't want to go to daycare today," he whined, and I could see tears forming in his big brown eyes. "I want to stay home with you today."

"Oh sweetie, please don't be sad," I tilted my head to the side and lifted my eyebrows in concern. My stomach was starting to sink as I began to feel guilty for being so excited to have a day without kids. "Mommy won't be home today, remember. I'm going back to work and Rhys is going to daycare with you."

"I don't want you to go back to work," he said sitting up and folding his arms tightly across his chest. "Humph," he grunted to emphasize his displeasure.

"I'm sorry, buddy, but Mommy has to go back to work. And I need you to be a big boy and keep an eye on sister for me today. I'll need you to tell me what she does at daycare since she can't talk yet, okay?"

Somehow we got out of the house on time and without too much trouble. I managed to drop off both kids with only a few tears (from both Theo and me) and was soon inching through rush hour traffic.

* * *

Stepping off the elevator, I took a deep breath as I looked around at the familiar surroundings. There was the usual morning bustle as people caught up on what had happened over the weekend while waiting for their coffee to brew. It felt great to be back to work and surrounded by the sounds of the city.

There was my desk, waiting for me to sit down and get back to work. Everything was just where I had left it three months before. And just like I did after returning to work from my maternity leave with Theo, my first call was to the IT Department. I had once again forgotten my password. Instead of feeling annoyed, I laughed, it was great to be back. *Clearly some things don't change.*

Coworkers greeted me throughout the week as I passed them in the halls or joined them in meetings.

"Kim, you're back! How's the baby doing?"

"Hey Kim, great to see you. How old's the baby now? How's she doing?"

"Kim, where've you been? I haven't seen you in forever!"

Many of the women asked to see pictures and I smiled broadly as I bragged about my kids. I was proud of the family Nate and I created. *See acting like everything is great isn't that hard,* I told myself.

Starting back to work was also the beginning of what came to be known as 'the awkward phase.' For the previous three months the only people who asked questions about Rhys's adoption were close friends and the doctors we had seen. Strangers we met when we were out and about cooed at the baby in the infant seat or asked how old she was. There was no outward sign we had adopted a child.

But in returning to work, where there was a mix of people, some who knew and some who didn't know that we had adopted, I experienced the first of many awkward conversations about our daughter. I had been back for a few days when I ran into someone I hadn't worked with much but had seen around the building several times a week.

"Did I hear you were out on maternity leave?" she asked.

"Yeah, I just returned this week," I said smiling as I thought about my kids.

"But I never saw you pregnant."

I was totally unprepared for that. A series of responses flashed through my mind in rapid succession. What was the right response? What can I say that won't end up embarrassing one, or worse, both of us? Was I obligated to tell her that we'd adopted our baby? If I don't tell her we had adopted was I hiding something? Did I care if people knew our daughter was adopted? Or more importantly, would our daughter someday care if people knew?

So many questions I didn't know the right answer to. And I only had a second to think about.

"Um," I paused as I felt myself begin to blush. "That's because I wasn't." My coworker looked at me, her eyes widened as she tilted her head down and leaned in towards me. Her body language said *tell me more.*

"We adopted our daughter," I clarified, unable to think of anything else to say.

"Oh, that makes sense," she said shrugging her shoulders. "See ya."

Ugh. I felt slightly nauseous as I turned and walked in the opposite direction. *That makes sense? Glad my family makes sense to you,* I thought feeling defensive. Once again the devil and the angel appeared, one on each shoulder.

You can't blame her for being confused. There was no swollen belly or swollen ankles, no baby shower. Remember, there were none of the usual signs alerting people a baby was on the way.

But on the other hand, how our daughter had joined our family was nobody else's business and feeling an obligation to tell people felt like a breach of privacy. If I told someone Rhys was adopted I felt like I was letting her down, giving information she would someday consider only hers to share. That certainly wasn't my intention. Or worse, when I shared how she came to be part of our family, was I inadvertently adding an asterisk next to her in our family tree?

These awkward moments always caught me off guard and left me wondering whether I handled them correctly. Once again I felt like I was ill-prepared for this unexpected phase of our adoption journey.

I wasn't close enough to the few people I knew who had adopted to ask them about how they reacted or what they encountered. So I just felt my way blindly through, hoping for the best and trying not to cause too much embarrassment or harm.

Those awkward moments didn't only happen at work, they happened with total strangers as well. One Saturday morning, when Rhys was about six months old, I decided to take her shopping with me at the mall. She loved riding in the baby carrier on my chest facing outward so she could see and interact with people.

Rhys loved watching people and people responded to her. They were charmed by her big blue eyes, framed by her long, perfectly curled lashes. Or her head filled with curls that shot off in multiple directions, her porcelain white skin accentuating her chubby pink cheeks. Like all new mothers, I thought my baby was the most beautiful baby in the world and was delighted when people stopped to meet her.

Our first stop was the make-up counter at Macy's. My skin was rebelling and I hoped that the women at the Clinique counter could recommend a concoction that would help me get it under control.

"Hi! How can I help you?" The cheerful sales lady asked as she reached out to touch Rhys's hand. "Hi sweetheart. Ooh look at those eyes!"

"Um, hi," I said suddenly feeling embarrassed and reflexively reaching up to hold Rhys's hands as I started to sway side to side. "I'm hoping you have something to help me deal with an increase in blemishes."

"Sure, no problem," she said before leading us over to a display filled with a mix of soaps, lotions, and toners. "A woman's skin often changes after having a baby." She turned and flashed me a knowing smile as she reached for a pamphlet.

Oh no, not again, I thought. Do I correct her? If yes, what do I say? Would my answer really change her product recommendations? *Ugh!*

"Um, well yes. I did have that problem after my son was born, too," I said sounding apologetic. I walked away with a bag full of products I hoped would return my skin to normal. "That was awkward," I said to Rhys as we left the store.

I reached for one of her hands with my free one and bounced her arm up and down as we walked. I loved the feeling of her tiny fingers wrapped tightly around my index finger.

We walked through the mall looking at the brightly lit window displays, Rhys smiling at everyone who made eye contact with her.

"Let's stop in here, baby girl," I said kissing the top of her head as we slowed in front of a colorful store window. "We can see if they have a gift for your cousin."

"Hi, how can I help you?" The question came from a tall, skinny man in his early twenties. He smiled brightly and looked eager to help.

"Oh, we're just looking right now," I said with a smile as I continued walking further into the store. I paused to look at a display of soaps, body scrubs, and bubble baths in assorted floral scents. I picked up a sample to smell and heard another question come from just over my right shoulder.

"That one's nice, but Heirloom Rose is my favorite. Are you selecting a scent for yourself?" There he was again, smiling at us. He reminded me of a dog waiting for its owner to throw the ball in a game of catch.

"Oh, thank you for the recommendation. Not sure what we're looking for, we'll just continue to look around." I smiled once again and hoped another customer would arrive soon to distract him.

We continued deeper into the store and with each step I hoped we'd lose our friendly pursuer. It seemed to work and a few minutes later I found something my niece would like. As we stepped up to the counter, there he was again, this time ready to ring up our purchase.

"You found some very nice selections," he said as if we were buying fine wines. "Would you like these gift-wrapped perhaps?"

"No thank you, no gift wrap is necessary," I swung the diaper bag off my shoulder and began to hunt for my wallet.

"We have a special on our samples, they're three for six dollars or six for ten."

"No thank you, just our items please." I opened my wallet and grabbed my debit card. *Just ring us up please,* I thought. I knew he was just trying to be helpful but at the same time, he was beginning to get on my nerves.

"Sure, no problem. You're total is $24.79. Will that be cash or credit?"

"Debit please," I said handing him my card. I began to bounce gently as Rhys started to kick her legs excitedly.

"Can I ask you a question?" he asked handing me my debit card with one hand as he continued to hold our items in the other.

Um, no, I thought as I felt myself blush. My gut told me something uncomfortable was about the happen.

"Um, sure?" I stammered.

"Did your daughter get her bright blue eyes from her father?"

Whoa, wasn't expecting that. Where is this guy headed? I wondered. "Nope, my husband has dark brown eyes like me," I said with a smile as I reached for our bag. It was time to go.

"Do her grandparents have blue eyes?" He cocked his head to the side as if trying to solve a riddle.

"Nope," I said shaking my head slowly back and forth. "It was nice meeting you," I said reaching my hand further across the counter for our bag. My previous gesture hadn't worked; I hoped this more obvious one would.

"Well, where did her blue eyes come from then?"

Man, this guy is persistent. *I'm sure you're just trying to be nice, but SERIOUSLY guy.*

"She's just lucky I guess," I said trying to hide my growing annoyance. "Can we have our purchases please?"

"Well, eye color is genetic and if neither you or your husband..."

That was quite enough, I wasn't going to tell this total stranger anything about my daughter's genetics. It was none of his business. Rhys's eyes were amazingly beautiful and people constantly commented on them. But this young man's curiosity had crossed a line.

"Please hand me our purchases, we need to get going," I said cutting him off mid-sentence. "Have a nice day," I said as I grabbed the bag, turned, and walked briskly out of the store.

My heart raced and I felt short of breath. I felt guilty for possibly hurting the man's feelings, but his persistence was too much. I wondered if we would start getting questions like that more regularly. The thought that I'd forever be confronted with strangers challenging my daughter's genetic background was disturbing. I felt a surge of empathy thinking of all the looks and questions families who adopted children of a different race received. If eyes color was enough to entice a total stranger to comment, what must it be like when skin colors differed? Or when both parents were the same sex? I knew I wasn't the first parent to be asked an invasive question, but I felt alone. I felt like people saw a difference in my family that they felt free to ask about.

Each of these situations made me feel backed into a corner and stuck in an unwinnable situation. I didn't want to let people into our family business and more importantly invade Rhys's privacy.

Logically I knew that the makeup of my family wasn't anyone else's business and that people were just trying to make sense of what they saw. But emotionally, it felt like I was keeping a secret and being evasive.

I also didn't want to hurt anyone's feelings. Once again, in trying to protect other people, I found a new way to hurt myself.

Was there any way to feel prepared for all the uncomfortable, unexpected surprises that adoption continued to deliver? Where could I go for answers? Was I the only one unprepared for these encounters? I wanted to share my experiences with someone who understood, someone who had been there, too. I wanted someone to talk things over with and brainstorm responses without negative consequences. But I didn't know where to turn – and the agency was clearly not going to be any help.

I wanted to know I wasn't alone. Friends and family tried to help, all offering well-meaning advice. But they didn't understand. In the end, their responses always included some form of "Well all you need to do is…" or "Just stop …" or "Just start …" or "Why don't you just …." Possibly the worst of all was, "Just ignore it and it will go away." "Just" became a four-letter word that I all but banned from my conversations.

Not knowing what else to do, I did a few Internet searches but came up empty handed. All the groups I found were located thousands of miles away and the sites I found were focused on celebrating the wondrous miracle that was adoption—or condemned adoptive parents as lacking a "primal bond" that only the birthmother could provide.

The bond between me and my daughter was every bit as primal and maternal as the bond between me and the son I'd given birth to. And both of my kids were wondrous miracles. It was the reality of our adoption that was not so miraculous.

It all left me feeling as if I was stranded on a deserted island in the middle of the ocean. There was nothing but water for as far as I could see. The weather above my island was stormy and the seas were rough. I yearned to find someone else navigating similar seas and successfully sheltering from the storms that adoption created. I hoped to find someone to come to my rescue before there was too much more destruction.

Chapter 33

Severn Four Day

The day had finally arrived. Years in the making, and almost five months since we first met her, it was Rhys's adoption finalization day. We would legally become her parents, her name changed on all documentation, and our names added to her official birth certificate.

"Well hello everyone. Rhys, it's your big moment!" Our attorney, Samuel's voice boomed down the hallway and echoed off the walls, as he walked up to all of us gathered beside the courtroom doors.

He invited us inside and asked us to take seats on the sturdy wood benches similar to the ones lining the hallway. My parents, Nate, Theo, Rhys and I sat in the first row just behind the wooden waist-high bar that separated the gallery from the area where the official proceedings took place. My sisters and their families sat in the row behind us.

Danielle and Mark had relinquished their parental rights five months before, the agency had done their part of the paperwork and therefore they weren't required to attend. That left just us, our family, our attorney, the judge and his staff.

"I'll go check in with the judge and make sure everything's ready to go," Samuel said, looking at me and Nate. "You guys ready for this?" he asked smiling. I could tell he was enjoying his role in our special day.

"More than ready," I said feeling a lump form in my throat.

My dad and Nate stood to take pictures of everyone while we waited to get started. Theo sat next to me tickling and making funny faces at Rhys who laughed. I felt tears begin to build behind my eyes as my hands began to sweat. I was nervous and so grateful that the day had finally come.

The last piece of the puzzle was about to be put into place. Within an hour our family would no longer be living with a footnote next to our daughter's name. Our beautiful baby girl, who captured our hearts and became a member of our family even before we laid eyes on her, would legally have our name. We would forever be her parents. It was a responsibility, an honor, that I'd been longing for.

Ten minutes later we all stood as the judge, his assistant, and the court stenographer entered the courtroom and took their places on the wooden dais. My legs started to shake, and I tried to dry my hands on the receiving blanket laying in Rhys's infant seat. This was it, we had finally reached the summit of this long, stressful, exciting journey.

The judge sat down in his tall, black leather chair, dressed in the standard black judge's robe, the top of his balding head just a few inches below the bottom of the State seal that hung on the honey stained oak wood wall behind him. Without a bailiff in the room, as I'd seen in so many procedural dramas on television, I wasn't sure what I was supposed to do.

"Good afternoon, Your Honor," Samuel said as he walked through the swinging gate in the bar to officially greet the judge. "I hope you're having a great day. We're excited to be here with you."

"Good afternoon, Samuel, looks like everything is in place," the judge said, looking through a stack of papers sitting to his right on the large, imposing desk.

"We are ready Your Honor. If it pleases the Court I'd like to introduce you to Nate and Kimberly Severn," he turned and extended his right hand in our direction, "and their children Theo and Rhys. It is Rhys that we are here for today."

"Good to meet you all. I hope you are excited for this special day," he said with a soft smile that created creases at the outside of his dark eyes. The judge looked so imposing sitting high atop the dais, the years of difficult cases having carved deep grooves in his brow. But when he smiled, his entire face lit up as he leaned forward and seemed to hold the entire room in a comforting embrace.

"We are, Your Honor," Nate and I said in unison first looking at the judge and then at each another. The lump in my throat grew and I instinctively put my arm around Theo's shoulder as Nate patted his knee.

"It's wonderful to see the support you have with you today. Nate, would you like to introduce your guests?"

"Yes, Your Honor." Nate rose and stepped into the aisle. He angled his body, so he could easily see both the judge and our family. He looked so handsome in his green cotton button-down shirt, khaki pants, and leather loafers. "This is my father-in-law, Scott," he said as he gestured in my dad's direction.

I could hear the nervousness in his voice as it shook slightly, and he spoke more slowly than usual.

I tried to catch his eye, to give him a reassuring smile. After introducing my mom, Nate found his groove and introduced my sisters, their husbands and kids.

"Thank you all for coming and supporting Nate and Kimberly on this important day. There is a lot that this court deals with that happens because of a lack of familial support. It is a pleasure to be presiding over court business such as the reason we are here for today. Nate and Kimberly, if you'd like to bring Rhys forward and join Samuel at the table," he gestured to the wooden table that sat across the room from him and to his left.

Nate and I rose, and I turned toward my mom. I needed reassurance as my hands continued to sweat, and my heartbeat quickened. My mom looked back at me and smiled, her eyes filled with tears. *She loves me and will support me to the ends of the earth,* I thought. I felt lucky to have her and was grateful she was able to share the day with us.

"You stay here with Grandma, okay?" I bent down and kissed the top of Theo's head. "Daddy and I will be right up there with Rhys," I said, pointing to the table.

"It's okay," the judge said, his voice filled with kindness. "This is a family occasion. He's welcome to join you."

Nate and Theo walked hand in hand toward the table as I carried Rhys, one arm around her waist and the other beneath her bottom. I bounced her gently up and down as we walked.

"Please remain standing and raise your right hand," the judge said and waited.

I quickly adjusted Rhys to free my right hand while Nate bent gently pushing Theo's left hand down and pointed to his right.

With everyone in proper position the judge asked us to take the oath and swear we were indeed the people named in the paperwork. Oath taken, and assurances given, Nate sat down and pulled Theo onto his lap. I sat with Rhys facing forward, bouncing her slightly on my knee. I could feel her body tensing and knew she needed a nap. I silently hoped we'd make it through the proceedings without any major breakdowns. I was also glad the finalization was a part of the adoption process just for us.

"Nate and Kimberly, I've reviewed all of the paperwork submitted to the court and it appears everything is in order," he said officially and smiled again. "I have presided over several adoption finalizations during my time on the bench, officially forming families in the eyes of the law. What I learned from my experience is that children seem to find a way to their forever family."

In response, Rhys began to fuss, and the judge paused and looked at Nate and me.

I was trying to reposition Rhys and find her pacifier to help calm her down. I turned her to face me and cradled her in my left arm, as Nate placed a pacifier in her mouth.

"Shhh, Rhysie, it's okay," Theo said, patting her back.

"Shh," I whispered close to her ear as I gently swayed back and forth. Seeing her heavy eyelids begin to close I looked up at the judge. "Apologies, Your Honor," I said nervously. He sat with his hands folded on the desk, leaning slightly forwarded watching our family. He continued to smile, and I noticed a glint in his eyes. *Are his eyes watering,* I wondered?

"And I know," he said, his voice smooth as he continued, sounding like a wise sage, "that parents receive the children who God created especially for them. Sometimes parents give birth to these children, and sometimes, through a multitude of circumstances, parents and children find one another. It is my honor to preside over these matters."

The judge paused again to let his words sink in. All of the heartache of the last couple of years flashed through my mind. But instead of leaving me shaken and profoundly sad, everything felt as if it had happened for a reason. Our lives were meant to work out this way. We were exactly the family we were meant to be.

This is what it feels like to experience destiny, I thought. I let tears of relief and happiness fall down my cheeks. I let myself feel a multitude of the feelings in rapid succession: anger, sadness, resentment, jealousy, envy, fear, happiness, excitement, disappointment, exhaustion, contentment, and finally peace.

As the judge signed and embossed the State seal on each of the documents that made up the inches tall stack of paperwork, I felt at peace. The world was right. The child I had wanted so badly, I had loved with every ounce of my being since I first learned of her, the child I was ready to give my life for, was now legally part of our family. The reward for all those days, weeks, and months of waiting was an overwhelming feeling of peace. And more than an ounce of relief.

"Nate, Kimberly, Theo, and the now sleeping Rhys, will you please rise," he paused while we pushed our chairs back and stood. "Nate and Kimberly, you are now and forever the parents of Rhys Makenna Davis Severn. Responsible for her, the good, the bad, and the ugly," he chuckled.

"It's our pleasure and honor," I said, looking directly into the judge's eyes. I had never meant anything more. I reached up and wiped the tears from my cheeks.

"Please turn and face your family," he continued. "It is my pleasure to introduce you to Miss Rhys Makenna Davis Severn, her parents Nate and Kimberly, and her big brother Theo."

I smiled, a new round of tears fell down my cheeks as I reached down and patted Theo's back. I leaned over and kissed Nate. "We did it, babe," I whispered.

"We're all done here," the judge said. "Feel free to remain and take pictures. Your attorney will file the signed paperwork and I'm sure he'll be happy to get you the copies you need so you can apply for Rhys's new birth certificate."

The judge stood and left the courtroom to a cacophony of thanks from Nate, me and my family. We took pictures with Samuel, the judge's bench in the background. All moments captured, we thanked Samuel, and headed to my parents' house for dinner, before the plane ride home.

* * *

The day of Rhys's adoption finalization became one of a handful of extra special days in my life. As I laid down in bed that night I thought about my high school and college graduations, my wedding, Theo's and Rhys's births, and everything that had transpired that day. I went to bed thinking about all the future Severn Four Day celebrations to come.

I fell asleep with a smile on my face wrapped in the feeling of peace. I was filled with hope that everything regarding Rhys's adoption would finally begin to smooth out. Now that the footnote that had hung metaphorically after our daughter's name had been erased, things would be simpler, our relationship with Mark and Danielle would become easier, the boundaries now clearer. After all, it had to be. The adoption was final, and we were Rhys's parents, for the rest of her life.

If only it were that simple. Instead, I was to discover that we had merely stepped off an emotional roller coaster at the adoption theme park, and soon we would find ourselves on a whole new ride, this one even scarier than the last.

Chapter 34

Me, Depression, and Babies

Once the adoption was finalized, and I was legally Rhys's mother, my heart swelled with relief. We had settled in to our daily routine. Nate and I were both working full-time and had arranged our schedules so I woke the kids up, got them ready to go, and dropped them off at daycare. He went to work early and picked them up in the afternoon and most nights had dinner ready when I got home from work at six.

I had also hoped the finalization was the missing piece to a puzzle that would finally help us smooth out our tumultuous relationship with Danielle and Mark. I had naively hoped that with the paperwork finalized they would finally understand that parenting Rhys was our responsibility, not theirs. I wanted the finalization to be the light switch that illuminated the boundaries of our relationships, a light that would bring clarity to everyone's roles and bring peace to our relationship.

But my expectations were unrealistic. The finalization did nothing to change their frequent demands. Instead, it was the fire to ignite their desire to constantly test the boundaries of their role in Rhys's life. They continued to call constantly, to demand more and more photos, to criticize our parenting, and to remind me that they regretted ever choosing me as Rhys's mom—or more accurately, as Sara's caretaker. As their efforts to punish me and tell me how to raise my daughter increased, so did my worries about whether I was strong enough to handle the constant challenges from them.

I realized that if we had a chance of making our relationship with Danielle and Mark work, I had to learn to understand and communicate with them effectively. The only experience I had with concrete thinkers was with my kids. But communicating with them like they were five-year olds was both inappropriate and disrespectful. I didn't have any experience trying to communicate about complex emotional issues with adults who experienced the world in the stark black and white terms they did.

The way they experienced life also meant they were unable to see someone else's point of view. They were incapable of considering the needs and feelings of others. All they knew was what they wanted. And they were both very determined to fulfill their wants and needs.

I spent countless lunch hours searching for resources that would help me to better understand how their brains worked and looking for tips on the best ways to deal with it. I needed to find a way to improve our relationship and take the stress and dread out of our face to face meetings. It was up to me to find the solution, as it was clear the agency wasn't going to respond to our requests for help. So I continued my quest for logic-based solutions to improve my emotional reaction to Danielle and Mark.

* * *

Nate and I felt it was important that Rhys know she was adopted. It was part of her creation story. We would tell her about the night she was born, how grateful we were to her birth parents, and how much they loved her even though they couldn't care for her. I would answer her questions about the people who conceived her and the 'tummy' she grew in whenever the time came.

Theo asked me when he wanted to hear about the night he was born, and I figured Rhys was likely to do the same. I would be ready to tell her whenever she decided to ask. But I was terrified of the conversation and the questions that might follow. What if I screwed it up? What if I said the wrong thing? What if she no longer wanted me to be her mom?

I would often lay awake after her two a.m. feedings, hot tears of fear running down my cheeks and dampening my pillow, at times barely able to breathe. I loved our daughter so much and still mourned the loss of the opportunity to birth her myself. I laid in the black of the night and felt myself sinking further into a deepening depression. There was no time during the day to feel sad or indulge myself in my growing distress. I had work to do, a career to nurture. In the evenings I had a five-year-old and seven-month old who needed my care and attention. There wasn't time to curl up in a ball and hide from the world.

The turning point came on an ordinary Tuesday morning. I pulled my car into the parking lot at work, put my car in park, and unplugged my cell phone. I quickly glanced at my schedule, hoping I had time to grab a cup of coffee before my first meeting.

The line at Starbucks was almost out the door. I thought about leaving, but I really wanted the extra boost of energy the combination of caffeine and sugar was sure to deliver. After glancing over the headlines of a *New York Times* left deserted on a nearby table, I pulled out my phone to check for any emails that had arrived overnight. It wasn't unusual for my coworkers to get a burst of inspiration at three in the morning.

After quickly triaging my work email I looked to see if there was anything interesting in my personal account. I expected to see the usual mix of promotions from retailers and announcements from blogs I followed. I rapidly scanned down the list and then my entire body froze. There was an email from Mark. My breath caught in my chest and my stomach clenched.

I took a deep breath as the line moved forward a couple feet and then opened the message:

We are excited to see Sara at our next visit. You need to tell us when that is going to be so we can be ready. And we want to know what she looks like. You need to send us pictures. And at Halloween you will send us pictures of Sara in her costume. Call us and tell us when we will see Sara.

Mark and Danielle

What the hell?! *They don't get to tell me what pictures I take and when to send them.* I was instantly outraged at Mark and Danielle, and at myself. I was fed up with their continued demands. Even when they only wanted something reasonable, like Halloween pictures, by instructing me to do it like I was their nanny, it made me want to dig in my heels and refuse. But what bothered me more than anything was that they were still calling her Sara. Their refusal to refer to her by her name was more than just a power play, it felt like they were disrespecting who *she* was.

I had tried everything I could think of to work with them. Finally, a month before, I had stopped giving in to their demands. I felt incredibly guilty about it, but something had to change. The status quo wasn't working. And with their demand for Halloween pictures, my inner child wanted to give them the middle finger. I had tried hard for months to carefully select pictures I thought they would enjoy, pictures that showed Rhys's many important firsts.

Although the open adoption agreement stated we only needed to send pictures twice a year, I had gone along with Joyce's suggestion and began flooding them with pictures. I sent several pictures, in duplicate, every four weeks or so. It didn't work. The more I sent, the more they wanted, and Joyce's response was always, "This is how this population parents."

They weren't parenting. They were putting me through a special kind of torture I wasn't prepared to handle. I had sent the additional pictures in an attempt to help our relationship and also ease my guilt over the ever-present anger and resentment I felt that was fueled by their relentless demands.

I was also outraged with myself because I should have just deleted the email. I knew it would do nothing to improve my day and was likely to send me into an emotional descent that I would waste precious energy fighting my way out of.

"Good morning," said the chipper cashier. "What can I get for you this morning?"

"Venti iced vanilla latte with an extra shot please," I said smiling. The smile was my first attempt to stop the downward spiral. She jotted my order on the cup and completed my transaction.

"Have a great day," she said.

Great day. Whatever, I thought, wanting to punch her in her cheerful face. My hostility was followed quickly by shock at my reaction to the innocent woman just trying to do a good job. *Ugh, I am losing my mind! I have to do something.*

Fortunately, my employer covered short-term counseling. I didn't want to reach out for help. Reaching out meant I wasn't strong enough to handle the situation on my own. And possibly worse than that, it meant I had taken on something that I wasn't good enough, strong enough, or prepared enough to handle. Logically I knew none of this was true and I was taking the next step I would advise any woman who felt like I did to take. But that didn't matter. The situation had landed me back to when I was five and got the first N, N for not satisfactory, on my report card for my terrible handwriting. Back then I had failed at properly writing my letters and numbers. And now the stakes were higher, I had failed at building a relationship with the people who birthed my daughter.

"If this is an emergency or you feel you are in immediate danger, please hang up and dial 9-1-1," the recorded voice instructed.

I sat in the small phone room, slouched on the built-in banquet with my feet propped on a chair, my laptop open in front of me. I scrolled down the *New York Times* homepage as I listened to what was supposed to be soothing hold music. The wait had me debating whether asking for help was really what I needed to do.

Maybe I just need to tough it out? Maybe my expectations are too high and I need to just give in to the

*situation? Maybe I'm a horrible person and need to realize
that the sacrifice Danielle made is greater than my need to
mother my child without their intrusion?*

A few minutes later the music was interrupted
by another recorded message: "The information you
provide is confidential and will not be shared without
your permission."

Finally, I was connected with a counselor, for
whom I summarized the stress of the last nine months
since Joyce had asked us about meeting Mark and
Danielle.

I completed my monologue by saying "So they
are causing me no shortage of stress and I've hit my
breaking point. I need to get out of my funk. Maybe
there's someone who could help me with that?"

"Oh, Kim, it sounds like there's a lot going on," the
counselor responded. "I agree it would be good for you
to talk to someone. Let me take a look at who we have
in your area and we can get an appointment scheduled
for you." I could hear the compassion in her voice and
it was nice to know there was something I could do,
an action I could take, that would make the situation
better.

* * *

A week later I sat on a couch as a man in his
mid-thirties glanced at an appointment book on his
desk. With his back to me, I took the opportunity to
familiarize myself with the office. The warm beige
walls were sparsely decorated. A calendar hung above
his desk next to the door, a painting of a mountain
scene hung between two floor-to-ceiling windows, and
another sat atop a small bookcase next to an overstuffed

chair. The small bookcase and an end table on the other side of the chair held a range of books. The office left me with the impression that the man thought deeply about what he surrounded himself with and that each item had a specific meaning for him.

"Hello Kimberly, I'm Matthew Simons. It's nice to meet you," he said with a smile as he sat down in the chair and adjusted his wire-framed glasses on the bridge of his nose. "He went over how many sessions were covered by my insurance, his education and professional experience, and how the cancellation policy worked. *Seems reasonable enough*, I thought as I fidgeted and began bouncing my leg up and down. I shifted my position, hoping to look more comfortable, and disguise more of my nervousness and apprehension. Then he asked about what had brought me to seek counseling.

I provided him the same information I had given the counselor on the phone. He listened intently with his head tilted to one side. He nodded from time to time encouraging me to continue. I took this as a sign the information I provided made sense. I began to feel a hint of relief.

"Thanks for sharing, Kimberly," he said. "There's something I feel I need to disclose to you before you decide whether or not you'd like to come back."

Oh no, what had I done? I wondered as my stomach fell. Had I said something wrong? *I knew I should've just powered through,* I thought, beating myself up for reaching out and asking for help.

"My brother was adopted. So I have experience with adoption and this might bias me in our work together." He stopped talking and leaned back in the chair, his arms resting on the armrests. He waited for me to respond.

I was momentarily speechless, my worries instantly washed away. I sat dumbstruck by the sudden feeling of relief. *He might understand what I'm going through!* I was filled with hope as the possibility dawned on me that I had made the right choice.

I cleared my throat and smiled. "Thank you for telling me that. I believe if we're aware of our biases they're less likely to be harmful." I paused giving him opportunity to respond. When he said nothing I moved to the edge of the couch and said, "So I'll see you at the same time next week?"

Every Monday at 11:30 I walked the eight blocks to Matthew's office. For the first few weeks we talked about my continued anxiety about our next visit with Mark and Danielle and our turbulent relationship. He offered no solutions, instead asking questions that made me think and search deeper and deeper for the cause of my distress.

Near the end of my sixth or seventh session he asked a question that would become a major turning point in my healing. Once again tilting his head to the side and leaning forward slightly as he always did when he was going to ask a question he wasn't sure I was ready for, he asked, "Do you think you're depressed?"

"I've thought about that and I don't think so," I instantly responded, then hesitated. Matthew looked at me and waited. I looked away and stared at the painting on top of the bookcase. It was a watercolor of a single canoe, pushed up on a sandy beach, oar resting across the top. There were trees just beyond the beach and across the water on a mountain. I studied the canoe and wondered where it's occupants had gone. I also thought back to when my OB had asked me the same question six weeks after Theo was born. I had been too embarrassed about it to answer honestly, thinking I was weak and broken for not feeling cheerful and energized.

"Actually," I said after a minute or so, "I've thought a lot about it. And I feel a lot like I did after Theo was born, when I had postpartum depression. But this can't be that," I paused again before continuing. "I didn't have her."

"I know you didn't have her, but hasn't your experience been much the same?" Again he waited, allowing me time to consider what he had just said.

"But I didn't have all the hormones rushing through me that I had back then. I thought postpartum depression is caused by hormones." I felt myself beginning to question my assumptions.

"Let's talk about the hormones in a sec," he said, leaning forward. "Do you care for Rhys any differently than you did Theo?"

I leaned forward, too, as if changing my posture would allow me to see where he was going with the conversation before he got to his point.

"If Rhys has just fallen asleep in your arms and you suddenly have to go to the bathroom, do you move?"

"Oh God no!" I said chuckling as I thought about how many times I waited until the last moment before I might wet my pants to get up and go to the bathroom, hoping the delay would allow her to fall into a deep enough sleep that she wouldn't wake up when I set her down.

"And if you're starving and just sat down to eat when she starts crying and needs you. What do you do?"

"I get up, figure out what's wrong, and take care of it." I began to understand where he was headed.

"If you need something and Rhys needs something at the same time, who wins?"

"She does," I said, smiling with pride at my ability to put my kids' needs before my own.

"Now let's talk about the body's chemical reaction to caring for children. What do you think would happen if your brain didn't respond by depressing your reaction to the stress of caring for young children?"

"I've thought about that before," I said. "Whenever I hear about a parent hurting an infant, like the stories of a parent shaking a baby, I'm horrified. But there's part of me that understands how it can happen." My voice trailed off.

He nodded and pursed his lips together. "As humans, our brains release chemicals to dampen our urges when we care for our young so we can bear to put their needs first. Otherwise, well as we know, bad things can happen. So even though you didn't give birth to Rhys, you're her mother. You care for her just like you did Theo, and your body is responding just the same."

"So maybe I have postpartum depression?"

"Well, post-adoption depression is a possibility we should consider. You've been through a lot."

Even as I struggled to admit it to myself, I knew I was experiencing depression in the months following Rhys's birth. But I had never heard of 'post-adoption depression' as a recognized condition, caused by experiences similar to what caused the more widely-recognized postpartum depression.

Tears spilled down my cheeks and relief flooded over me as I sank back into the couch. The euphoria I'd felt when Rhys was born had reached its peak and I had plummeted into the depths of depression. I was still overcome with joy and gratitude every moment that I thought of her or held her in my arms. But as all mothers know, the dopamine high of new motherhood wears off once those sleepless nights and exhausting days take hold. Add to that the stress of dealing with Danielle and Mark, and the constant worry that Rhys could have a seizure at any moment and I had more than enough ingredients for the depression cocktail.

There was a reason why I felt the way I did. I wasn't special, broken, or crazy. I was struggling, for sure, but I knew I wasn't alone in what I was experiencing. And maybe most important of all, it was because I was doing so much right that I felt so damn horrible.

"What a relief," I said. laughing softly through my tears as I reached for a tissue to dry my eyes. "Matthew, I think you just made my month."

The revelation that I was suffering from post-adoption depression was a relief. There was a defined problem I could now begin to work on addressing and I felt strongly that with Matthew's help I would recover faster than if I tried to do it on my own. I had been here before and was confident I could overcome the sadness just as I had done four years before.

* * *

Confident as I was that the depression wouldn't last forever, life in the following months was not always easy. With the continued stress of the thrice-yearly visits with Mark and Danielle and the still constant worry that Rhys would suffer a seizure, there were definite ups and downs. There were times I made progress and then times when I would sink back again as feelings of hopelessness nearly overwhelmed me.

It was mid-November; the air was cold and what had started as a gentle breeze was quickly working itself into a brisk wind. I turned a corner and decided to cut through a small park on the way back to my office after my weekly appointment with Matthew.

I walked with my head down and concentrated on the uneven ground covered in the original cobblestones from a century ago. I kept my mind occupied by wondering how women of the time hadn't regularly broken their ankles or worse trying to traverse such a hazardous surface. The rain dripped down the brick exteriors of the four and five story late nineteenth century buildings that surrounded the cobblestone square.

The discussion of the past hour had left me feeling unsettled. I felt as if everything I had ever known about family was no longer true, and there were no words to describe my new reality. I shivered as a gust of wind blew through my now damp slacks. I reached up to hold my hood closed beneath my chin trying to keep it from blowing off my head.

As I continued to walk I began thinking again about the story I had shared with Matthew. It had been a particularly hot July night, four months before, when we were getting ready for our second trip to visit Danielle and Mark. I had received a text from Danielle telling me she was Sara's real mom and once again, saying how much she wished she hadn't chosen me as Sara's adoptive mother.

As I read the text heat rose from my belly to the top of my head, panic and anger filling my body. The hurt of her words sunk in and shock was replaced by a devastating insecurity.

My nausea had worsened as I continued to panic. As Rhys grew older, would I be able to look her in the eye and say without wavering that I was her mom? Did I have the right to be the sole honoree of that title? Was it my responsibility to remind her of her birth parents, to always add them in to conversation about family? If so, when were the right times and how would I figure that out?

That night as I tried to calm my tattered nerves, I tried to find the logical answer I was looking for. I searched for the language I needed to know for sure that I was undeniably Rhys's mom and she was, unquestionably, my daughter. Legal papers and feelings couldn't provide the certainty I was looking for. I needed the words to prove it. I needed language that everyone agreed upon to back me up.

In a near desperate search for answers, the only thing I could think to do was look up the definition of mother, child, and daughter in the dictionary. This is what I found:

> **moth·er**: 1. Female parent: a woman who has a child 2. Woman acting as parent: a woman who acts as the parent of a child to whom she has not given birth

> **child**: 1. Young human being: a young human being between birth and puberty 2. Human offspring: a son or daughter of human parents

> **daugh·ter**: 1. Female child: somebody's female child

The definitions provided mixed comfort at best. What I secretly hoped for was definitive proof that only I had the right to call Rhys my daughter and that only I had the right to be called, or call myself, her mom. The definition of mother buoyed me, until I read the second definition...was I only acting as her parent?

My reaction to the definition of child was much the same. Definition one was straightforward enough, but that second one... technically she wasn't my offspring. That made me feel even worse than when I started the exercise.

Bottom-line, I wished someone had told me the intimate details of mothering when there are two women who can rightly claim the word mother. And two women, unrelated, not married to each other and certainly not in love with one another, who could claim a single human as her child.

Words had a profound and powerful impact as I worked my way back to a healthy me. At times it was words that caused the greatest distress, while at other times were the cure I searched for to soothe my aching soul.

I was coming to realize, it wasn't just me searching for the right words to describe what was, or what should be, the relationships for the many people impacted by Rhys's adoption. As we continued to traverse through our adoption journey, our search for the right words and definitions came up short. It was all very complicated and there were so many people, each with their own wants, needs, and opinions on how things should be.

Stepping through the main entrance of my building I took off my hood and tried to gently shake off the rain and my somber mood. I was wholly unprepared for even language to fail me in the first tumultuous year of my daughter's life.

I tried to distract myself by mentally building Rhys's family tree. What was the right way to represent all the people connected to her? How did I show us, her forever family, and also represent her genetic roots? There were so many different types of relationships, some known, some unknown, and some still developing. If I couldn't make sense of it, how would I ever help her to?

Chapter 35

The Definition of Family

As the months went on and Rhys began to crawl and babble, our relationship with Danielle and Mark wasn't getting any easier. In our case, we not only struggled to form a healthy relationship with Rhys's birthmother but with her birthfather as well. In all my fantasies of a warm and fuzzy relationship with my baby's birthmother, and all the discussions Nate and I had had about negotiating this emotionally tender relationship, we simply never expected our child's birthfather to continue wanting a relationship with the baby. But Mark was making it just as clear as Danielle was, that he wasn't letting go of his "Sara," and we had better toe the line and please him.

The weekend before Rhys turned one we traveled across the state to see my family and make the first birth parent visit of the year.

Mark and Danielle were waiting in the reception area when we walked through the door of the agency, where we held our scheduled visits. Nate walked in ahead of me holding Rhys. I had dressed her up in turquoise leggings and a white and turquoise cotton shirt with a bow at the collar. She wore a pair of white socks that a friend had sewn with colorful beads around each ankle. We didn't bother with shoes because she hated wearing them and she hadn't started walking. She looked adorable and was happy and excited for what she could tell was something special.

Before we could even say hello to the receptionist both Mark and Danielle were up and out of their chairs and just inches from Rhys. My heart pounded in my chest as my anxiety grew. Then once again, as if waiting above the door jamb to land on me as soon as I entered, the angel and the devil were each perched on a shoulder battling back and forth once again.

Give Rhys some space! The devil insisted, nudging me to hold my daughter tighter.

Give them a break! The angel replied. *They're excited to see her, cut them some slack.*

But don't they know they'll freak her out? The devil asked.

Chill out, they mean no harm. She won't break for Heaven's sake, the angel continued.

I took a deep breath, "Hi guys. Let's check in and see if it's okay if we use the room upstairs. Okay?" I smiled and put my arm around Nate's shoulder guiding him to the side so I could shut the door and make eye contact with the receptionist.

"Hi," Lynn said in our general direction. "There's another family upstairs for a birth parent visit, so go ahead and use whichever room is free. And take as long as you'd like."

"Thanks," Nate and I said in unison and turned toward the stairs.

"After you," I said to them, extending my left hand in the direction of the staircase. "We'll be right behind you." They both glared at me.

The five of us headed up the stairs and once again entered the big room that extended across the front of the old house. The room felt dark and depressing and I wondered again why the windows were covered. It was like we'd entered some place sealed off from the world where the rules no longer applied.

"Why don't you guys go ahead and have a seat," I said while I set Rhys's diaper bag on the table behind one of the large overstuffed couches.

Nate stood, still holding Rhys, waiting for me to take a seat. As I turned to survey the room and figure out the best place to sit down, Rhys lunged at me.

"Mama!" she yelled with her arms outstretched.

"Whoa kiddo," I said with a laugh. "Daddy might have dropped you," I continued while I took her in my arms and kissed her on the cheek.

"I'll take her," Danielle said, stepping toward us.

"Why don't we all have a seat and give Rhys a couple minutes to get comfortable." I knew if we pushed her too quickly Rhys would get upset and there might be no recovering. She had become quite a mama's girl in the last few weeks and we'd experienced more than one meltdown. She'd even begun crying when I dropped her off at daycare in the morning, something she'd long before stopped doing. It seemed that as she gained new skills, she feared her independence and clung to me ever more tightly.

I saw the disappointment in Danielle's face and the annoyance on Mark's. I didn't want them to have a bad visit and I knew they had looked forward to seeing Rhys. I also wondered if this was a particularly hard time for them since it was near the first anniversary of giving their baby up for adoption.

"I'm sorry guys, it's just the stage she's at right now. If we're patient, I'm sure she'll warm up." I gave them a reassuring smile. For as uncomfortable as these visits were I truly did have compassion for them. I wasn't sure I would be strong enough to endure the visits if I was in Danielle's shoes.

"Why's she wearing socks with beads? Those are a choking hazard!" Mark asked as soon as we were all seated, Mark and Danielle on one couch, Rhys and me on another directly across from them, Nate in an overstuffed chair at the end of the room.

"These are fancy socks one of my friends made for her. Rhys loves them because she can shake her feet and they make noise." I picked up Rhys's ankles and shook them up and down making her laugh.

"She could choke on the beads. They're dangerous," he replied.

"The beads are sewn on very tight," I said pulling on one of the beads to demonstrate. "If we thought she could hurt herself we wouldn't allow her to have them," I tried to reassure him. "And we take them off before naptime." I hoped that final piece of information would put an end to the admonitions.

"We've been showing our daughter's pictures to all of our friends," Danielle said with a smile.

"You have?" I said trying not to visibly bristle at the reference to Rhys as their daughter. *At least she didn't call her Sara,* the angel pointed out. I was glad to see that the pictures had made her happy as her face brightened when she talked about showing them to her friends.

"Yeah, and they all say how pretty she is," Mark said. "And that we better watch out cause boys are going to be after her."

Whoa there doggy, what are you talkin' about? She's barely a year old!

"She is a beautiful baby. But there's a long time before boys will be anything more than playmates."

"Well boys are going to want to date her and she can't date until she's 18," he declared.

"Rhys, do you want to show Danielle how you can clap?" I asked Rhys, trying to change the subject. I tickled her belly and made her laugh again. I wanted desperately to change the subject. Mark probably didn't understand how inappropriate what he was saying was, but he'd said it nonetheless. He was setting the rules for my daughter.

Before they could answer I wrapped my arms around Rhys and placed my hands where she could see them. "Clap, clap, clap," I said as I brought my hands together each time. "Now Rhys does it, okay big girl?"

"Clap, clap, clap," I said again and Rhys clapped her hands together, her smile blossoming. "Yea Rhys! Good job, big girl!" I said hugging her tightly and kissing her soft chubby cheek.

Feeling Rhys's body relax I put her down on the floor between my feet and invited Danielle to grab a toy for her to play with from the basketful sitting next to the couch. She found a rubber giraffe and after a few minutes Rhys was interacting with Danielle on the floor. Danielle smiled broadly and her cheeks glowed with pleasure.

"Take our picture!" Danielle demanded of Mark in a tone that clearly showed she was accustomed to telling him what to do. She pulled her phone out of her pocket and tossed it to him. "Don't use your phone, use mine," she insisted.

He began taking pictures, and I relaxed, letting the angel on my shoulder take over. A few minutes of playing with the baby they'd created wasn't a threat to Nate and me and was clearly a joy for them.

The visit went well until it was almost time to leave. "About fifteen more minutes guys and then we need to head out. We need to make sure to get Rhys some lunch before her afternoon nap," I explained.

"We haven't gotten enough pictures yet," Mark protested as he narrowed his eyes at me.

"Well now's the time," I said, trying my best to hide my irritation as I looked over at Nate. I was hoping he'd read my thoughts and pick up on my plea for help, as he usually did.

Throughout the visit Nate stayed pretty quiet, only responding when they spoke to him, which wasn't too often. From their perspective, I alone remained the enemy, the person who was blocking their ability to parent their daughter.

And in that moment it took me to shoot Nate a look, Danielle stood up, grabbed Rhys off the floor, and sat down next to Mark. When I turned back, Mark was pulling Rhys onto his lap and Rhys was arching her back in protest.

"Whoa, guys, be careful," I said starting to stand.

"Guys, she's not a doll," Nate said as soon as he saw what was happening.

"It's okay Rhys," I said, hoping to avoid a full-scale tantrum. "Danielle and Mark want to get some pictures with you." But my efforts to explain to a one-year-old what was happening met with little success. I hoped the tone of my voice would calm her down. "Nate, why don't you grab their phones and take a couple pictures. *Quickly*," I urged. I wanted them to have a good visit, but I also needed to protect my child.

"Look at Mama," I said trying to get Rhys to sit still and smile. "Hey Rhys, silly girl, I'm gonna getcha!" I leaned in and acted like I was going to tickle her tummy. It was a game we often played and luckily it worked. She settled down and we got a few pictures for them.

After a couple minutes Rhys started to fuss and arch her back again. "Why don't you let her slide down your legs and on to the floor," I suggested. "That way you can watch her crawl before we go."

Mark reluctantly let go and let Rhys slide down his long, jean clad legs. Her diaper-covered bottom hit the floor with a muffled thud and she crawled over to me and put her arms in the air.

"Nate, why don't you go over there and we'll have her crawl to you so Danielle and Mark can see her crawl a little more."

"Sure," he said, in a voice that rang with strained delight. I knew he was as uncomfortable with them as I was but trying his best to keep things as pleasant as possible.

He walked over to the entrance of the room and I set Rhys back down on the carpet. "Go over to Daddy, go on, go over to Dad," I encouraged. But Rhys would have none of it. She turned and put her arms in the air for me to pick her up again.

"I'm sorry, guys," I said. "I think it's time we get packed up and head out."

"But we want more time with Sara," Mark said. "We don't have enough pictures yet with our daughter." He gave me an icy stare.

Ignoring his demands, we packed up our daughter and brought the visit to an end.

That afternoon when Rhys woke up from her nap she was extra clingy and didn't want Nate or me to be out of arms reach. She also slept poorly that night and was clingy again the next day. At first we chalked it up to being in an unfamiliar place. She had only been seven months old the last time we stayed at my parents' house, she was too young to remember, so we didn't think much of it.

It wouldn't be until seven months later, after our third visit of the year with Mark and Danielle, that we would recognize the pattern in these same behaviors for several days after each visit.

* * *

The open adoption agreement spelled out the minimum amount of communication we would have with Danielle and Mark each year. It didn't say anything about the other relationships that are potentially created through open adoption.

When Rhys was born, and in the days immediately following, we had met Danielle's mom, Kathy, and her stepdad, Dan, Danielle's siblings, and her dad. And I had met Mark's parents during that single, short encounter the morning Rhys was born. In the months following, during our visits to see Danielle and Mark, we also met Dan's mother, Danielle's paternal grandmother, a couple of Kathy's sisters, and a few of Danielle's cousins. They were all very kind and gracious people. They welcomed us and were excited to get to know Rhys.

Kathy was wonderful to us. She was warm, loving, open, and patient. I am certain I said some really stupid things in those early days that probably stung. But Kathy was gracious enough to never let me know it. We did a graceful tap dance around each other, both knowing that we were dancing for a beautiful baby girl.

My relationship with Kathy was as close to my fantasy birth family relationship as I could hope for.

There were a variety of people who wanted to know Rhys and be part of her life. The fact that she was so loved and adored delighted me. I felt she was lucky to have so many people who wanted to watch her learn and grow.

At the same time, it was also really overwhelming to try to figure out how to develop and manage all these new relationships. There were so many potential landmines. I had no idea who to trust, who to let in, or who I was "supposed" to keep up to date. It quickly became terribly complicated and overwhelming. The day to day management of relationships felt like a lead vest, pressing on my heart and lungs and making it hard to breathe. I would suddenly be panic stricken that I had over-shared or the reverse, that I had kept information from someone who had the right to know it. I would feel a jolt of electricity run through me as guilt overcame me, seemingly out of nowhere, worried I had done something wrong or said something to offend. I was not prepared for any of it. Once again, nobody had warned me about the emotional and pragmatic complexity of this extended family, so I could try to be prepared.

Managing all the new relationships and family dynamics was a nearly overwhelming feat and was the subject of my appointment with Matthew on a rainy December day. I was still struggling to comprehend Rhys's new family tree and it had left me feeling like a rudderless ship floating dangerously through a rock-filled ocean, not knowing when I would hit one and do irreparable damage. How do I draw her family tree? Who do I include? How do I connect the branches to the trunk? A family tree built based on genetics is completely disconnected from one created through open adoption.

I wondered how I was going to find the energy to think it all through and try to figure everything out. I felt like I needed to know so I could explain it to Rhys when the time came. I was once again an island in the ocean all alone. I didn't know anyone dealing with a similar set of questions and didn't have anyone to ask how they were answering the questions Rhys would someday have.

The other frustrating part of managing all the relationships was the fact that Nate was oblivious. It wasn't that he was oblivious because he wasn't paying attention. He was oblivious because our roles as Rhys's parents were perceived as vastly different. Nobody contacted Nate to see how Rhys was doing, to schedule a visit, or request pictures. This all seemed to fall under "family management" and that was a role I was expected to fulfill.

My experience mothering Theo wasn't helpful when it came to this particular problem. When he was born, who we shared information with was simple. We shared information with our 'inner circle.' Inner circle members included people related by blood or marriage, or friends Nate or I had known for years or spoke with on a regular basis.

During Theo's first couple years, my mom tended to get more information about how he was doing and was often the first person I called if I had questions about his well-being. She was my mom, he had come from me, and we had genetics in common. I shared a lot with my mother-in-law, too. She was a wonderful woman and always willing to help, although I was more guarded with her because I felt more vulnerable, and I didn't want her to think that I wasn't taking good care of her son or grandson.

When there were questions about a rash, timing of a developmental milestones, or sleep habits I would ask both my mom and mother-in-law. Our connection was strong, there was a bloodline to follow. I was comforted by the wisdom of our genetic connection when I was puzzled by parenthood.

With Rhys, however, it was no longer clear at all. I kept our 'inner circle' up-to-date as we had with Theo. But *what about Rhys's birth family?* The question nagged at me with every milestone. Mark's parents had made it easy, letting us know they had no interest in "the baby." But sharing with Danielle and Mark was problematic because any additional information I provided set off a new storm of demands. And it didn't feel entirely safe bringing Kathy fully into the circle. *Was I supposed to develop a relationship with her? Did she want to be involved? What would she think of me?*

Kathy had been a savior to us during the first months of Rhys's life. She was a tremendous help as she tried to help Danielle through the transition from her pregnancy to role of birthmother. She had even reached out to the agency to try to get them to help Danielle transition to her new role. But she had as much success as we'd had, which is to say, none at all. Yet her many efforts to be involved in Rhys's life, while not at all threatening to me, left me feeling confused about the boundaries of our relationship.

Before we went for our first trip to Children's Hospital to meet with the geneticist, Kathy had talked to the doctors and sent Danielle's health history. She clearly loved Rhys deeply and was willing to do just about anything we asked of her. *But was it fair for me to ask?* I wondered. I was never able to come up with an answer I was entirely comfortable with.

When it came to Rhys's health, I was comfortable asking Kathy questions and requesting relevant medical history. Our children's health, safety, and development were our primary concern and I would do whatever it took to ensure they grew into happy, healthy, successful adults.

After the first few months I *tried* not to talk to her about our relationship with Mark and Danielle. I wanted to respect the fact that Danielle was her daughter and she didn't need to hear about the struggles or the difficulties I was having trying to develop a healthy relationship with them. But I slipped from time to time and I always felt guilty about it. I also couldn't shake the feeling that if asked to take sides between me and Danielle I was certain to lose; just like I continually lost when I tried to get support from the adoption agency. I was glad nobody asked her to take sides.

Torn and confused, I started to pull back on the visits we had with Kathy, Dan, and their extended family. At first whenever we went for a visit with Mark and Danielle we would make time to see Kathy's family too. But the added visits made our agenda tighter and took time away from my family, which in turn caused tension between us.

I wasn't strong enough at the time to talk about ending the visits with Kathy or discussing the tension it caused with my mom or my sisters who often felt we didn't have enough time for them. I hate conflict, am terrified of hurting other people's feelings, and didn't know how to start the conversation.

Nate and I talked about it a lot, but he and I are similar in our tendencies to avoid conflict if at all possible. And this wasn't something he was willing to get into. He supported me and whatever I thought was best. At the same time, it was only a tension he felt three times a year when we went for visits. That just wasn't enough discomfort for him to do something about.

I didn't know how to be more open with Kathy about how the visits were affecting me, so we could have worked together to find a solution. And I didn't know how to talk to my mom about her feelings. Understanding her feelings might have helped me to understand mine better, but at the time, I was too confused and overwhelmed to see the benefit.

Trying to understand and define the roles of all the people involved in adoption was a challenge that never occurred to me until I was in the midst of trying to manage it. I suddenly felt like I had to establish a new boundary. Danielle and Mark couldn't understand that Rhys was no longer their child, couldn't respect our role as Rhys's parents and without that, I had to create a boundary to make it clear we were responsible for Rhys's health, safety, and development.

Language failed me and traditional family roles and responsibilities failed me too. In the end, I did the best I could to stay in touch over email and Facebook with Kathy and her extended family, while at the same time beginning to build a wall that would provide the boundaries I was comfortable with.

It wasn't until after several months working with Matthew that I was able to tease apart my fear of letting Danielle and Mark get further entwined in our lives, and the blessings that came with so many people lovingly interested in supporting our family.

I limited our communication with Danielle and Mark. I stopped sending pictures as often and when I did send them I mailed them to the adoption agency, rather than directly to Danielle's apartment. As expected, they resented me all the more, and although I was still complying with all the terms of the open adoption agreement, the agency did nothing to support us in setting boundaries with birthparents who demanded we go far and beyond the adoption agreement. It was clear we had to re-evaluate our plans and reinforce the boundaries we had established.

Chapter 36

Back to Court

Rhys sat in the middle of the living room floor playing with her Little People Zoo and occasionally glanced up at the television to see what Dora the Explorer was up to. Theo sat at the dining room table cracking jokes as he recorded himself on the webcam.

We were in a new era of parenting. Our kids could entertain themselves for a few minutes giving Nate and me a chance to put dishes in the dishwasher, fold a load of laundry, or talk to each other without having to entertain a child at the same time. It was a freedom experienced in 15-minute increments we hadn't enjoyed since Theo was born. Rhys was two and a half and Theo seven; family life was entering a new phase.

Our kids were finally both at an age that included using the toilet, asking for what they wanted, and sleeping through the night on a consistent basis. While we didn't have to keep either child within arm's reach at all times to keep them safe, we were hesitant to have them out of our sight and had to be careful what we said. Our coded language of spelling out key words had been cracked.

"Hey Nate, do you think we should go to the p-a-r-k?" Would prompt a nearly immediate "Yes!" from

Rhys as she dropped whatever it was she was doing and ran to my side.

We had survived the baby phase and more importantly, Rhys had survived her first two years without a seizure. The day of her second birthday I began to hold my breath once again, as I often had in the days after she was born. I was fearful that fate would play an evil trick on me in an attempt to prove medicine was in fact a mix of art and science. Even though she had survived her first two years seizure-free, I was once again on edge, afraid that one would pounce upon her, ravaging her brain at two years and one week, or would it be two years and two months? After all, two years in medical speak does not necessarily mean 730 days. It means two years, more or less.

Rather than relieve my fears, that two-year mark only heightened them. Just as I'd done for the first six months of Rhys's life, once again I worried constantly that any sound, any sickness, any crying fit, was the sign of an impending seizure. But finally my anxiety began to ease little by little, dying away altogether before she was two and a half.

The danger had passed. Rhys was healthy. There weren't going to be any seizures. There wasn't going to be any brain damage. My daughter was going to be just fine.

* * *

It was time for another visit with Mark and Danielle, our eighth, and the second since Rhys turned two. The visit three months prior hadn't gone well. Tensions continued to be high between Danielle, Mark, and me as they both continued to try to put me in my place. If not constantly managed, the conversation would veer into uncomfortable territory. And Rhys was becoming increasingly hesitant to leave my side during the visits. She continued to have a hard time returning to her usual self after the visits. She would have trouble sleeping, started biting her nails, and cried when I was out of her sight.

I became increasingly anxious as the visit approached. One evening after a busy day at work and an evening entertaining our energetic kids, with the next visit only a few weeks away, I plopped down on the couch exhausted. I needed to let the agency know it was time for our next visit and make sure there was a room available for us to use. My hands shook and my palms were damp with sweat as I typed out the email.

Why am I still feeling anxious? Why do I feel like I have everything figured out, only to have the thought of seeing them send me into a tailspin? Why am I still letting this bother me so much? It doesn't make sense! I was frustrated that my anxiety level and discomfort with the visits hadn't abated over the years. It was a constant topic between Matthew and me during my weekly appointments as we talked through the complexities of the relationships we were trying to build with Danielle and Mark.

"I don't think I can do this anymore," I said to Nate as I closed the top of my laptop with a thud. "There's no end in sight to the visits and things continue to stay the same." I paused before continuing as I leaned forward and put my head in my hands. "Actually, things feel like they're getting worse."

Nate closed the mountain biking magazine he was reading and moved from his recliner to sit on the couch next to me. "What can we do about it?"

"I don't think they're going to change. They just want to see *their daughter*." My words were dripping with sarcasm. "And the agency is totally worthless. They dropped this whole thing in my lap." The anger grew unexpectedly until the heat of the situation boiled over inside of me and I felt my cheeks burn. "And you don't seem to want to do anything, letting me deal with all of this shit by myself."

I knew my words stung Nate as soon as I said them. But I had chosen to keep my feelings and frustrations mostly to myself for years. The resentment and anger mixed together and caused an unexpected explosion. I looked at Nate, ready to continue my assault. And then I saw the hurt in his eyes. I bit my lip and tried to stay silent until the anger abated.

He sat next to me for several minutes, neither of us speaking. My anger remained and I wanted to strike out. I wanted to yell, jump up and down, and kick something. I wanted to do anything to help me release the energy stuck in my belly, the frustration held captive in my muscles, the sadness and fear lodged in my heart. I knew it wasn't fair to take it out on Nate, but he was the only one around. And for as terrible as it was to knowingly hurt him, I also knew he would forgive me when I wasn't sure anyone else would.

"I realize how much you have on your plate, Kim," Nate said as he reached out to put his hand on my knee.

"Do you," I asked jerking my head up and swiftly moving his hand. "I don't think you get it. You don't get the insults. You don't get the demands. You don't get the suggestions from the agency in a tone that makes it sound like you're a selfish bitch whose heart isn't big enough to appreciate what you have." I was so angry I nearly spat.

"You're right, I'm not in the line of fire like you are," he said. I could tell he was trying to stay calm and while on one hand I appreciated it, on the other I just wanted to fight.

"And did it ever occur to you," I paused and narrowed my eyes, "even for a second, to step into the line of fire to give me a break? Did it ever occur to you I needed time to crawl away and lick my wounds? Huh? Did it?" I felt ugly and mean — I knew I was being horrible but at the same time the tantrum was providing me the release I had needed for months.

"Kim, I," he stammered and shook his head. "I don't want to fight with you. I'm happy to help."

We sat again in silence, tears streamed down my cheeks. I was so sick of crying, of feeling weak and alone. I was tired of feeling angry, resentful, and incompetent.

"I'm sorry," I said reaching out to put a hand on Nate's arm as he stood up. "Please sit down. That wasn't fair. This all just sucks so much." I fell to the side, my head lying on his chest, and I cried. "It wasn't supposed to be this way," I sobbed. "I'm not supposed to hate seeing Danielle and Mark. I'm not supposed to feel anxious for weeks before every visit. And I shouldn't have to comfort our daughter for days afterward."

"I know, it wasn't what we signed up for," he said as he kissed the top of my head and gently rubbed my back.

"And it's not just about me," I said. "Rhys doesn't want to leave my lap during the visits. Then they get more and more upset and think it's my fault. I can't make her go to them." I looked over at Nate, my eyebrows knitted together with worry.

"I hear you," he said. I knew he wanted to provide a solution but the truth was neither of us had one.

"I think we should consider stopping the visits." My stomach did a summersault as I said the words, guilt rushing over me. I knew how much Mark and Danielle looked forward to the visits. I knew how much they loved Rhys and wanted to spend time with her.

But the problem was, they wanted more than that. What they yearned for was impossible. They wanted to be mom and dad to a little girl, even if it was only for a few hours a year.

"Can we do that?" Nate asked, leaning back on the couch as if opening his mind to the idea for the first time.

"I remember reading something about it in the adoption finalization paperwork," I said. "I remember I looked a year or so ago when we were joking about me taking a job in Cambridge." I looked over at Nate and saw a look of surprise on his face. His eyes were wide and he'd turned his head slightly to one side. "I know we were just joking, but I wondered if the open adoption agreement would prevent it."

"I had no idea you'd done that," he said, clearly still surprised. "I think we should look into it and see what our options are."

"Okay, I'll call the attorney tomorrow and see what the next steps might be."

We sat in companionable silence for a couple of hours, while Nate surfed between a baseball game, Food Network, and *Survivor*. I tried to browse a recent issue of *Architectural Digest*, but in all honesty I was rolling the idea of stopping the visits around in my mind.

I felt a mixture of relief, guilt, and failure. The feeling of failure was bigger than the others. There was a challenge I'd taken on when agreeing to the open adoption agreement that I'd been unable to live up to. I'd built a life and a successful career around defining and solving problems. But our relationship with Danielle and Mark was a problem I was unable to solve.

Emotionally, it was a very personal failure. In my mind, it was a failure of my character, a failure of my gratitude. Logically, it was a shared failure. Relationships, by their nature, involved more than a single person and success can only be achieved if everyone is working at it. Logically I knew the failure was based on the gap between what we felt was best for Rhys and what Danielle and Mark wanted.

I had tried to bridge the gap with compassion and putting our needs aside. Yet I knew that approach would never work. But it was the only thing I knew to do and for years it felt better than hopelessness. For as horribly as I felt, it was time to accept defeat and figure out what to do next.

* * *

When we signed the open adoption agreement, sitting beside Joyce in the maternity ward waiting room, Rhys barely a day old, I had given more than my word. Nate and I signed a contract agreeing to three visits a year with Mark and Danielle ... forever—or at least until she turned 18, which certainly felt like forever. Having already fallen in love with our baby girl, we relied on trust when we signed the agreement. We'd hired the agency and they were the experts. They'd told us the agreement was standard but that visits typically lasted less than two years because the birth parents would lose interest. It was that information that stuck in our minds when we glanced over the agreement, our minds filled with the excitement of meeting our baby for the first time. And so, eager to go home with our new baby, we signed the agreement.

It didn't matter that we hadn't fully grasped the permanence of the contract, when Nate and I were given the impression that visits would only be for the first couple of years. It didn't matter that the visits caused me to suffer from severe anxiety for weeks before and days after. It didn't matter that the agency hadn't held up their commitments to properly support either the birth parents or our family. None of the realities of our experiences mattered, because it wasn't about us. It was about two birth parents who wanted to see the little girl they had created.

It wasn't just about me and that was why I was willing to suffer the consequences of the visits and try to ignore my feelings. But it also couldn't be all about what Rhys's birth parents wanted. We were all legally adults. It had to be about Rhys. And it was time to realize that during the visits, and in the days following them, our daughter changed.

We knew our daughter well. She was a happy, outgoing little girl who loved people. When we were out in public she was constantly trying to get strangers' attention, and she was good at it. She made eye contact, said hi, or waved. She batted her eyelashes, smiled, and giggled. When we played at the park she went up to other children and began to play. And unlike her brother at a similar age, she was unafraid to be left with the nursery ladies at church.

During our visits to see Mark and Danielle, we stayed with my parents, spent time with my family, and for a couple years, saw Kathy and her extended family as well. Rhys saw these people at the same intervals as she saw Mark and Danielle. Her behavior stayed consistent and she only became timid, needy, and anxious during our visits with her birth parents.

I just couldn't do it any longer. It had been over two years and things weren't getting any better. In fact, in some ways they were getting worse. Rhys was now old enough to pick up on the inevitable tension that remained firmly embedded in our interactions with Mark and Danielle. And now she could understand more of what they said as well. And what they said each time we visited, was that she was their daughter, her name was Sara, and they were her parents. And that we were keeping her from them.

Our child's well-being had to be our primary concern. If Rhys's behavior hadn't changed during the visits, and for days following, I would have sucked it up and continued to find a way to deal with my negative reactions. But it wasn't about me. It was about our daughter.

While I couldn't deny that I wanted desperately to end the visits for my own well-being, there was no denying that Rhys was frightened of Mark and Danielle. She didn't like the way they clung to her, grabbed at her, or held her, and she could sense their anger toward me whenever we visited.

If the agency wouldn't establish some boundaries, then it was up to me to do so.

* * *

With less than two weeks to go before the visit, our attorney told us that in order to start the process of altering the open adoption agreement, we had to have a child development specialist observe the visit. According to the finalization paperwork, unless they voluntarily agreed to change the open adoption agreement, we'd have to petition the court. And for the judge to rule in our favor, the burden of proof was high. We had to prove the visits were causing Rhys harm.

We had to submit evidence to the court, documented by an expert, that our daughter was being harmed by the visits with Mark and Danielle. I felt sick.

"Hey babe," I said to Nate one night after the kids were both finally asleep. "I need to talk to you about what it means to try to change the open adoption agreement." I swallowed hard already finding it difficult to control my emotions.

"What's up?" he asked in an overly casual tone. I'd heard that tone before and knew he was uncomfortable.

"I talked to the attorney again today," I took a deep breath. "We need to move the location of our next visit. If we're going to move forward with changing the agreement, we have to have the visit observed by a licensed early childhood development expert."

"Okay," he said tilting his head and gesturing for me to continue. He stood and leaned over the back of his recliner. He was trying to look casual, but I could tell by the set of his jaw and the rigidity of his shoulders he was tense.

"See, the thing is, in order to get the agreement changed we need to go back to court. And for the judge to consider changing the agreement he needs proof of harm." My chin began to quiver as the familiar mix of emotions rushed over me. Once again, I was swimming in the turbulent sea filled with waves of guilt, sadness, fear, and shame. If we petitioned to change the open adoption agreement and the expert felt Rhys was fine with the visits, we'd be even worse off. The court would rule that we were wrong, and Mark and Danielle would be even angrier and feel even more justified in asserting their "parental" rights. But if we didn't petition to end the in-person visits, I knew Rhys would pay the price. And I couldn't do that to her.

"Okay," Nate said again. This time he moved to sit at the edge of the recliner and leaned forward, his elbows on his knees. "And then?" he prompted.

"And then we wait to see what the expert says. He or she will write up a report and we'll go from there." Nate continued to look at me as I swallowed hard trying to dislodge the lump that had formed in my throat. "Oh, and we're paying the attorney by the hour and we'll have to pay the child specialist as well," I paused. "Sorry, that was crass. It just all feels surreal and so frustrating. Like we're waiting for our baby all over again."

"Well, I think it's something we both agree we need to do. Right?"

"Yeah. But I feel so badly. How are they going to feel?"

"Kim, it's not your job to worry about how Mark and Danielle feel. You've done everything you can do." He paused for several seconds. "The agency hasn't done shit to help the situation and Rhys is the one paying the price." He was angry now. It took a lot for Nate to get angry. I was shocked and filled with love for him.

He does care! He has been paying attention! I'm not the evil one! I was overcome with relief. It was the first time he'd shown his frustration with the situation. Until then he'd shown empathy and annoyance, but never anger. I knew he was taking my lead as I navigated our family through the adoption journey, but now it was different. I felt like we were partners and he was more than just along for the ride. We were in this together.

"I know you're right, but I just can't imagine how horrible I would feel if I were in their situation," I said, trying to explain.

"Kim, you already feel horrible because of the situation we're in. More to the point, you feel horrible because of the position *they put you in!*" Nate was on a roll now. Part of me wanted to stop him from getting wound up, and part of me wanted him to keep going. It felt good to hear his point of view about what we'd been through over the past few years and to feel his validation of my experience. "You've gone above and beyond. Nothing is changing. We need to do what's best for Rhys. It's gonna suck, but it has to be done."

It took another week to find the expert we needed to observe our visit and it meant extending our trip by a day to squeeze into her schedule. The plan was to meet in her office for a one-hour visit with Mark and Danielle.

I needed to let them know the time and location of our visit had changed and let the adoption agency know we wouldn't need to meet there.

Fearing a letter wouldn't reach them in time, I decided to send an email, hoping they each still had a working computer. As a back-up, if I didn't receive a reply in the next day or two I'd call the agency and ask them to call Danielle.

Dear Danielle and Mark,

We hope you're enjoying your summer. I'm writing to let you know that we'll be there for our next visit on July 22nd. We won't be meeting at the agency this time. Instead we'll be meeting at County Family Services located at 223 South Main Street. We'll meet you in the lobby at 10 a.m.

See you in a couple of weeks,
Kim and Nate

A few hours later there was a reply in my inbox.

We are having a good summer. We don't want to meet there. We'll meet you at the agency. And 10 is too early, we'll be there at 11.

Mark

My heart raced as I wondered how to reply. I felt guilty and deceptive. I hadn't told them why we weren't meeting at the agency, I didn't know how to tell them, and I was afraid of what would happen if I did. I didn't owe them an explanation and Samuel, our attorney, had advised me against it. But I felt bad not offering one. *What do I say? What if they don't show up? What if they call the agency and tell on us?*

I took a deep breath and prepared myself to respond. *You're doing nothing wrong. You promised to care for Rhys forever and that's what this is about, taking care of Rhys.*

Mark,

We will be at County Family Services at 10:00 a.m. for a one-hour visit on the 22nd.

Kim and Nate

There was another reply waiting in my inbox the next morning. Before clicking it open I wondered how long the back and forth was going to last.

We aren't available. You need to change the time. Was all the email said.

You have over a week to rearrange your schedules. That is the only time available. See you then or see you in October, I replied.

I wasn't playing games. It was summertime so Mark didn't have classes and I couldn't imagine either of them had any appointment or plans that couldn't be changed. If Nate and I could take extra time away from work with little notice, they could surely change their plans too. They didn't get to call the shots anymore. I'd been through too much, hurt too deeply, and given in too many times.

* * *

We walked into County Family Services at 9:55 a.m. on July 22nd and they were already seated in the crowded waiting room. They both narrowed their eyes and scowled at me as the three of us walked in, Rhys in between me and Nate, each of us holding one of her hands. As soon as she saw them she stopped, turned, and reached up to me.

"Up, Mama, up," she demanded.

"It's okay, Sweetheart. Take my hand," I offered trying to reassure her everything was okay.

"Up, Mama. Up!"

"Come here big girl," I said as I picked her up and swung her on to my hip. I looked up and Danielle's eyes were narrowed even more and anger spread across Mark's face. They both stood and walked toward us.

"Let's have a seat guys," Nate said as he took a step in front of Rhys and me. "I'm sure Terrie will be down soon to get us."

Terrie was the expert our attorney had found. I'd spoken with her briefly over the phone explaining the situation, the concerns we had, and why we were asking her to observe the visit.

We waited in silence. Mark and Danielle sat glaring at us. Nate was between me and Danielle. When we first sat down I tried to get Rhys to face outward on my lap only to have her wiggle around and bury her face in my hair. I rubbed her back and rocked gently from side to side. Feeling her little heart beating rapidly against my breast I worried she wasn't feeling well. I kissed her forehead to check for fever. She didn't have one, but she was certainly acting as needy as if she were sick.

The small waiting room was chaotic as adults and children came and went. Kids fidgeted and parents tried to keep them distracted. The room itself was dim with the blinds all drawn to keep the bright summer sunshine from heating up the room. Chairs lined the walls and well-worn toys and magazines were scattered on all unoccupied flat surfaces, chairs and end tables alike.

A heavy-set young woman with a bright smile entered the waiting room and briefly looked around. Making eye contact with me she took a few steps forward and extended her hand "Kim I presume," she said.

"Terrie?" it came out as a question. "Yes, I'm Kim. This is my husband, Nate. And this is our daughter, Rhys." I stopped short, hoping my calling Rhys our daughter hadn't stung them. I was still trying to protect them and did my best to avoid referring to Rhys as our daughter during our visits. "And this is Danielle and Mark, Rhys's birth parents."

"Nice to meet you all," Terrie said shaking everyone's hand but Rhys's. She bent down and gave Rhys a quick smile, getting a brief one in return. "Why don't you follow me up to my office and you can have your visit." She nodded as if agreeing to her own suggestion, turned, and walked toward a long staircase.

Her office was an eight by twelve room with large windows at the far end that overlooked the freeway a few blocks away. With a variety of toys lining the walls and all the chairs sized to fit a child no older than six, I quickly surveyed the room for the best place to sit. Still holding Rhys who clung to me like a little koala bear, I sat in one of the small chairs next to an equally small table. Nate leaned against a post on the opposite side of the room. Mark and Danielle each chose to sit on the floor next to some toys. Terrie rolled an office chair in from another room and closed the door. She removed a clipboard from the chair and sat down.

"Go ahead and have your visit. Try to just ignore me."

"Do you want to find a toy to play with, Rhys?" I asked, trying to pry her from my chest. I was feeling increasingly alarmed. Her shyness had never been this bad before.

"No," came a tiny voice muffled by my sweatshirt.

"Sorry guys," I said looking over at them. "Toddlers can be kinda unpredictable."

"We're here to see our daughter," Mark said, staring back at me and then looking at Terrie as if asking for her intervention. He sat with his legs folded in front of him and fiddled with the laces on his black leather combat boots.

"Yeah, we want to spend time with our daughter," Danielle said, also looking in Terrie's direction.

"Just give her a few minutes, she'll warm up," Nate said. "So, what have you guys been up to?" he asked, trying to break the ice and take their attention away from Rhys. Maybe if she saw Nate interacting with them she'd warm up faster.

Mark and Danielle talked about going to the mall to check out the latest video game he wanted to buy, riding the bus around town, and hanging out with their friends at the city bus terminal.

As we listened to stories about their summer adventures Rhys slowly began to warm up. She started to play with a set of plastic animals in a container near the table where we sat. But even though Danielle sat next to a doll house that had clearly caught her eye, Rhys wouldn't venture over no matter how much we tried to move her in that direction. Knowing the likely consequences of the visit, we wanted them to have time with Rhys and we wanted Rhys to have the best experience possible with them. Even with everything we'd experienced, I still clung to an infinitesimal grain of hope that we could make the relationship work.

They took pictures with their cell phones of Rhys playing from a few feet away and commented on the fact they'd lost their digital camera and needed a new one. "That stinks," I said trying to empathize.

"Yeah, well, we need a new one," he said.

"Maybe you'll get one for your birthday," I suggested.

"That's not for months."

I kept my mouth shut. I knew he was hinting that we should be the ones to replace it and that wasn't going to happen.

"Your visit has come to an end," Terrie said after an hour.

"We haven't held our daughter," Danielle said.

"Yeah, we didn't get pictures with our daughter," he added.

I stood up and smoothed the creases in my shorts. "I'm sorry guys," I said, feeling badly for them. "I think you got some good pictures of her playing though." I turned to grab my purse off the floor.

"Give me a hug," Danielle said, picking Rhys up and pressing her cheek next to Rhys's.

"I want a hug too," Mark said, taking Rhys out of Danielle's arms.

"Whoa, guys. She's not a doll," I said, stunned. I seemed to have to say that to them at least once a visit. I wanted to pull Rhys away, but Nate was closer and I didn't want to make matters worse.

"Alright, guys. Time for us to go," Nate said. His voice was deeper than I had ever heard it. He leaned over and took Rhys from Mark and headed out the door.

I stood still, unable to move, suddenly feeling the entire visit had been a catastrophe. After what felt like minutes but was no more than 10 seconds I found my voice. "Thanks for your time Terrie," I said in a near whisper.

"You're welcome Kim, I'll send my report to your attorney."

Nate was at the front door and Mark and Danielle were almost all the way down the stairs by the time I reached the staircase. *Thank God they hadn't heard her reference the attorney*, I thought as I walked down the stairs to join them.

We stepped outside into the bright sunshine. The day was going to be a hot one. In little over an hour the temperature had risen enough that I was instantly uncomfortable in my sweatshirt.

"We're not meeting here next time," Mark declared.

412

"Our daughter didn't want to hang out with us because we weren't at the agency," Danielle said, her voice filled with hurt. "We're going to meet you at the agency next time."

"Rhys is changing guys, she's getting older and she doesn't always do what we want her to."

"You decided we'd meet here. You took our daughter away from us," Mark said and Danielle nodded in agreement.

Yes, we had decided to meet them there but we hadn't taken their daughter away. They had chosen adoption months before we met them, we were the couple who agreed to be Rhys's parents.

For the first time in nearly two and a half years, I accepted that I hadn't caused their pain. I wasn't to blame for how they were feeling or reacting to the adoption. Furthermore, no matter how much the agency had tried to make it so, it wasn't my responsibility to help them come to terms with the consequences of their decision. None of us could give them what they wanted. And most importantly, it wasn't Rhys's responsibility to ease their pain.

* * *

Three months later we had one final visit with Mark and Danielle at Terrie's request. During the first visit Terrie had observed enough to show the visits weren't beneficial to Rhys, but she hadn't seen evidence of harm. After the second visit she did.

For the second visit we arrived 20 minutes early to allow Terrie the opportunity to observe Rhys without seeing her birth parents first. Rhys greeted Terrie with a wide smile, playing freely with the toys in Terrie's playroom. She found the plastic animals again, showed

Terrie each animal and made animal noises for her when Terrie asked her to.

When Terrie escorted Mark and Danielle into the room, Rhys jumped on my lap and tried to hide her head in my cardigan sweater. She asked me where Theo was and said she wanted to go home. It was heart-wrenching. After the appointment she once again started biting her nails and bit them so short they were bright red and sore.

Between what she observed in the combination of the two visits, Terrie wrote a letter to the court stating there was a basis for modification of the open adoption agreement. Instead of feeling the relief I'd expected, I again faced dueling emotions. I was excited to have the stress of the in-person visits gone from our lives. But at the same time, I was sad that we had failed in creating a healthy relationship with our daughter's birth parents. I was disappointed we hadn't found a way to make them a part of her life going forward.

With the letter from Terrie, Samuel drew up and filed the paperwork requesting the court amend the open adoption agreement, removing the in-person visits. We agreed to continue to send pictures twice a year.

Samuel reached out to Mark and Danielle a couple of times trying to get them to settle out of court by voluntarily agreeing to the new terms. We were hoping they might come to see that their visits were frightening and confusing Rhys. But they weren't interested and I understood why; it was a profound loss to them and the truth was, they lacked the cognitive capacity to consider Rhys's needs. Before serving them with the court papers, a necessary step prior to our hearing with the judge, Samuel contacted both Kathy and Frank, Mark's dad, to explain what was happening.

Kathy told him she understood but didn't think she could help. She hadn't spoken to Danielle in some time. If Danielle reached out, she would encourage her to agree to the change. Frank said that he would talk to Mark and tell him he should agree as well, but couldn't force him to do it. Unprompted, he added that he didn't think Mark continuing to see "the baby" after she was born was ever a good idea. It was the one and only time I agreed with him.

Two weeks before we were scheduled to be in court, our attorney reached out with a compromise offer.

"Hi Kim, I received a call from Joyce at the agency yesterday afternoon and she has some questions about our petition," Samuel explained.

"Why is she even involved?" I said, my anger instantly beginning to rise.

"Mark and Danielle called her and told her you were taking away their visits."

"Isn't that great that Joyce decides to give a crap now," I said, closing my eyes and leaning my head back on my office chair. "I'm sorry. We tried for years to get the agency to help with the situation and they laid it all at our feet."

"Joyce would like to know if you'll agree to one visit a year."

"Are you kidding?" Now I was angry with him. "Harm is harm, Samuel. You read the reports Terrie wrote. Once a year, three times a year. The answer is no. I'm not going to knowingly hurt our daughter!" I could barely breathe I was so angry. *Did he forget who we were doing this for? Has he forgotten who's paying his bill?* Although I knew he had a legal obligation to tell us of the compromise offer, I still felt that Rhys was the one being compromised. Even if we took her only once a year, she would still be afraid of them. And I'd still feel like I was betraying her, by making her see them, making her engage with them, and letting them hold her against her will. No, even once a year was once a year too many. I couldn't do that to her anymore.

"They mean well, Kim, and she's just trying to come to an amicable solution."

"I don't care that they mean well. They're hurting Rhys, that's the bottom line," I took a breath trying to stop my rising anger. "The time for them to make a difference was nearly three years ago. The answer is no."

"I guessed that's what you'd say. Joyce suggested that if you weren't happy with meeting at the agency, maybe we could find a location with a one-way mirror? They could watch her play with you. She wouldn't know they were there."

Everything went white, I was blinded by my anger. I quickly turned to make sure my office door was closed because I feared I would scream my response. If I hadn't been at work, I likely would have. There were times during the adoption process I had been angry, but I had never felt anything like I experienced in that moment. I was barely holding myself in check.

"You've *got* to be joking!" I tried to take a long deep breath to calm myself down and regain control of my emotions. My face was burning and tears streamed down my face. *Did he think we took this lightly? Did he think we wanted to be in this position? Was he crazy?* I spoke very slowly, carefully choosing every word.

"Our daughter is a human being. She is *not* an animal at the zoo. I will absolutely not, under any circumstances, have my daughter used by them."

"I think you're..."

"Stop, just stop!" I yelled. I couldn't take it any longer. "Unless you're going to say you think I'm right you should just stop talking." I was suddenly eerily calm yet my tone was barely civil. "You have what you need prepared for review by the judge?"

I was all business. He needed to know there was no wiggle room, no time for negotiations. We'd been through three years of visits. The process to change the open adoption agreement had taken eight months and thousands of dollars. I hadn't taken any part of the adoption process lightly. I had stayed awake nights making sure I was doing everything I could for a successful open adoption. And we hadn't taken the decision to end the in-person visits lightly. It had been another emotional rollercoaster that I felt grateful to have survived.

"Yes, we have everything and the court date is scheduled for February 17th."

"Good. I'll get our plane tickets as soon as I hang up and we'll be there. Please let me know if anything changes." I hung up the phone in disgust.

I sat at my desk trying to make sense of the call. I was surprised at the severity of my reaction. The tension and frustration of more than three years had finally exploded. I felt strangely relieved.

I was also dumbfounded. I couldn't believe Joyce had suggested we allow our child to be watched by someone from behind a one-way mirror. How could these two adults put Mark and Danielle's needs ahead of Rhys's? Rhys was a child and her needs came first.

To our surprise and great relief, just three days before we were set to go to court, they unexpectedly agreed to the changes to the open adoption agreement.

There would be no more in-person visits and we would continue to send pictures twice a year via the adoption agency.

Our decision to remove the visits was the right one, but I still felt sad about how things had turned out. I couldn't help wondering, had the agency done their job clarifying the boundaries with Danielle and Mark once it was clear they didn't understand them, if things might have turned out differently. Instead, Joyce and Barbara had made the boundaries even fuzzier by referring to their behavior as "parenting," by requesting we send more pictures and schedule additional visits, and perhaps worst of all, by continuing to refer to Rhys as Sara—even when they communicated privately with us.

I also wondered what I would tell Rhys when she asked about her birth parents. What would I tell her when she asked me if she'd ever met them? And how I would answer when she asked when she could see them again?

But before any of those conversations happened, we needed to share with her that she was adopted. I figured that the time was coming. She was over three, an age when children are often curious about where babies come from. I knew the conversation would come sooner rather than later. And with one of Rhys's preschool friends announcing to the class she was going to be a big sister, it was likely the questions would be sooner rather than later.

I hoped I understood enough about being Rhys's mother to handle what I felt was our next big test in this crazy journey.

Chapter 37

Where Do Babies Come From

Rhys was a healthy, creative, energetic four-year-old and I loved her more than I ever thought possible. With the pressure of trying to manage a relationship with Danielle and Mark in the past, and our kids increasingly independent, capable, and trustworthy, life had a lightness I hadn't experienced in years. I was exhausted on a daily basis balancing motherhood with a successful career but it was no longer the dark exhaustion that depression delivered. It was a contented exhaustion that left a smile on my face when I closed my eyes. There were challenges, but I had the energy to successfully navigate them. I had the life I'd yearned for.

* * *

Rhys and I hung out while the boys slept in. I tried to catch up on work email that had gone unread from the week before. Rhys watched *Olivia*, a cartoon about an active pig whose mix of creativity and smarts was a constant source of trouble for her mother. Rhys was a lot like Olivia. Too active to sit still, she buzzed between activities. She played at her kitchen, making play cupcakes and scrambled eggs, which I would dutifully pretend to eat. We pulled out craft paper, glue, paint, markers, and scissors so she could create another artistic masterpiece. The dining room table was perpetually covered with an explosion of art supplies we'd have to move aside before we could sit down to eat.

"What should we have for breakfast?" I asked once the caffeine from my coffee kicked in.

"Snowman pancakes, bacon, and cheesy eggs," she said looking over her shoulder at me. "And I'll help!"

"Okay, let's get started," I said as I summoned the energy to keep up with her. "Grab your stool so you're high enough to stir," I reminded her as I walked into the pantry to grab the pancake mix.

We busied ourselves making breakfast. I measured the ingredients as she stirred, the first wild motion of the whisk spraying flour out of the bowl and onto the counter. "Wow! You're too strong, slow down, big girl." In response, Rhys smiled with pride.

"Head upstairs and wake up your dad and brother," I asked, quickly adding *"NICELY!"* as she ran full speed up the stairs, each footstep pounding on the floor as if she were an elephant rather than a 35-pound preschooler. Nate and Theo, woken by the sound of her not so subtle approach, were up before she entered their rooms.

Once breakfast was cleaned up I headed for the shower, hoping to have a few minutes to myself. Inevitably, as I rinsed the conditioner from my hair, I felt a rush of cold air as the shower curtain was pulled back and there stood Rhys, with an emergency. I had hoped to be spared the interruption this time. But I was not so lucky.

"I don't want to get dressed!" came the loud protest from Rhys as she stared in at me.

"Dad said it's time to get dressed," Theo yelled back from the door of the bathroom. At eight, Theo often tried to be the third parent.

"I'm trying to take a shower," I said. "Please put the shower curtain back," I told Rhys, "And go work it out with your dad."

This same situation occurred almost every weekend and my pleas rarely worked. It was nearly impossible to get any time to myself. Every time I sat down I had a kid, a husband or a dog, vying for my attention. I was constantly bouncing between requests for snacks, help getting craft supplies, or intervening in the bickering between Theo and Rhys. Even if Nate was sitting next to me, all requests came to me. And with my working mom guilt in full effect, I tried to dutifully respond and manage it all.

I'd taken to referring to our kids as the Bickersons. Just like I had when they were babies and my patience was running low, I injected humor into the situation whenever I could. It seemed to calm us all down and helped me maintain perspective. But their bickering seemed constant whenever they were within 10 feet of each other. If love was measured by the number of things a person found to fight about, then our house was overflowing with it.

Finishing my shower as quickly as possible, I pulled on a pair of yoga pants and a t-shirt from a recent 5k. This was my weekend uniform. I could do just about anything in these clothes and the running shirts reminded me that I could fit in time for personal goals.

Theo, Rhys, and the dog appeared in the bathroom as I pulled on my socks. Deciding the best place to be was under my feet, I hopped on one foot trying to finish getting dressed as I attempted to avoid them all.

"But I wanted to wear a dress," Rhys complained.

"Dad asked you to pick out your clothes and you said no so he did it," Theo shot back.

"But I…" Rhys started to whine.

"Guys, please. Take the dog downstairs and let me finish getting ready," I pleaded. "I just need to brush my teeth, pull my hair in a pony and put on my shoes. Give me five minutes."

"But we want to be with *you*," they said in unison.

"Fine, but please stay out from under me." I smiled. I was lucky to have two happy, healthy kids who just wanted to spend time with me. As frustrating as it was, I knew that it wouldn't be like this forever. I tried my best to enjoy it while it lasted.

I had been lucky that Nate hadn't added himself to the fray as he often did. With the kids upstairs, he often figured he was free to get cleaned up. He would come to see what was up, then jump in the shower once he saw I was fully clothed. Out of the shower he'd brush his teeth, grab his deodorant, and reach for a comb all the time reaching around and bumping into me.

Just as I was about to leave the bathroom, he came wandering in.

"Looking great sweetie," he said leaning in to give me a quick kiss.

"Oh please," I replied, rolling my eyes.

"That's gross!" Theo said squirming as he stood in the doorway.

My family had felt incomplete without two children, but now that I had two children, most times, it would feel like I had three.

Giving up on putting on even the slightest amount of make-up, I laced up my running shoes and steered the kids into the hallway. We went into each kid's bedroom to make sure their dirty clothes were in their hamper so I could start the laundry.

After running errands and completing a few loads of laundry it was time for lunch. Feeling like a short order cook, I made a sandwich for Rhys, cut into triangles without the crust, and Kraft mac and cheese for Theo. Cooking something special for each kid took extra time and energy, but felt better than the inevitable whining if I tried to convince them to eat the same thing. It was just another example of my preference for a moment's peace, over the long-term solution with only the remote possibility of a lasting truce. And it was also another example of the impact of working mom guilt in our ordinary day.

I loved my career and would feel incomplete without the challenge and people it brought with it. But with both of us working full time there was always more to do than time in the day. Tradeoffs had to be made and spoiling my kids with attention when I was around was one I could live with.

With the lunch cleaned up and the kids both happily distracted, I walked into the kitchen and whispered to Nate, "I'm going upstairs to get a little time to myself." With everyone busy entertaining themselves, I hoped I could get thirty uninterrupted minutes.

"Okay, I'll try to keep them down here," he whispered back as he continued to unload the dishwasher.

I grabbed my cellphone, a magazine from the top of a pile threatening to topple and tiptoed across the living room. I walked quietly up the stairs and closed the door to our bedroom behind me. Propping pillows against the headboard, I stretched out, and opened a months old copy of *Architectural Digest*.

423

An article featuring the condo of a New York City socialite caught my eye. I read the photo captions and tried to picture what a day in the life of the residents was like. *Did they hit the snooze button one too many times each morning, hoping the extra eighteen minutes of sleep would make them feel well rested?* I doubted it.

The residents of this million-dollar residence with a sweeping Manhattan view probably had an army to help them with the typical day to day activities of a modern family. *How else could a home be picture perfect, everything in its place?* I took a deep breath and reminded myself that the condo looked so amazing because it was expertly decorated, professionally cleaned, and staged for the photo shoot. Reality was a cold comfort. I was tired, my energy depleted, the list of to-dos was long. I wanted to find a way to quickly recharge.

The pages that followed contained more inspiration for the perfect city dwelling, followed by lakeside retreats designed to pull you away from the grind of everyday life. They looked both inspiring and relaxing. I could picture myself sitting at the rustic wooden desk overlooking a tree-lined lake writing for hours on end while the kids played on the emerald green lawn.

My daydreaming turned to an imaginary world full of summer weekends spent playing outdoors with nightly fireside chats. My mind, completely distracted by the fantasy life I had created, was jolted back to reality when Rhys jumped onto the bed beside me.

"Whatcha doin'?" she chirped.

"Just trying to relax and look at my magazine," I said, smiling as she cuddled up next to me.

"Can I relax too?" she asked.

"Sure babe, but you have to be quiet. Mom is trying to have some downtime."

"Okay," she said looking up at me with a sparkle in her eye. Her skin was milky white, with perfect rose-colored circles on her cheeks, her strawberry blond hair a wild mess of curls around her face.

She cuddled quietly beside me for a minute looking at the pictures of the next weekend retreat. "Theo grew in your tummy," she said, breaking the silence.

"Yes he did." I laid the magazine across my lap and put my arm around her pulling her even closer.

"I grew in Danielle's tummy," she stated matter-of-factly. Rhys had a first year book that we looked through from time to time. We would go through each of the pages and we'd talk about who was in each of the pictures and how they were part of her story. There was a picture of Nate, Theo, Mark, and me with Danielle holding Rhys in her book.

"That's right," I said with a lump growing in my throat. *Here it comes,* I thought feeling a mixture of anticipation, fear, and regret.

"Why didn't I grow in your tummy?" she asked looking me in the eyes, her eyebrows raised.

At four and a half we'd had bits of this conversation before. I always tried to stop whatever I was doing and give her my full attention; trying my best to answer whatever question she was wondering about.

"When Mommy and Daddy tried to have another baby my body just didn't know how to do it anymore," I said, working hard to keep my voice steady. I felt the tears building behind my eyes and a tightness in my chest. I was still mourning the fact that I'd been unable to have another baby. I still felt robbed of the opportunity to try again for the perfect pregnancy and delivery. It didn't matter how irrational the feelings were, it remained my reality.

"Oh," she said looking up at me and tilting her head so it rested against my chest. "So I grew in your heart?"

"Yes, sweetie. You grew in my heart."

My friend Mary, who had adopted her daughters twenty years before, had given us a framed poem that hung on Rhys's bedroom wall. It read:

Not flesh of my flesh
Nor bone of my bone
But still miraculously my own.
Never doubt for a single minute
You were made not under my heart
But in it.

~Anonymous

The poem was the best written expression I'd found to describe the ferocity with which I loved our daughter. I hadn't had the privilege of making her or carrying her in my womb. But I felt certain she was made *for* me, created and put on earth for me to be her mother. These feelings were as ponderous to me as was the ability for a woman to create another human. I thought of all of the millions of things that had to go just right to birth a healthy baby, and I thought of all the millions of things that had had to go just right for our adoption to finally become a reality. Both were miracles, in my mind.

"So your body didn't work anymore?" she asked after a minute.

"Yep, that's right." I hugged her tighter.

"That must have made you very sad," she said. Her voice was filled with compassion. She sounded more like a wise sage than a four-year-old. A tear slipped down my cheek.

"It did make me very sad," I said, my eyes continuing to fill with tears. "But I wouldn't have you if my body still worked. And I want *you* as my daughter." I didn't even try to stop them. I allowed the tears to stream down my cheeks as I pulled her into my lap and hugged her tightly the curls on the top of her head tickled my chin. "*You* are my daughter and I love *you!*"

"I love you too, mommy," she said snuggling into my neck.

We sat on the bed for a few more minutes, the sun streaming through the windows. I'd survived the big "where did I come from" conversation. It wasn't as scary as I feared, and I didn't feel like I'd failed. I had done okay.

Rhys seemed satisfied with the answers I was able to provide. We would take these talks one step at a time and I knew I would continue to do the best I could to give her the answers she sought.

I pondered how such a little person could have wisdom that was only now beginning to dawn for me. I wondered about the crazy series of events that led up to our conversation. I thought back to the moment I decided we had to say yes to the baby girl who could possibly have seizures that would wrack her brain. That was possibly the biggest and scariest decision I would ever make in my life.

And having made that scary decision, I finally had the life I had dreamt of. We were an ordinary family working together to keep everyone as healthy and happy as possible. I smiled as I thought ahead to the milestones to come.

Epilogue

Rhys and I sat down on my bedroom floor by the window, the late August sun shining brightly on our bare toes. We unzipped the bag holding a couple dozen bottles of nail polish preparing to paint our toenails.

"And my fingernails, Mommy, so I look pretty for school tomorrow," Rhys declared.

"You always look pretty," I said with a smile. I was excited to see her finally looking forward to the start of school. For a month she had alternated between an excited, "I can't wait to meet my teacher!" and a defiant, "I'm *never* going to school!"

We looked through the colors. Rhys was having trouble deciding, so she had seven colors lined up beside her.

"Do you want to pick one color for your fingers and one for your toes?" I asked.

"Nope, I want a pattern," she said, smiling as she changed the order of the bottles. A rainbow of pinks, purples, and blues sat side by side, along with a bottle with silver glitter.

"Well, I think seven is too many colors," I said gently. I didn't want to risk destroying her good mood and have her positive attitude about the first day of school turn negative too. "Why don't you pick out four. There are plenty of patterns we can do with four."

"Five Mommy!" She smiled brightly, the sunlight sparkled in her eyes. *"Please!"*

"Okay, five, but only if the fifth is the sparkles. We can put the sparkles on top of the other colors."

Five it was. We ended up with an alternating pattern of fuchsia and royal blue on her fingers and magenta and lilac on her toes. We added the clear coat with silver glitter on top of all her fingers and toes. Rhys held her hands in front of her as we admired our work.

"They look a-mazing!" she said as she wiggled her fingers six inches from my nose.

"You are a-mazing, Rhys!" I said as I reached out and tickled her tummy, making her giggle.

"Stop tickling, silly Mommy!"

"Okay, I'll stop," I said instantly pulling my hands into my lap. "Now, what're we gonna do to sit still while your fingers and toes dry? We don't want polish all over the place." I knew I needed to remind her not to run off, likely smearing nail polish somewhere along her path. It was hard for her to sit still. She was always busy doing something. She loved to sing, dance, and draw. She'd also spend hours running around the backyard playing on our wooden playset or in the sandbox. And at five and a half, maybe her favorite past time was getting a rise out of her almost 10-year-old brother. It seemed the only time Rhys sat still was when she slept.

Her nails done and dried, we enjoyed the last day of summer vacation. We ran around in the backyard, I pushed her on the swing, and she played in her sandbox while I sat on the deck and read a book. All the while Theo kept himself busy playing video games on the Xbox or watching other people play video games on YouTube.

"Alright guys, 15-minute warning," Nate warned, looking at the clock on the microwave. "It's a school night so it's an eight o'clock bedtime."

"But I'm not tired," Rhys whined as she looked up from her Play-Doh.

"I'm sorry you're not tired sweetie, but it's a school night and you need to have a good night's sleep before your first day of kindergarten," he said with a smile.

"I'm *not* tired!"

"Rhys, please don't talk to your daddy like that. I know you don't want to go to bed, but eight o'clock is bedtime. Do you want Mommy to read to you tonight or Daddy," I asked hoping to avoid a fight.

"You," she shouted as she extended her arm and pointed at me with a determined look in her eye.

"You got it. Ten minutes and we'll go up, brush teeth, and pick out three books."

"Five books," she said as she turned to face me from her chair at the dining room table.

"Three books," I said walking over to stand beside her. "Three's a lot," I continued, cutting off her next argument before she had time to make it.

Bedtime went smoothly. Nate and I sat companionably on the couch and enjoyed what was left of the evening together.

The day had finally arrived and there was no need for an alarm to wake us up. It was Rhys's first day of kindergarten and her internal alarm had woken her just before six like it did every morning. I heard her bound into the bathroom before appearing at my side of the bed.

"Let's go downstairs, Mommy," she said smiling. She was definitely a morning person.

"Why don't you come snuggle your mama," I asked pulling her onto the bed and hugging her tightly. "I want to snuggle my baby."

"I'm not a baby, I'm a big girl," she declared loud enough to wake her dad.

Nate rolled over and threw his arm over us. He was not a morning person and I wondered whether I should insist he get up, too, or let him sleep for another half hour.

"Ugh, Daddy, you're squishing me!" Rhys giggled and wriggled to get free.

"Alright big kid," I said. "Let's head downstairs and feed the dog!"

The morning went smoothly. I made Rhys's favorite breakfast of pancakes, bacon, and scrambled eggs with extra cheese. And hoping to make it extra special, I made her pancake in the shape of a flower. I offered to make a special pancake for Theo too, but he just rolled his eyes and said, "normal pancakes are fine Mom."

Rhys picked out a white cotton sundress with bunches of tiny neon pink and purple flowers. The early September morning brought with it a chilly breeze so I managed to convince her to wear a sweater. She bounced down the stairs with a bright purple cardigan with sequins dots and pink sandals. I loved her funky style.

"How do you want your hair today?" I asked, picking up a comb.

"Super fancy," she said, her voice filled with excitement.

"You want me to curl your hair for you?" I wasn't sure what super fancy hair meant.

"Nope, I'll pick out the hair stuff and you can make my hair fancy," she skipped off toward the stairs in the direction of the kids' bathroom.

She came back with a handful of barrettes and ponytail holders. I wasn't sure what to do. I tried to figure out how to work her selection into her thin shoulder-length hair.

"I want two ponies, and then you can decorate the ponies with these," she held the barrettes in my direction.

"Alright, let's see what we can do." I smiled and raised my eyebrows at Nate who was in the kitchen making the kids' lunches.

"Good luck," he said, shrugging his shoulders.

"Better watch what I'm doin'," I laughed, "Startin' tomorrow it'll be all you, mister!"

When I was done she had two ponytails, one on each side of her head with a series of barrettes down each one. *So long as she's happy,* I thought.

"Hey, buddy," I hollered at Theo who was relaxing on the couch playing Xbox. "Did you at least run a comb through your hair?"

"Yes, Mom," he said, turning and giving me a cheesy grin. *That kid,* I thought laughing to myself.

"Alright guys, let's go out front and get first day of school pictures," I said to both kids. I felt the prick of tears forming behind my eyes.

"In a minute," Rhys said, looking up from the variety of stuffed animals she had set up in a semi-circle around her. "We're right in the middle of a tea party."

"One minute, but then we need to get some pictures. We have to leave for school in fifteen minutes. Okay?" I raised my eyebrows at her.

"Come on Rhys," Theo said as he stood up and walked over to her. "This is important to Mom, let's go outside and get it over with." He sounded the perfect 50/50 mix of big brother and parent.

"I said in a *minute*, Theo," Rhys said, putting her hands on her hips and looking up at him.

"There's no need to be nasty," Theo shot back.

"Alright guys, enough. These pictures *are* important to me. It'll only take a couple of minutes."

"Did your mom take first day of school pictures when you were little?" Rhys asked me.

Rhys had been asking me questions like that a lot lately. She was constantly asking whether I had done this or that when I was little or whether my mom had made me do something. Every time a bright smile would spread across her face as I said yes. She would then prompt me for details. A couple of times when she wasn't sure she wanted to do what I asked her to do she asked if we could call my mom to confirm that I had, in fact, done the same thing when I was little. It felt good that my daughter wanted to have experiences like mine. She was my girl, forever and for always.

Nate pulled into the gravel lot across from the school. As the car came to a stop my heart started beating faster and my palms began to sweat. I rubbed my hands up and down my jeans to quickly dry them. I remembered feeling sentimental when we'd dropped Theo off on his first day of kindergarten, but with Rhys it felt even a little more meaningful. Whether it was because she was the baby of the family, or because of the journey that brought us together, I wasn't sure.

Mrs. Anderson was at the doorway to the classroom greeting the students as they arrived.

"Hi Rhys," she said with a bright smile. "Hi Kim, hi Nate. Go ahead and find a seat for Rhys. You can hang her bag on her chair."

"Where do you want to sit?" I asked, looking down at Rhys.

She led me over to a table where another girl sat coloring. She pulled out the chair, hung her backpack on it, and sat down just as the teacher had asked her to.

I knelt beside her, suddenly not ready to leave. Rhys reached over to the middle of the table, grabbed a coloring sheet and a handful of crayons.

"Have a great day at school sister," Nate said, leaning down to give her a kiss on the cheek. He looked at me, widening his eyes and raising his eyebrows as if to urge me to say good-bye too.

"Have a great day!" I said, my voice sounding overly cheerful. "We'll see you this afternoon." I gave her a hug and a kiss.

"Rhys, this is Cynthia," Mrs. Anderson was suddenly at our side. "You two have a great day and we'll see you this afternoon," she said to Nate and me.

"We'll leave you to it," I said. My eyes filled with tears that refused to be contained.

Nate took my hand and we walked out the backdoor of the classroom and into the asphalt courtyard. I didn't try to stop the two tears that escaped and ran slowly down my cheeks. Nate squeezed my hand and leaned over to kiss my temple.

"She'll be just fine," he whispered.

"I know," I said, smiling and wiping away the tears. "I know everything will be fine."

Back at home, as I sat reading a magazine, I noticed how relaxed I felt. In a rush of clarity, it dawned on me that I'd worried for years this day would never come.

There had always been a little part of me, for the past five and a half years, that thought the seizures would start, seizures that would rob me of my perfectly healthy, 100% normal kid. As a result, I had worried I wouldn't be able to sit on the bedroom floor painting nails with my daughter. I worried I wouldn't be brushing her hair and putting it in ponytails. I worried I wouldn't see my daughter's smiling face looking up at me while I told her to have a wonderful day at school.

I had fought hard for a baby growing in the belly of a woman I didn't even know. I loved her with a fierceness I never thought possible. Kindergarten is a new beginning for lots of moms and kids. It's a start of a new time in their lives where both mother and child are forced to let go of each other a little more.

As hard as letting go was, I thought for Rhys and me, it might never happen. Dropping Rhys off for her first day of kindergarten I knew we were just another mother and daughter beginning a new phase of life. Maybe I could finally let go of the worry and begin to make room for whatever motherhood brought next. Whatever it was, I knew there would always be another something. But I'd grown more confident in letting go of the things I couldn't control. I'd grown more certain that I could control what needed controlling—or ask others for help when I couldn't do it on my own. And I'd grown more relaxed in accepting the imperfections that come with every journey.

It hadn't been easy and it hadn't gone as I'd planned. I'd stumbled and faltered and made mistakes every step of the way. But I'd finally achieved my dream of the perfect family, and I loved it, imperfections and all.

Acknowledgements

To my husband, my partner, my best friend. Thank you for your love, support, and for saying yes when I asked you to join me in achieving my dreams. I'm forever grateful for the life we've built. And to our kids, I couldn't ask for a more amazing son and daughter. I am so proud to be your mom.

Thanks to my parents and siblings who helped me become who I am today. Thanks for loving and supporting my family as we continue to make the most out of life. I love you all.

Thanks to my friends for your support, encouragement, and the many nudges that motivated me to keep going. To those who read early drafts, thanks for sharing your feedback and ideas.

Thanks to my two weekly heroes who helped me make sense of my journey. My gratitude runs deep.

Thanks Robin for introducing me to Renee. I never would have started writing without this introduction. Thanks to Renee for helping my pen start moving and for introducing me to Suz, who then connected me with Amy. Thanks Suz and Amy for helping me understand that adoption experiences are as diverse as the people who enter into them.

And to my writing coach, Janice, thanks for helping me find the words to share my story.

Thank you for reading *The Making of a Mom: My Unexpected Journey through Birth & Adoption.*

Made in the USA
Coppell, TX
03 January 2020

14039968R00246